THE DYNAMICS OF RENTAL HOUSING IN NEW YORK CITY

THE DYNAMICS OF RENTAL HOUSING IN NEW YORK CITY

Michael A. Stegman

CENTER FOR URBAN POLICY RESEARCH

RUTGERS UNIVERSITY • P.O. BOX 489
PISCATAWAY • NEW JERSEY • 08854

Published in the United States of America
by the Center for Urban Policy Research
Building 4051-Kilmer Campus
New Brunswick, New Jersey 08903

Library of Congress Cataloging in Publication Data

Stegman, Michael A.
The dynamics of rental housing in New
York City.

1. Rental housing—New York (N.Y.)
I. Rutgers University. Center for Urban Policy
Research. II. Title.
HD7288.85.U62N57 363.5 82-4248
ISBN 0-88285-088-1 (pbk.) AACR2

TABLE OF CONTENTS

CHAPTER

LIST OF EXHIBITS

CHAPTER 2: THE RENT REGULATION SYSTEM IN NEW YORK CITY

CHAPTER 3: POPULATION AND HOUSING IN NEW YORK CITY

CHAPTER 7: THE LEVEL OF RENTS

CHAPTER 8: THE INCOME OF NEW YORK CITY RENTERS

CHAPTER 9: RENTAL HOUSING MARKET DYNAMICS

LIST OF TABLES

CHAPTER 9: RENTAL HOUSING MARKET DYNAMICS

FOREWORD AND ACKNOWLEDGEMENTS

Because continuation of rent regulations in New York is conditioned upon the continuation of a serious housing shortage, the most important purpose of our study is to document the net rental vacancy rate across the City and in various market sectors, as of the first quarter of 1981. In addition to this narrow purpose, however, we hope that this report will help frame the larger continuing debate concerning housing needs and housing conditions in New York City and the appropriate public and private responsibilities to meet the needs. We attempt to accomplish this latter objective by providing accurate, current and easily understood information on the City's supply and location of rental housing, including data on rents and housing conditions; and on housing needs, including information on the incomes, socioeconomic characteristics and housing expense burdens of the City's nearly two million renters. As with previous reports in this series, wherever possible we compare current housing and market conditions with those of various times in the past to help gauge whether things are improving or getting worse over time.

Two important additions to the 1981 report should be noted. First, Chapter 2 presents a history of rent regulation in New York City from World War II to the present which, among other things, discusses the relationship between rent control and rent stabilization. The review also analyzes operating costs of rent stabilized apartments in New York City since the inception of rent stabilization. The second addition is a chapter devoted to the special problem of In-Rem, or City-owned housing taken by the City for back-taxes. Chapter 10 provides a detailed description of the In-Rem stock and the nearly 34,000 households that continue to live in this landlord-abandoned housing.

Given the highly emotional, ideological and political content of the rent regulation debate and because this study is intended to be useful to individuals and organizations who hold widely differing views, we have tried to remain policy and program neutral in our presentation. For this reason, too, the data we used was limited to the 1981 Housing and Vacancy Survey carried out by the Census Bureau under contract to the City and to such other surveys as the Bureau of Labor Statistics annual survey of operating costs for rent stabilized apartments. Where necessary, these data were supplemented with information from various City Departments or, as in the case of building permits data, from the New York State Division of Housing and Community Renewal.

Finally, while we are familiar with the large and growing literature on the market effects of rent control, we do not rely heavily upon it. This is because many of the studies are dated, others do not pertain directly to New York City, while those that do tend to treat just a single facet of the City's comprehensive rent regulation system. Rather than assessing the quality of their respective data bases and judging on a case by case basis the areas in which their respective findings can be accepted with a high degree of confidence, we decided that our study would be more useful to more people if we left that task to others, or for another time.

Not counting the time during which the 1981 Housing and Vacancy Survey was conducted and the data processed by the Bureau of the Census, the preparation of this report from initial outline to delivery of final copy to the City was completed in just six months. To accomplish such an enormous task on time and within budget required an extraordinary degree of coordination and cooperation among two governmental agencies and many individuals to whom I owe a substantial debt of gratitude. First, in the Bureau of the Census, Art Young, Chief of the Housing Division, did whatever was necessary to expedite the processing of the Housing and Vacancy Survey data. Betty Kent of the Housing Division, who so ably supervised the implementation of the 1981 Housing and Vacancy Survey as she has each of its predecessors, patiently explained what was and was not part of the Bureau's contract with the City, set a data delivery schedule and met every deadline. Peter Fronczek, also of the Housing Division, was our day-to-day technical contact with the Bureau and very ably assisted us through the thicket of multiple sample frames, standard errors, interpretation of data on housing losses and longitudinal analyses. By giving us quick responses on our countless calls for help, he made it possible for us to meet our ultimate project deadline.

Many individuals in the New York City Department of Housing Preservation and Development assisted us. Commissioner Anthony B. Gliedman demonstrated by example that our work was important to the City. He provided staff assistance when we needed to verify some elusive numbers and personally reviewed early analyses for which we are very grateful. His extensive knowledge of the City's rent regulation sytem was helpful to us in revising drafts of the early chapters of the report. Commissioner of Rent and Housing Maintenance, Daniel Joy, was also very supportive of our work. He made our effort far more rewarding than it might otherwise have been by assigning oversight responsibility for our study to a very talented staff member, William Bernstein, who is Director of the Management Support and Systems Analysis Unit of the Rent Control Division. It is hard to imagine how we could have proceeded without Bill Bernstein's day-to-day efforts on our behalf; helping us understand the intricacies of the City's rent regulation system; guiding us through MBR, providing the necessary continuity with earlier studies; backing up our analysis with his own; and finally providing a very perceptive and constructively critical assessment of our work. His patience and attention to detail have made this study far stronger than it would have been without his highly professional presence.

Good people tend to work with other good people. Because of their demonstrated interest in improving our report, commitment to accuracy and attention to detail, we would like to acknowledge the contributions of three members of Mr. Bernstein's small but highly capable staff. Ron Osmundsen, Senior Research Associate in the Management Support and Systems Analysis Unit, is a storehouse of information on changes over time in the size, composition and conditions in each regulated market sector. He also shared with us his own analyses of Housing and Vacancy Survey Data and long term changes in controlled and stabilized rents which we used in our report. Ms. Denise Herron and Ms. Chaw-Wha Wang, two new staff analysts, carefully reviewed our draft chapters, uncovering many errors, omissions and confusing prose. We thank them for their thorough and timely reviews.

Finally, there is the University of North Carolina Rent Control Project staff housed at Chapel Hill, about whom I cannot possibly say enough. To appreciate the importance of the resident staff to the success of this project, one must recognize that the 1981 Housing and Vacancy Survey data the Census delivered to the City was not on computer tape but in the form of 6,000+ individual tabulations and crosstabulations which filled 18 separate looseleaf binders. Each table included in this report was developed by hand from one or more of these Census tabulations. Because of the massive amount of hand copy involved, the thousands of separate hand calculations that had to be made to construct the final tables, and the countless chances for miscalculations, running the percentages in the wrong direction, failing to adjust for "not reporteds" and the like, the quality of this report is a function of the level of quality control built into the analysis. No better system of quality control could have been devised for this work than that which is rooted in the dedication and commitment to excellence of this highly professional group of young people who never tired of checking on their own calculations and verifying those of their colleagues.

The University of North Carolina staff, directed by Linda Convissor, consisted of six people. As Project Director, Linda -- a 1981 graduate of UNC's Department of City and Regional Planning -- trained and organized the staff of Research Assistants, was responsible for preparing all statistical materials for analysis, designing and overseeing the quality control system and for supervising the production of the final report, including designing the cover. On a day-to-day basis, Linda kept in touch with the Rent Control Division in New York and the Census Bureau in Washington to keep our work on course. It is a pleasure to have worked with a person whose high sense of professional commitment belies her young years and who intuitively grasps the importance of having pride in, and feeling good about, her own work.

The staff of Research Assistants consisted of five second-year graduate students in the Department of City and Regional Planning at the University of North Carolina. Karen DeLoach, Dick George, Hilary Greenberg, Linda Hoke and Steve Smotherman, none of whom is from New York City, have each developed a high level of expertise on the inner workings of the City's rent control and rent stabilization programs. More important than these substantive skills, which are probably not highly marketable, are a set of professional work standards that certainly will be. Together, these five people carried out virtually all of the statistical analyses necessary to produce the final report, and performed all quality control work, read and re-read every draft chapter I prepared and saved me from more of my own careless mistakes than I care to remember. Working with such a fine group of students is what academic life is all about.

In addition to the work of the immediate project staff, I conducted a workshop on rent control during the Fall semester in which a larger group of students analyzed the New York City Housing and Vacancy Survey data. While my work with all of the students in the workshop provided additional insights into the New York rental housing situation, I want to single out three students in particular whose work is partially reflected in the study.

Priscilla Cobb examined the beneficiaries of rent controlled housing; Anne Hafrey analyzed housing needs using the residual income approach, and Susan Hyman analyzed real income over time and changes in the spatial concentration of the rich and the poor in New York City. I would also like to acknowledge the excellent graphics work of Julie Shambaugh. She responded to our request for aid without any hesitation and delivered more than a dozen fine quality graphs and maps on very short notice.

Finally, I owe a special debt of gratitude to my colleague Mary Pettis who, under the most difficult and trying circumstances produced early drafts and the final text of the report. Her sophisticated use of the word processing equipment not only made it possible for me to recover from countless errors and malapropisms, but is responsible for the high quality of the design and readability of the report. In addition to her typing and production responsibilities, Mary shared with Linda the keeping of the books and many of the contracting requirements involving payroll, procurement and the like. For this, too, I would like to acknowledge her assistance.

As the sole author of the report, I want to acknowledge my full responsibility for its entire content and accuracy. I also want to acknowledge the excellent editorial assistance of Anne Hafrey, whose charge to make what I wrote more readable has been a truly thankless task.

Michael A. Stegman
Chapel Hill, North Carolina
February 12, 1982.

SUMMARY

Organization of the Report

The report begins with a review of the major findings from the 1981 Housing and Vacancy Survey, which is presented below. Statistics keyed to these findings are presented in a summary table at the end of this chapter.

The body of the report contains nine chapters. The first substantive chapter (Chapter 2) brings the reader up-to-date on the City's rent control and rent stabilization programs and the rent increases that have been permitted under their respective regulations since 1970. Chapter 3 provides another kind of overview necessary to an understanding of New York City's housing situation: the important changes that have occurred in the size and composition of the City's population since 1970. The analysis contained in Chapter 3 is based on the results of the 1980 Census of Population. All other chapters use data from the 1981 and earlier Housing and Vacancy Surveys. An appendix to Chapter 3 describes some of the differences between the results of the 1980 Census and the 1981 Housing and Vacancy Survey.

Chapter 4 presents an overview of New York City's housing market, including data on homeowners and the owner-occupied stock. Most of the chapter is devoted to a description of the size and characteristics of the rental stock, its location, vacancy levels and distribution according to its rent control or stabilization status. This chapter provides a broad introduction to the detailed analysis of conditions in the rental market in the remaining chapters. Chapters 5, 6 and 7 deal in considerable detail, with, respectively, rental vacancies, housing quality and the level of rents. In each of these chapters attention is paid to changes over time and within various rent control classes. Chapter 8 discusses the incomes of renters and relative housing expense burdens of different population groups.

Important elements of the supply and demand sides of the market are brought together in Chapter 9, which analyzes the components of inventory change, new construction in the City, and losses from the inventory. Demand-side analyses include changes in household composition resulting from changes in the status of housing from rent controlled to rent stabilized. Chapter 10 deals with the inventory of occupied *in rem* units i.e., city-owned housing which was taken for back taxes. The characteristics of both the stock and the households who occupy this housing are described in some detail.

Each chapter contains statistics upon which the analysis is based. Although many tables contain rounded numbers, computations were carried out using unrounded numbers wherever possible. Exceptions to this rule, and other limitations of the data, are explained in the "Notes" presented at the bottom of the tables. In the tables 'N.A.' is used as an abbreviation for "not applicable", and "--" indicates an amount less than 500 or .05 percent. The reader should also consult the Appendix to the report for detailed information on the design of the 1981 Housing and Vacancy Survey, and definitions of technical and specialized terms.

Finally, frequent references are made in the text and tables to earlier reports in this series. A full citation is given the first time a report is mentioned, after which it is cited by reference to the author's last name and the page number of the report from which the data were taken.

Rent Regulations

- Between 1970 and 1981, under the Maximum Base Rent (MBR) system, landlords of rent controlled apartments have been permitted to increase their rents on a compound basis a maximum of 137 percent, assuming collection of all maximum annual increases.

- Over the same period, the Rent Guidelines Board has allowed owners of rent stabilized apartments to raise their rents by an average of 91 percent.

- The Guidelines Board's most recent rent increase order for leases entered into between October 1, 1981 and September 30, 1982 permits landlords the following maximum rent adjustments:

	Renewal	Turnover
1-year lease	10.0 percent	25.0 percent
2-year lease	13.0 percent	28.0 percent
3-year lease	16.0 percent	31.0 percent

- The price index of operating costs for rent stabilized apartments has more than tripled since 1967, and between 1978 and 1981 alone, the price index rose by 38.6 percent.

- The fuel and utilities component of the price index has increased over 700 percent since 1967 and by 116 percent since 1978. The price of labor has more than doubled since 1967, and the combined charges for taxes, fees and permits rose 74 percent.

- The average operating and maintenance ratio for rent stabilized apartments rose from 55 to 70 percent between 1971 and 1981. This means that the fraction of the rent roll available to offset vacancy losses, pay debt service and provide for a return on investments has declined by 27 percent since 1971.

Population

- New York City had slightly more than 7 million inhabitants in 1980, a 10.4 percent decline since 1970.

- Due to declining household size, which at the average is just under 2.5 persons, the total number of households in New York City fell by less than 2 percent since 1970, to 2,788,000.

- The number of households in the Bronx declined by 14 percent and in Brooklyn by 6 percent. Household populations in all other boroughs grew: Manhattan by 2.5 percent, Queens by 3.2 percent, and Richmond by 32.9 percent.

- Since 1978, the size of the City's population in households, which excludes special places such as college dormitories, prisons and hospitals, declined by 1.1 percent. The number of White persons in households fell by 4 percent, Blacks by 1 percent and Puerto Ricans by around 5 percent. Alternatively, the size of the population in households classified as "other" which in New York City is predominantly Asian, grew by 28 percent.

- During the 1970s, New York City witnessed a continued net outmigration of the nonhispanic White population and a continued growth in minority populations. The former are estimated to have declined in number by 25 percent since 1970, while the Black population grew by 7 percent and the Hispanic population by 17 percent. In 1980 Whites accounted for 51 percent of the population, Blacks for 25 percent and Hispanics for 20 percent, and Others for 3 percent.

The Housing Market

- Since 1978, the size of new York City's total housing stock has scarcely changed.

- The proportion of homeowning households remained virtually constant at 27.8 percent. Owner occupancy rates vary substantially by borough, ranging from a low of 11.4 percent in Manhattan to a high of 63.6 percent in Richmond.

- More than one-fifth of all homeowners in New York City live in cooperatives or condominiums.

- Ownership rates also differ by race and ethnic origin. While 34 percent of all White households in New York City own their homes, 23.3 percent of all Black and just 8.6 percent of all Puerto Rican households do.

- Notwithstanding a slight decline in the total renter stock, the occupied rental inventory grew by 4,000 units between 1978 and 1981, and the number of available vacancies fell by 17,000 units.

- The size of the rent controlled inventory in 1981 was 286,000 units, a decline since 1978 of 29 percent. The stock of decontrolled apartments, which now stands at 282,000 units, has grown by 5 percent since 1978. There are nearly 64,000 more pre-'47 rent stabilized apartments in 1981, an 11.5 percent increase over 1978. Post-'47 rent stabilized apartments have declined by 7,000 units since 1978, or by 2.2 percent.

- As of the first quarter of 1981, controlled and decontrolled apartments each account for around 15 percent of all occupied rental units in the City. Pre-'47 stabilized apartments make up 31.8 percent of the total occupied stock, and post-'47 units make up 16.2 percent of the inventory.

- Old and New Law tenements continue to house many of the City's renters. There are still 185,000 occupied Old Law and 553,000 occupied New Law tenements in New York. The number of Old Law tenements has declined by over 1,000 units since 1978, while the inventory of New Law tenements dropped by 22,000 units. Most of the New Law losses were in the Bronx.

Vacancies

- There were 42,000 vacant available rental units in New York City as of the first quarter of 1981. This represents a reduction of 17,000 available vacant units since 1978, and explains why the net rental vacancy rate in New York City declined from 2.95 percent in 1978 to 2.13 percent in 1981.

- Though quite low throughout the City, the rental vacancy rate varies by borough and is the lowest in Manhattan at just 1.9 percent, and highest in Richmond at 2.6 percent. The 50 percent decline since 1978 in the net vacancy rate in the Bronx is not due to increased demand but to a sizable loss in the number of habitable vacancies there. The number of available nondilapidated vacancies in the Bronx fell by 10,000 units.

- The net vacancy rate also varies by asking rent, although the range across rent classes is quite narrow. Vacancy rates range from a low of less than 1 percent for apartments renting at less than $150 a month, to a high of 3.74 percent for apartments with asking rents of $1,000 or more.

- Net rental vacancy rates for decontrolled, pre- and post-'47 rent stabilized apartments each average between 1.9 and 2.4 percent.

- Not only is the vacancy rate down from what it was three years ago, but so are vacancy durations, i.e., the length of time vacant units have been on the market. Since 1978, the median vacancy duration has declined from 2.3 to 1.9 months. Vacancy durations are shortest in Queens where half of all available vacancies have been on the market for just one month, and are longest in Richmond where the median vacancy duration is 3.3 months.

- Vacant available apartments in New York City are likely to be located on streets on which there are boarded-up buildings. This is truer for decontrolled and pre-'47 stabilized vacancies than for post-'47 stabilized vacancies. Nearly half of all decontrolled and pre-'47 stabilized vacancies are near boarded-up buildings, compared to 24 percent of all post-'47 stabilized vacant apartments.

Housing Quality

- The number of occupied dilapidated apartments in New York City has increased by 17,000 since 1978, raising the dilapidation rate from around 3 to 4 percent of the occupied rental stock.

- Excluding public housing and "other" rental housing, fifty-five percent of all dilapidated housing is in the pre-'47 rent stabilized sector of the market, 17.6 percent is in the controlled and 20 percent is in the decontrolled sectors.

- The likelihood that a family will live in a dilapidated apartment varies by race and ethnic origin. Just 2.5 percent of all White renters live in dilapidated units, compared to 5.9 percent of all Black and 9.4 percent of all Puerto Rican households.

- Most dilapidated apartments were built before 1947 (73,000), but 6,000 were built after that date.

- Less serious than dilapidation, which involves the presence of one or more health-threatening conditions, is the problem posed by multiple maintenance deficiencies of a non-health-threatening nature. Far more New York City renters live in housing with three or more maintenance problems than occupy dilapidated housing, including:

  20.6 percent of all renters
  12.5 percent of all Whites
  34.5 percent of all Blacks
  38.1 percent of all Puerto Ricans
  15.6 percent of all single people
  24.9 percent of all female householders
  14.1 percent of all elderly householders.

- The problem of overcrowding (1.01 or more people per room) has remained constant since 1978 at 6.5 percent of all renters. Serious overcrowding (more than 1.5 persons per room) has also remained stable at less than 2 percent.

Rents

- The median gross rent for all apartments in New York City in 1981 was $265, an increase of 26.2 percent since 1978. Rent controlled apartments had a median rent of $213, while pre-'47 rent stabilized apartments had a median rent of $262. The three-year increase in controlled rents amounted to 30 percent, compared to a 25 percent increase for pre-'47 stabilized apartments.

- Despite these very substantial rent increases, the cost of living as measured by the Consumer Price Index rose at a rate of 32 percent, with the result that in real terms, rents declined over the last three years. In 1967 dollars the median gross rent in New York City in 1981 was $104.

Incomes

- The median household income in New York City in 1980 was $12,687, 22 percent higher than three years earlier. The median income of renters increased 23 percent to $11,001, while the median income for homeowners grew 31 percent to $20,333.

- The gap between the incomes of homeowners and renters has widened over the past three years. In 1977, renters had a median income 58 percent as high as owners. By 1980, it was just 54 percent as high.

- White and Black renter household incomes have grown at roughly the same rates since 1977, although Black incomes are still only 68 percent as high as White incomes. The median income for Puerto Rican households was less than $6,500 in 1980, an increase of just 10.5 percent since 1977. This is equal to 71 percent of the Black median and 48 percent of the White median income.

- The incomes of all racial and ethnic groups have declined in real terms since 1977, although Whites almost held their own, losing just 2 percent in purchasing power, and Blacks slipped a little further behind, losing nearly 4 percent to inflation. The biggest losers in the fight against inflation were Puerto Rican renters whose real incomes fell 14 percent in three years. In 1980, the median Puerto Rican household had the purchasing power of $2,723 in 1967 dollars.

- The incomes of older householders who have reached their 65th year are around half those of their younger counterparts ($6,037), and while indexing of Social Security benefits has helped them keep abreast of inflation, in absolute terms older households are more likely than others to be living at the economic margin of survival.

- The growth of household incomes in New York varied substantially by borough and was highest in Manhattan. Since 1977, the median income of renters in Manhattan grew by 27 percent, compared to just 8 percent in Richmond and 17 percent in both Queens and the Bronx. This means that Manhattan's renters more nearly held their own in the battle against inflation since 1977 than did residents of the other boroughs.

- In 1980 one out of every four renter households in New York City had an income below the official poverty level. This represents an increase of more than 12 percent in the incidence of poverty since 1977.

- The median rent-income ratio for all households in New York City was 28 percent, the same as in 1978. More than half of all renters now spend at least 25 percent of their incomes for rent, while 31 percent spend over 40 percent of their incomes on housing.

- Rent-income ratios do not differ much for Whites and Blacks, the former being 26 percent and the latter 29 percent. Due to their substantially lower incomes, however, Puerto Rican households have a much higher relative housing expense burden. The median rent-income ratio for Puerto Rican renters in 1981 was 36 percent.

- Households headed by women are much more likely to have high rent-income ratios than those headed by males. The median rent-income ratios for male households in 1981 was 24 percent, versus 35 percent for female households.

<u>Market Dynamics</u>

- The total housing inventory in New York City grew by 9,000 units between 1978 and 1981, compared to a net decline of 56,000 units between 1975 and 1978.

- Additions to the inventory through new construction, loft and other conversions, totaled 40,000 units since 1978.

- Gross losses to the inventory since 1978 totaled 81,000 housing units, which represents a lower rate of gross losses than in the 1970 to 1978 period. Of the 81,000 losses, nearly 9 percent were owner-occupied in 1978, 63 percent were renter-occupied and 17 percent were vacant available apartments.

- In addition to the above additions, 33,000 housing units which were classified as losses to the inventory in 1978 were back in the market supply by 1981. Most of these "returning losses" have come back into the rental inventory. Between 1975 and 1978, another 38,000 units which had previously been defined as losses also returned to the inventory.

- Returning losses represent a significant proportion of gross additions to the inventory. Between 1975 and 1978, returning losses equalled 84 percent of new construction. Between 1978 and 1981, returning losses exceeded the number of housing units added to the supply through new construction.

- When a rent controlled apartment is vacated and reoccupied, it is either decontrolled if it is in a building with fewer than six units, or becomes rent stabilized if it is in a larger building. The transition of an apartment from controlled to stabilized is accompanied by substantial changes in rent and occupancy characteristics. The median age of the household head declines by more than 20 years, and the likelihood that the new tenant will be Black or Hispanic and/or a recipient of public assistance increases.

In Rem Housing

- The City owns 33,816 occupied apartments that are in buildings taken for back taxes. Nearly 40 percent of this in rem stock is in the Bronx, one-third is in Manhattan and one-quarter is in Brooklyn. Queens contains less than 4 percent of the in rem stock, while Richmond has hardly any at all.

- Nearly 60 percent of all occupied in rem units are in New Law tenements and 23 percent are in Old Law buildings.

- The rate of dilapidation in the in rem stock is around four times higher than in the City as a whole (18 vs. 4 percent).

- More than 60 percent of all occupied in rem apartments are located on blocks with boarded-up buildings.

- In rem tenants are much more likely than New York City renters in general to be nonwhite or Hispanic: 54 percent of in rem households are Black, 24 percent are Puerto Rican, and only 19 percent are White.

- A larger proportion of in rem households are headed by women (57.9 percent) and include children (41.5 percent) than in the City as a whole.

- *In rem* households have a median income of $6,865, which is only 62 percent that of all renters.

- The median gross rent for *in rem* housing is $210, just $3 less than that for occupied rent controlled apartments.

- The median gross rent-income ratio is much higher for *in rem* tenants (36 percent) than it is for all renters in the City (28 percent) because of their lower incomes.

SUMMARY STATISTICS

CHAPTER 2. AN OVERVIEW OF RENT REGULATIONS IN NEW YORK CITY

Rent Increases, 1970-1981

Controlled (Maximum Allowable)	137.0
Stabilized (Average)	90.9

Maximum Rent Increases for Leases entered into between Oct. 1, 1981 - Sept. 30, 1982, for Rent Stabilized Apartments

	Renewal	Turnover
1 year lease	10.0%	25.0%
2 year lease	13.0	28.0
3 year lease	16.0	31.0

Price Index of Operating Costs for Rent Stabilized Apartments, 1967-1981
(1967 = 100) 305.7

Consumer Price Index for New York-Northeastern New Jersey, 1967-1981
(1967 = 100) 255.4

Percent Price Increases for Operating Cost Components of Rent Stabilized Units, 1967-1981

	1967-1981	1978-1981
Taxes, fees and permits	+ 74.2	- 0.5
Labor	+213.6	+ 27.7
Fuel & Utilities	+721.5	+116.2

Percent of Rent Devoted to Operating and Maintenance Costs for Rent Stabilized Units, 1971 and 1981

1971	55.0%
1981	70.0%

SUMMARY STATISTICS (All numbers in thousands)

CHAPTER 3: POPULATION

New York City	1970	1980	Percent Change
Population	7,895	7,071	-10.4
Households	2,837	2,788	- 1.7
Households by Borough			
Bronx	497	429	-13.7
Brooklyn	876	828	- 5.5
Manhattan	687	704	+ 2.5
Queens	690	712	+ 3.2
Richmond	86	115	+32.9
Racial and Ethnic Composition of Total Population*			
White	4,847	3,638	-24.9
Black	1,668	1,784	+ 7.0
Hispanic	1,202	1,406	+16.9
Other	178	243	+36.8

*Exhibit 3-1 explains how the 1980 population figures were derived.

SUMMARY STATISTICS (All numbers in thousands)

CHAPTER 4. HOUSING MARKET

	1978	1981	Percent Change
Total Housing Units	2,783	2,792	+ 0.3
Total Owner Units	735	755	+ 2.7
Occupied	727	746	+ 2.6
Vacant	8	9	+12.5
Total Renter Units	1,989	1,976	- 0.6
occupied	1,930	1,934	+ 0.2
vacant	59	42	-28.2
Vacant, Not Available	59	62	+ 3.9
Percent Owner-Occupied	27.4%	27.8%	
Percent Renter-Occupied	72.6%	72.2%	
Percent Owner by Borough			
Bronx	20.7%	21.3%	
Brooklyn	27.5%	27.4%	
Manhattan	10.2%	11.4%	
Queens	41.7%	42.2%	
Richmond	64.6%	63.6%	
Vacancy Rate			
Renter-occupied	2.95%	2.13%	
Owner-occupied	1.09%	1.14%	
Percent Owner by Race and Ethnic Origin			
All households	27.4%	27.8%	
White	34.6%	34.0%	
Black	22.1%	23.3%	
Puerto Rican	8.4%	8.6%	
Total Occupied Rental Housing Units	1,930	1,934	+ 0.2
Controlled	402	286	-29.0
Decontrolled	268	282	+ 5.2
Pre-'47 Stabilized	552	615	+11.5
Post-'47 Stabilized	320	313	- 2.2
% Rent Controlled	20.8%	14.8%	
% Decontrolled	13.9%	14.6%	
% Pre-'47 Stabilized	28.6%	31.8%	
% Post-'47 Stabilized	16.6%	16.2%	
Old Law tenements	186	185	- 0.8
New Law tenements	575	553	- 3.9
Post-'29 multiple dwelling units	712	717	+ 0.6

SUMMARY STATISTICS (All numbers in thousands)

CHAPTER 5. VACANCIES

	1978	1981	Percent Change
Vacant Units for Rent	59	42	-28.2
Vacant Units for Sale	8	9	+12.5
Number of Dilapidated Vacant Housing Units Not Available for Sale or Rent	14	16	+13.0
Net Rental Vacancy Rate	2.95%	2.13%	
Net Rental Vacancy Rate by Borough			
Bronx	5.18%	2.40%	
Brooklyn	3.07%	2.11%	
Manhattan	2.29%	1.90%	
Queens	1.88%	2.23%	
Richmond	2.57%	2.64%	
Net Vacancy Rate by Contract Rent			
Less than $150	2.19%	0.87%	
$150-$199	3.75%	2.10%	
$200-$299	2.58%	1.95%	
$300 or more	3.12%	2.02%	
Net Rental Vacancy Rate By Control Status			
All Stabilized	3.19%	2.27%	
Pre-'47 Stabilized	3.49%	2.22%	
Post-'47 Stabilized	2.32%	2.43%	
Decontrolled	3.17%	1.94%	
Median Duration of Vacancies by Borough (in months)			
New York City	2.3	1.9	-17.4
Bronx	1.7	2.3	-35.3
Brooklyn	2.4	1.9	-20.8
Manhattan	3.6	2.2	-38.9
Queens	2.6	1.0	-61.5
Richmond	1.7	3.3	+94.1
Percent of All Vacant Units Located on Streets with Boarded-up Buildings	44.7%	45.0%	
Decontrolled	43.6%	48.6%	
Pre-'47 Stabilized	54.9%	48.9%	
Post-'47 Stabilized	29.4%	23.8%	

SUMMARY STATISTICS (All numbers in thousands)

CHAPTER 6. HOUSING QUALITY

	1978	1981
Occupied Dilapidated Rental Units	62	79
Dilapidated Rental Units by Control Status		
Controlled	14	14
Decontrolled	11	16
Pre-'47 Stabilized	33	37
Post-'47 Stabilized	1	--
Dilapidated Rental Units by Age of Structure		
Pre-'47	60	73
1947-1959	2	4
1960-1969	--	1
1970-1977	--	1
Percent of Racial or Ethnic Group Who Occupy Dilapidated Housing		
White	1.2%	2.5%
Black	6.1%	5.9%
Puerto Rican	8.6%	9.4%
Percent of Occupied Units with Boarded-up Structures on Street		
Controlled	25.3%	20.4%
Decontrolled	28.3%	27.9%
Pre-'47 Stabilized	34.1%	30.8%
Post-'47 Stabilized	8.6%	8.4%
Maintenance Deficiencies		
1 or more deficiencies	53.7%	55.4%
3 or more deficiencies	17.8%	20.6%
Percent of Rental Units with 3 or more Maintenance Deficiencies by Borough		
Bronx	26.3%	26.8%
Brooklyn	18.5%	24.2%
Manhattan	18.6%	21.1%
Queens	9.3%	11.4%
Richmond	8.0%	9.4%
Percent in Housing with 3 or More Maintenance Deficiencies		
White	11.6%	12.5%
Black	30.9%	34.5%
Puerto Rican	30.2%	38.1%
Single Person	14.0%	15.6%
Female	21.6%	24.9%
Elderly	12.7%	14.1%

Chapter 6 (continued):

	1978	1981
Percent Overcrowded		
1.01 or more persons per room	6.5%	6.5%
1.51 or more persons per room	1.5%	1.7%

SUMMARY STATISTICS

CHAPTER 7. RENT LEVELS

	1978	1981	Percent Change
Median Gross Rents (Current Dollars)			
All Units	$210	$265	+26.2
Controlled	$164	$213	+29.9
Decontrolled	$222	$271	+22.1
Pre-'47 Stabilized	$209	$262	+25.4
Post-'47 Stabilized	$296	$368	+24.3
Consumer Price Index (1967 = 100)	192.2	253.9	+32.1
Real Median Gross Rents (1967 Dollars)			
All Units	$109	$104	- 4.6
Percent of Units with Gross Rents			
Less than $200	44.8%	25.5%	
$200-299	36.6%	37.6%	
$300 or more	18.6%	36.9%	
Median Gross Rents by Race and Ethnic Group:			
White	$223	$288	+29.1
Black	$192	$232	+20.8
Puerto Rican	$180	$225	+25.0

SUMMARY STATISTICS (All numbers in thousands)

CHAPTER 8. INCOMES

	1977	1980	Percent Change
Median Income (Current Dollars)			
All Households	$10	$13	+22.0
All Renters	$ 9	$11	+22.5
All Owners	$16	$20	+30.9
Median Income by Control Status			
Controlled	$ 7	$ 9	+21.5
Decontrolled	$ 9	$11	+32.4
Pre-'47 Stabilized	$ 8	$10	+26.0
Post-'47 Stabilized	$16	$19	+20.9
Median Renter Income By Race and Ethnic Origin			
White	$11	$13	+25.5
Black	$ 7	$ 9	+23.1
Puerto Rican	$ 6	$ 6	+10.5
Median Real Income (1967 Dollars)			
All Renters	$5	$5	- 4.2
White	$6	$6	- 1.9
Black	$4	$4	- 3.7
Puerto Rican	$3	$3	-13.6
Median Income by Borough (Current Dollars)			
Bronx	$ 7	$ 9	+17.2
Brooklyn	$ 8	$ 9	+21.9
Manhattan	$10	$13	+27.4
Queens	$11	$13	+17.4
Richmond	$11	$12	+ 7.7
Median Income by Age of Household Head (Current Dollars)			
Under 45	$10	$12	+20.0
45-64	$10	$12	+20.0
65 or more	$ 5	$ 6	+20.0
Median Income by Sex of Householder (Current Dollars)			
Male Head	$12	$15	+26.5
Female Head	$ 6	$ 7	+27.7

Chapter 8 (continued):

	1977	1980
Percent of New York City Renters		
Below 100% of the Poverty Level	22.5%	25.3%
Below 125% of the Poverty Level	32.1%	34.3%
Median Rent-Income Ratio		
All Renters	28.3%	28.0%
White	26.4%	26.3%
Black	30.5%	28.8%
Puerto Rican	36.3%	35.7%
Other	25.2%	28.0%
Male	23.5%	23.5%
Female	38.2%	35.1%
Percent of Households with Rent-Income Ratio		
In Excess of 25%	57.1%	56.7%
In Excess of 40%	31.7%	30.5%

SUMMARY STATISTICS

CHAPTER 9. HOUSING MARKET DYNAMICS

	1975-1978	1978-1981
	(numbers in thousands)	
Components of Inventory Change		
New Construction	+ 45	+28
Other Net Additions	+ 4	+12
Other Adjustments to the Inventory	- 8	+16
Gross Losses	-135	-81
Returning Losses	+ 38	+33
Percentage of Gross Losses Since 1978		
% Owner-Occupied in 1978	N.A.	8.7%
% Renter-Occupied	N.A.	63.2%
% Vacant For Rent	N.A.	17.0%
% Vacant For Sale	N.A.	0.8%
% Vacant, Unavailable	N.A.	10.3%

Longitudinal Analysis

	Controlled '78/ Controlled '81	Controlled '78/ Stabilized '81
Median Age of Male Head		
1978	61	57
1981	62	35
Percent White		
1978	79.2%	70.6%
1981	80.2%	55.0%
Percent Black		
1978	12.6%	12.7%
1981	12.0%	17.5%
Percent Puerto Rican		
1978	4.8%	10.4%
1981	4.8%	17.9%
Percent of Households Receiving Public Assistance		
1978	5.0%	7.2%
1981	4.0%	17.9%
Median Household Income		
1978	$7,529	$7,220
1981	$8,627	$10,440
Median Gross Rent		
1978	$167	$162
1981	$213	$265

SUMMARY STATISTICS (All numbers in thousands)

CHAPTER 10. THE SPECIAL PROBLEM OF IN REM HOUSING

	1981	Percent
Occupied *In Rem* Units	34	100.0%
Bronx	13	38.1%
Brooklyn	8	24.7%
Manhattan	11	33.5%
Queens	1	3.8%
Richmond*	--	--
Racial and Ethnic Origin of Household Head		
White	6	18.6
Black	17	53.5
Puerto Rican	8	24.1
Other	1	3.8
Median Household Income	$6,865	N.A.
Household Composition		
Single Person	11	34.4%
Female Headed	20	57.9%
Households with at Least One Child	14	41.5%
Households Receiving Public Assistance	--	29.7%
Households With Rent-Income Ratios Over 35%	--	51.2%
Structure Type		
Old Law	7	22.6%
New Law	18	57.7%
Post-'29 Multiple Dwellings	6	17.1%
Other Multiple Dwellings	--	0.7%
1- or 2-Family Houses	1	1.9%
Not Reported	1	--
Housing Condition		
Dilapidated	6	17.9%
Boarded-up Structure on Street	21	62.0%
Median Gross Rent	$210	

*See Chapter 10 for explanation.

CHAPTER 2

THE RENT REGULATION SYSTEM IN NEW YORK CITY

Federal, State and City Regulations

Rent control was one of many measures enacted by Congress to facilitate the rapid assembly of large civilian labor forces needed by the defense industry during the Second World War. By imposing a firm ceiling on rents, rent control not only dampened upward price pressures and speculation in the existing housing stock, but also had what was then considered the salutary effect of diverting the investment of capital from housing into productive sectors of the economy that were more closely allied with the war effort.[1] While the Emergency Price Control Act, which initally provided for wartime rent controls, was signed into law by President Franklin D. Roosevelt in January 1942, rent control was not administratively imposed on New York City until November 1943 (Exhibit 2-1).

As part of an anti-inflationary legislative program justified by wartime conditions, rent control was designed to be rigid, inflexible and restrictive. In New York's case, rents were rolled back to those in effect eight months before controls were imposed, with the explicit requirement that no diminution in housing services accompany the rollback.

After the war, the build-up in defense-related employment in major urban centers ended and the housing crisis worsened. Hundreds of thousands of families who migrated to the cities to work in the factories during the war remained there. "In Los Angeles for example, fewer than 15 percent of the 782,000 war workers left the city."[2] The combination of minimal residential construction during the war, migration of worker households to the cities and the return of veterans to their communities resulted in housing shortages of an extraordinary nature. "Throughout the nation many veterans and their families lived in attics, basements, chicken coops and boxcars. ...In Atlanta, 2,000 persons answered one advertisement of a vacancy, and a want ad in an Omaha newspaper read 'Big Ice Box, 7 by 17 feet. Could be fixed up to live in.'"[3]

Although the continuation of rent controls on existing housing could be justified due to the extreme shortage that persisted across the country, national policy began to encourage new construction. In October 1945, all wartime controls on the use of building materials were repealed. To discourage the building industry from emphasizing nonresidential construction and luxury housing which offered the greatest profit opportunities, President Truman placed a $10,000 ceiling on all new homes and ordered the Office of War Mobilization and Reconversion to channel no less than 50 percent of all construction materials into housing. In 1945, Truman also created the Office of Housing Expediter to direct a crash program to expand the housing supply.[4] As part of the series of moves to mobilize the nation's productive resources to alleviate the housing crisis, Congress enacted the Federal Housing and Rent Act of 1947 which exempted apartment units built after

February of that year from all forms of rent control.[5] Thus originates the distinction in New York City of pre- and post-1947 rental housing. Under the new law, pre-1947 apartments would be subject to continued controls; new apartments would have totally unregulated rents, and for the first time, procedures were established for decontrolling rents. However, decontrol procedures applied almost entirely to one-and two-family rental units.

With normalization of the national economy, federally administered rent control programs became less necessary and defensible. With the need for continued restraints on rents varying from community to community, the federal government passed on to state and local governments the prerogative to continue, eliminate, or modify the wartime system of rent control. Noting that market conditions continued to be abnormally tight and vigilance was needed "to prevent 'speculative, unwarranted and abnormal increases' in rents and evictions of tenants during a period of housing 'emergency'," the New York State Legislature established the Temporary State Housing Rent Commission in 1950 to oversee the systems of rent control in New York communities which saw fit to continue their programs.[6]

The extension of rent control in New York City was intended to be a temporary measure justified by continuing housing shortages related to emergency wartime conditions. Increases in supply through the normal workings of the market were expected to ease price pressures and allow the elimination of controls. "For this reason, a vacancy rate of 5 percent was established in the legislation as the criterion for the restoration of a normal supply-demand relationship in the housing market. Anything short of a 5 percent vacancy rate would be <u>prima facie</u> evidence of a continued 'housing shortage'."[7] Further underlining the temporary nature of the State's continued commitment to rent control, incoming-Governor Averell Harriman noted in 1955 that "rent ceilings do not bring roofs overhead. Rent control must be viewed as only a single aspect of a broader housing program and as an interim device until such time as an adequate housing supply makes it no longer necessary."[8]

New York was the only state in the country still administering a rent control program by the end of the 1950s. With growing political conflict between the City and the State over the continuation of controls, the legislature enacted the Emergency Housing Act of 1962, which passed on to the City all responsibilities for administering rent control.[9] That responsibility is presently carried out by the Rent Control Division of the New York City Department of Housing Preservation and Development. Under City Administration, post-'47 buildings continued to be free of any form of rent regulation until 1969, when the rent stabilization program came into being.* While imposition of stabilization on a previously uncontrolled sector of the rental market was criticized by industry representatives as a "shabby betrayal of trust," and blamed for the "virtual cessation of private new rental construction"[10] in New York, City officials justified their actions on

---

*Rents in post-'47 buildings of six or more units were initially exempt from controls by the 1947 Federal Housing and Rent Act. Rent stabilization not only brought these units under a modified form of control but also reinstated controls on rents in decontrolled pre-'47 buildings of six or more units.

EXHIBIT 2-1. CHRONOLOGY OF NEW YORK CITY'S RENT REGULATION SYSTEM

1942 President Franklin D. Roosevelt signed the Emergency Price Control Act, the enabling legislation establishing wartime rent controls.

1943 Rent control administratively imposed in New York City.

1947 Federal Housing and Rent Act of 1947 exempted apartments built after February 1947 from national rent control.

1950 New York State legislature passed the Emergency Housing Act of 1950 which established the Temporary Rent Commission to oversee New York City's rent control system.

1962 The Emergency Housing Act of 1962 gave New York City the responsibility of administering its rent control system.

1969 Rent stabilization program begun. Rents in post-'47 buildings and previously decontrolled units in buildings of six or more units were brought under rent stabilization, a modified form of rent control. The Rent Guidelines Board, Rent Stabilization Association and the Conciliation and Appeals Board were established to administer rent stabilization.

1970 New York City Local Law 30 was enacted, creating the Maximum Base Rent system and introducing the concept of economic rent to the City's rent controlled stock.

1971 The Vacancy Decontrol Law of 1971 was adopted providing for the decontrol of all controlled and stabilized units after a change in tenancy.

1974 The Emergency Tenant Protection Act terminated vacancy decontrol for rent stabilized apartments and required that vacated rent controlled units in buildings of six or more units come under rent stabilization after a free market rent (subject to tenant challenge as excessive) is negotiated with the new tenant.

1981 Emergency Tenant Protection Act extended until 1983.

the basis of what they deemed to be unconscionable increases in rents by owners of post-'47 buildings which landlords could not justify on the basis of cost and which their tenants could not afford.[11]

"Unlike the wholly government operated rent control statutes and regulations, the rent stabilization system combines industry self-regulation with supervision and control by both governmental and public bodies."[12] Three agencies were created to share administrative responsibilities under rent stabilization. The Rent Guidelines Board, composed of nine members appointed by the Mayor to represent tenants (2), owners (2) and the general public (5), establishes maximum rates for rent increases for lease renewals and new leases following vacancies. The City's housing agency, the Department of Housing Preservation and Development (HPD), oversees the system.

The Rent Stabilization Association (RSA) is an organization which all owners of apartments subject to the stabilization law are required to join.* It has three major responsibilities: enrolling building owners into the organization, drafting a code regulating the conduct of its membership consistent with the law, and levying and collecting sufficient dues to pay the costs of administering a substantial portion of the rent stabilization system.

The Conciliation and Appeals Board (CAB), the third party sharing rent stabilization responsibilities, was designed to be an independent public agency to enforce the law. Its operating budget is supported by the RSA. The CAB hears and resolves landlord and tenant disputes arising under the law. While orders of the nine-member CAB (four tenants, four owners, and an impartial chairman) are final and binding on all participants, they are subject to judicial review.

Annual rent increase orders of the Rent Guidelines Board rely heavily on estimates of changes in operating costs in rent stabilized buildings. These estimates are based on annual surveys prepared for the City by the U.S. Bureau of Labor Statistics.[13] Despite these surveys, however, there continues to be substantial disagreement between owners of stabilized buildings and the Guidelines Board, and between the Board and tenant organizations, over whether the Board relies too little or too much on the Bureau of Labor Statistics data and how much beyond the maintenance and operating cost area the Board should go in determining its annual rent decisions. One of several areas of disagreement with the Board's current procedures concerns its estimates of two- and three-year inflation rates. Such rates are necessary components of the Board's multiyear-lease rent increase orders. In the Guidelines Board's own words, "forecasting price changes is not an exact science."[14]

The intent of the stabilization system is to regulate rather than to rigidly control rents. It is somewhat representative of the new generation of moderate rent regulations which many cities have enacted recently to attempt to balance the interests of both parties to the lease. Stabilization

---

*If owners do not join RSA, the law stipulates that their properties will come under rent control.

is designed to permit property owners to earn reasonable returns on their equity investments. Whether it operates in fact as it is designed to in theory is a matter of continuing analysis and debate.

Another major piece of legislation was enacted at approximately the same time as rent stabilization. Local Law 30, of 1970, created the maximum Base Rent (MBR) system and represented the first major reform of the rent control program since 1950.[15] The MBR system is designed to eliminate the so-called rent gap, which was estimated in 1970 at $274 million a year, and to permit property owners, once rents cover operating costs, to keep up with costs over the longer term.[16] "By allowing landlords to receive sufficient revenues to maintain their buildings and by granting rent increases contingent upon maintaining acceptable housing quality, the new rent control legislation is designed both to encourage new investment in the controlled stock and to prevent further deterioration."[17] The MBR system centers around a formula for computing Maximum Base Rents for each rent controlled building. The MBR for each apartment is intended to approximate the actual rent that would be required to operate the unit under prevailing cost conditions, including generation of enough cash to return 8.5 percent of the equalized assessed value of the building. For apartments in buildings with no major outstanding code violations, in which all essential services are being provided and where landlords are investing appropriate amounts of money for operations and proper maintanence, rents are permitted to rise 7.5 percent a year until the MBR is reached. Under the original MBR law, new tenants would be charged the full MBR for the particular unit. However, vacancy decontrol was implemented before the MBR system had a chance to operate on vacancies.*

While the City was struggling to reform rent control through implementation of the MBR system, the State once again intervened by enacting the Vacancy Decontrol Law of 1971. Vacancy decontrol partially negated the need for the MBR system by providing for the decontrol of all controlled and stabilized apartments upon a turnover in tenancy. Thus, for the first time since stabilization began in 1969, the rents in a large and growing portion of the inventory would once again be permitted to rise to free market levels.

Just as steeply rising rents and substantial increases in evictions immediately preceded the enactment of the rent stabilization law in 1969, a similar rise in rents among decontrolled and destabilized units led directly to the New York State Emergency Tenant Protection Act of 1974 (ETPA). ETPA modified the concept of vacancy decontrol. Immediately after a free market rent was negotiated for a vacated apartment in a previously-controlled building of six or more units, said apartment would come under rent stabilization. Vacancy decontrol was terminated altogether for rent stabilized apartments in buildings with less than six units.[18] In 1981 the New York State legislature extended ETPA until 1983.

---

*The MBR system is to be distinguished from rent stabilization, in that the latter is not intended to close a rent gap, but to make sure that none arises by permitting landlords to charge economic rents.

EXHIBIT 2-2. TYPICAL SEQUENCES OF CONTROL STATUS CHANGES FOR SELECTED APARTMENTS

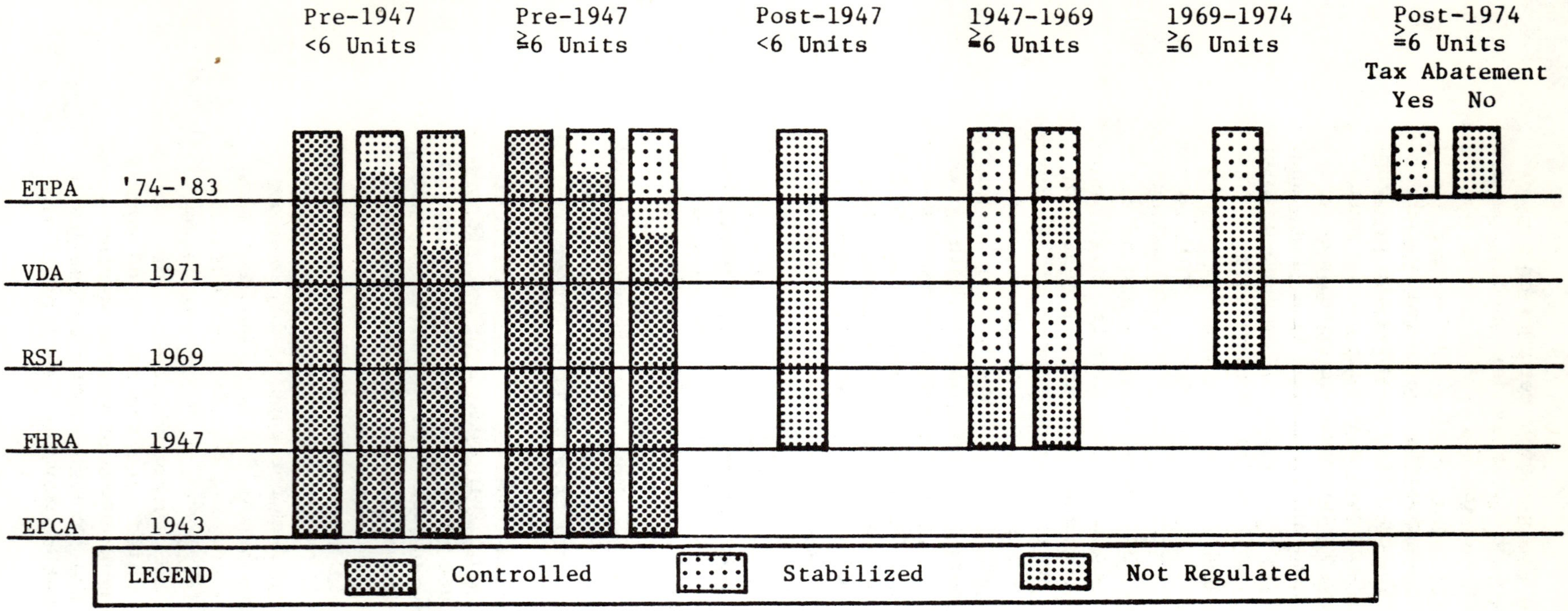

NOTES: 1. The abbreviations used above represent the following:

ETPA: Emergency Tenant Protection Act
VDA: Vacancy Decontrol Act
RSL: Rent Stabilization Law
FHRA: Federal Housing and Rent Act
EPCA: Emergency Price Control Act

2. This chart does not apply to public housing, state or city assisted apartments, apartments receiving special tax benefits, or apartments receiving City rehabilitation loans.

3. The chart outlines only the most common control status changes. Control status can also change under the following circumstances:

- High-rent apartments may have been decontrolled under rent regulations, for example, under luxury decontrol.
- Apartments in *in rem* buildings have their control status suspended.
- Stabilized apartments can become controlled if the owner is expelled by the CAB for cause, or by the RSA for non-payment of dues.

4. The control status changes shown above generally occur upon a vacancy. Several exceptions to this are:

- Apartments in buildings with six or more units which were decontrolled between 1971 and 1974 came back under rent regulation in 1974 with the enactment of the Emergency Tenant Protection Act.
- Apartments in buildings with six or more units which were built between 1947 and 1969 came under rent regulation in 1969 with the enactment of the Rent Stabilization Law.
- Apartments included in the categories listed in Note 3.

The following rent regulation system is now in place in New York City (see Exhibit 2-2): All pre-'47 apartments whose tenants were in occupancy prior to July 1, 1971, continue to be subject to rent control and the MBR system. All previously controlled and stabilized apartments which saw a turnover in occupancy between 1971 and 1974 were brought up to the then-market levels and entered the stabilization system. All stabilized units in which tenants have been in continuous occupancy since before July 1, 1971, or which have become vacant for the first time since 1974 remain under stabilization without having their rents brought up to market levels through vacancy decontrol. ETPA also provided that all apartments in buildings with less than six units which were subject to vacancy decontrol will remain permanently decontrolled rather than coming under stabilization. All rent stabilized apartments, both pre- and post-'47, are therefore in buildings with six or more units. Finally, the rents in privately-built structures constructed subsequent to the enactment of ETPA in 1974 remain totally unregulated unless they receive the benefit of some form of public subsidy, particularly real estate tax abatements or exemptions. Such buildings are subject to rent stabilization.

From the foregoing description, it can be seen that New York's system of rent regulation is complex, multidimensional, and dynamic. Under the current rent regulatory system, the size and composition of the City's inventory subject to each type of rent regulation will change each year. Since a modified form of decontrol remains in effect, the size of the controlled stock will continue to shrink as turnover in small buildings swells the permanently decontrolled stock and tenant turnover in larger buildings increases the size of the rent stabilized sector. Vacancy decontrol also means that some apartments in pre-'47 buildings will be subject to stabilization while others will continue to be subject to rent control. New and rehabilitated buildings which receive public subsidy in the form of tax benefits will add to the stabilized stock, while any new buildings built entirely without public assistance will increase the size of the never-regulated inventory.

Rent Control and Rental Housing Investment

The economic literature is full of complex theoretical and empirical analyses of how rent control distorts resource allocation decisions and market choices, encourages overconsumption because of below-market pricing, discourages new supply, and fosters undermaintenance and even the abandonment of physically adequate housing.[19] To better understand these arguments, it is helpful to review some fundamentals of rental housing investment.

There are four basic sources of profit in rental housing: net rental income; developer's fees; tax shelter benefits associated with depreciation allowances that exceed the decline in real value; and capital appreciation. The latter can be realized either through sale of the property -- the net proceeds of which are taxed at lower rates than ordinary income -- or through refinancing an existing mortgage, in which case the recovered equity is not taxed. The relative importance of these sources of profit varies according to the type, size and location of the structure, the income group it serves, the relative vitality of that market sector, and applicable tax regulations.

In federally assisted low-income housing projects the principal source of profit is the tax shelter from generous depreciation allowances. Development fees, which substitute for equity contributions, and high loan-to-value mortgages also attract private investment interest.[20] However, in order to attract equity capital into assisted housing, the above benefits must be large enough to offset fixed or regulated rent levels, restricted cash flows, and the limits on the possibilities of real capital growth.

Conversely, capital gains have traditionally been an important source of overall net investment returns in growing urban and suburban rental housing markets. In weak and deteriorating markets, though, particularly those serving low-income families, current rental income tends to determine the return on private investment. It is not uncommon in some inner city markets to find properties trading on a cash basis for as little as two and three times their annual rent rolls, compared to a multiplier of six or more for properties with secure, long term incomes. [21]

In real estate markets that function in reasonable accord with the principles of competition, individual investors can exert little influence on prevailing levels of market rents or on future capital values. They must accept the rent structure as given, project future market values as best they can and develop their operating, maintenance and improvement policies to maximize their overall investment returns, including net gains from sale. In vigorous markets where the outlook for long-term capital gains is positive, it may be economically prudent for investors to absorb inflationary increases in operating and maintenance costs without reducing their building services, even though market conditions might not support higher rents over the intermediate term. Any reductions in cash flow may be compensated for by rising capital values, which would be jeopardized by undermaintenance. On the other hand, where capital values are either not expected to rise or are expected to decline, investors would be less willing to hold services constant in the face of rising costs for fear of suffering irrecoverable losses in current income. Cutbacks in building services would be likely to occur where demand does not permit landlords to pass along the inflationary cost increases in the form of higher rents.[22] Indeed, where capital values are falling, net income from current operations would have to increase for net investment returns to just hold their own over the longer term.

Many of the theoretical arguments about the negative effects of rent control can be illustrated using these simple investment relationships. Some critics argue, for example, that rent control discourages new capital investment because, even if new construction is exempted from controls, investors fear that their buildings will be brought under controls at some later date, with the result that controlled rents will narrow future profit margins and lessen the possibilities of capital growth.[23] With respect to the existing stock, insufficient rent increases, particularly during periods of high inflation, cause current operating margins to narrow or disappear entirely, and cause capital values to decline and investor equity to erode where long-run opportunities for improved cash flow are not good. Finally, according to the argument, if investors seeking to recover as much of their sunk capital as possible from their properties have no other way out of their income-operating cost squeeze than to reduce building services, operating problems will eventually increase to the point where occupancy levels decline, income falls even more and the owner abandons the building.

According to some analysts, the process whereby rent control leads to abandonment sometimes includes a phase in which landlords virtually cease to screen their potential tenants, and pack their buildings with welfare families whose publicly supported rents, though fixed, are frequently higher than those which unsubsidized families are either willing or able to pay for housing in certain neighborhoods.[24] Here, abandonment is the end result of capital recovery through undermaintenance in which welfare rents are collected while building services are severely curtailed.[25]

In reality, of course, it is very difficult to untangle the cause and effects of complex housing market relationships. The demographic shifts in New York City since 1970, such as White flight and the increase of minority populations in many neighborhoods, combined with declining incomes, steep increases in operating costs for rental housing and an aging rental housing stock, make it even harder to separate the effects of rent regulations from demographic and social changes. A further complication is the diversity of regulation in New York today. In the past, when the City's rent regulation was rigid and insensitive to operating cost changes, documenting the independent effect of rent control was somewhat easier.

Not surprisingly, critics and supporters of rent control reach different conclusions about these effects. Longstanding critics of rent control, such as Frank Kristof, continue to argue that even moderate regulations have the adverse side-effect of discouraging both new supply and building maintenance.[26] On the other hand, supporters like John Gilderbloom suggest that, unlike earlier more rigid forms, "there is no empirical evidence that [moderate] rent control causes a decline in the quality or quantity of the housing stock."[27] However, it is not totally clear to what extent New York's hybrid system qualifies as "moderate" in Gilderbloom's terms.

<u>The Determination of Rent Increases</u>

When debating the continuation or modification of rent control and stabilization, it is important to know by how much and under what conditions landlords may increase rents. Unfortunately, a simple explanation of how rents are determined in New York City is impossible because the overlapping systems of regulation frequently apply different rules to different apartments in the same building, and establish different rent adjustments for new as opposed to renewal leases, and for leases of different terms. These rules are contained in the major rent adjustment decisions that have been made by the rent regulatory agencies over the last several years. In the following section the legal and administrative rulings which authorized those adjustments are described, and later chapters will discuss changes in actual rents since 1981, based on Housing and Vacancy Survey data.

<u>Recent Increases for Rent Controlled Apartments</u>. The analysis begins with apartments still under rent control. As already indicated, the maximum legal rent to which a controlled apartment is permitted to rise is its Maximum Base Rent (MBR). In eligible buildings, rents may be raised a maximum of 7.5 percent a year up to the MBR, and once that is reached no further increases are allowed until the legal MBR is raised. Once every two years the New York City Rent Control Division determines the maximum allowable rent increases to individual MBRs, based on estimated changes in operating costs. If the allowed MBR increase exceeds 7.5 percent, rents may be raised 7.5

percent in the first year, with the balance permitted in the second year, provided that it does not exceed 7.5 percent.

The MBR increase for 1978-79 was 9 percent. While precise data are not available, the Rent Control Division estimates that around two-thirds of the controlled stock qualified for the increase.[28] For the period 1980-81, MBRs were increased by another 10 percent. Although little is known about the rent controlled units not approved for MBR increases, they are likely to be either in older buildings with code violations that render them ineligible for the increase, or scattered in buildings that are predominantly rent stabilized, in which case it is scarcely worth the owners' time and expense to file for the MBR increase.

The maximum permissible rent increases for rent controlled buildings vary according to the past rental history of the building. Apartments already at their respective MBR limit before 1978, and still in the controlled inventory through 1981, could have rents raised by around 20 percent over the period. For the controlled inventory not at MBR at any time during these three years, rents have been allowed to rise by 34 percent.* Controlled units that have been vacated are subject to the modified decontrol program established by the Emergency Tenant Protection Act of 1974. Upon vacancy, if in a building of six or more units, they become part of the stabilized stock and their rents are raised to fair market levels.** The actual rent increases for these so-called vacancy leases are determined annually by the Conciliation and Appeals Board (CAB) based on the recommendations of the Rent Guidelines Board, and are subject to tenant appeals. The Rent Control Division estimates that less than one in four controlled units now rent at MBR.[29]

In addition to the biennial adjustments in MBRs and the rent increases permitted upon vacancy, the City began a fuel adjustment program in 1980 designed to distribute increased fuel costs between tenants and landlords. Under the program, up to 75 percent of the increased cost of heating fuel has been passed on to tenants in the form of higher rents. In 1980, 236,051 rent controlled units received fuel-cost adjustment rent increases averaging $12.06 per month, or $145 per year. At the median controlled rent, this amounts to an additional rent increase of 5.7 percent per year. By October 1981, 173,440 controlled units had been granted fuel cost rent adjustments averaging $4.18 per month for the first nine months of the year.[30]

---

*	12/31/77	100 (= MBR)	100 (below MBR)
	1/1/78	+ 7.5%	+ 7.5%
	1/1/79	+ 1.395%	+ 7.5%
	1/1/80	+ 7.5%	+ 7.5%
	1/1/81	+ 2.325%	+ 7.5%
	Total	+19.9%	+33.5%

**The Conciliation and Appeals Board will, upon appeal from a new tenant, determine a fair market rent for vacated controlled units based on the average of a specified percentage above MBR (for 1981-1982 this is 20 percent), a guideline set by the Guidelines Board, and a comparable rent for the unit.

Another way to summarize the rent effects of the Maximum Base Rent system is to develop a rent index, with the base period being July 1970, the month preceding implementation of MBR. Assuming that an apartment has remained in the rent control inventory since the MBR system began, which means that the same tenant has lived there for 11 years, and that the owner has qualified for all five MBR increases approved over the period, the approved rent would have increased by 137 percent between July 1, 1970 and January 1, 1981. If fuel pass-alongs are included, the approved rent would have increased by 153 percent (Table 2-1). The index shows a 33 percent increase in rents for the period January 1978 to January 1981, including fuel adjustments. This is equivalent to a 10 percent increase per year, compounded, compared to the pre-MBR rent control program where rent increases for apartments under continued occupancy were averaging about 2 percent a year.[31]

The assumption that all five MBR increases were approved for any controlled apartment is reflected in all these data and must be kept in mind when interpreting them. Disapproval of any of these increases would, of course, result in lower rates of increase over the period. If an apartment was approved for four out of the five MBR increases, maximum rents would have increased by 121 percent over the 10 year period, including fuel cost adjustments. If two MBR increases were missed, the overall rent increase would have been around 94 percent, while failure to receive any of the five MBR increases leads to a 10 year rent rise of just 30 percent, including fuel pass-throughs.[32]

Rent Increases for Rent Stabilized Apartments*

Unlike the rent control program, rent increases for apartments under rent stabilization are determined by the Rent Guidelines Board and are issued in a series of annual rent orders. The Rent Stabilization Law requires the Guidelines Board to consider the economic conditions of the residential real estate industry, prevailing and projected real estate tax rates, operating, maintenance and labor costs, costs and availability of mortgage financing, the annual supply of housing accommodations, and vacancy rates. In preparing its orders, the Board issues separate rent increase allowances for one-, two-, and three-year renewal leases with existing tenants and for vacancy leases with new tenants. The vacancy lease allowance is added to renewal lease increase allowances. Over the past few years, the vacancy lease increases have become progressively larger as the Guidelines Board has attempted to shift more of the burden of compensating landlords for rising operating costs from resident tenants to new ones. The vacancy lease allowance, which was 5 percent more than the increases permitted for renewal leases entered into in mid-1979, rose to 15 percent for leases entered into in late 1981.

The net effects of the different increases permitted each year under rent stabilization can be summarized through a weighted average rent index which takes account of factors such as the mix of lease terms in effect and

*The rent stabilization system also applies to certain classes of apartment hotels and rooming houses. These dwelling units are subject to different rent guidelines and are members of the Metropolitan Hotel Industry Stabilization Association (METHISA) and not the RSA.

the extent of tenant turnover. The Guidelines Board publishes such data for each year that the stabilization program has been in effect (Table 2-2). Assuming that the weighted average rent increases computed annually by the Board reflect the actual mix of new leases signed between 1971 and 1981, the

TABLE 2-1. SCHEDULE OF MAXIMUM ALLOWABLE RENT INCREASES FOR RENT CONTROLLED APARTMENTS, NEW YORK CITY, 1970-1981

Date	Rent Increase	Rent Index
7/31/70	--	100
8/1/70	15.0%*	115
1/1/72	7.5%**	123.63
1/1/73	7.5%	132.90
1/1/74	7.5%	142.86
1/1/75	7.5%***	153.58
1/1/76	7.5%	165.10
1/1/77	7.5%	177.48
1/1/78	7.5%	190.79
1/1/79	7.5%	205.10
1/1/80	7.5%	220.48
1/1/81	7.5%	237.02
7/1/80†	$12.06	
1/1/81††	$4.18	

*Represents the first year increase allowed under the MBR law. Provisions: a 15 percent increase is authorized if no 15 percent increase -- i.e., vacancy increase -- has been authorized since 1953. If one 15 percent increase had occurred an 8 percent raise was allowed, but if two or more 15 percent increases had taken place none was allowed. Furthermore, if the 7/31/70 rent was below $60, the increase for 4 or more rooms was $15 and for 1-3 rooms $10.

**Represents the annual percent MBR increase. Assumes that in each year the full 7.5 percent can be collected because the MBR had not been met.

***A temporary one-year fuel surcharge collectible for the period 7/1/75 to 6/30/76 is not shown. The increase was limited to $2 per room with a maximum of $9 per apartment per month.

†The $12.06 represents the average fuel cost adjustment for 1980 which became collectible on 7/1/80 retroactive to 1/1/80. The actual increase varies according to type of fuel used and amount consumed; fuel adjustments are not compounded by MBR.

††The $4.18 is the average fuel cost adjustment for 1981 collectible as of 1/1/81. A total of $16.24 is the total average fuel cost adjustment in 1981. Fuel adjustments are computed on an average of 3.4 rooms per apartment.

SOURCE: Rent Control Division, New York City Department of Housing Preservation and Development, October 1981.

the average rent in a stabilized apartment has been permitted to increase by 91 percent(Exhibit 2-3).* More importantly, perhaps, for the three years between 1978 and 1981, the Guidelines Board has let the average stabilized rent increase by one-third. The Guidelines Board instituted a fuel adjustment program for stabilized apartments prior to the institution of such a program for the controlled stock.**

On June 25, 1981, the Rent Guidelines Board approved a schedule for maximum permissible rent increases in vacant stabilized apartments, for lease renewals, and for controlled units which were vacated after October 1, 1981 (Table 2-3). For stabilized apartments, leases are renewed, rents may be increased by 10 percent if the renewal is for one year, by 13 percent for two years, and by 16 percent for three-year renewals. Maximum permissible increases are scaled up from this base schedule if electricity is included in the rent and are adjusted downward if the tenant pays for heating fuel.*†

Where there is a turnover in the occupancy of a stabilized apartment, the new rent may be increased by an additional 15 percent above the renewal guidelines. The Guidelines Board approved the large vacancy allowance as a "means of compensating for the drastic rise in mortgage financing costs ...," and chose the vacancy allowance over the usual rent guidelines increase route to "... minimize the burden on tenants in occupancy."[33] Thus, a new one-year lease for a stabilized unit may be as much as 25 percent more than it was before the last vacancy occurred, while new two- and three-year leases will produce immediate rent increases as high as 28 percent and 31 percent respectively.

While the stabilization and MBR rent indices presented above are not wholly compatible because the former depicts average, and the latter reflects maximum, rent increases, neither program now in effect in New York City is similar to the wartime program that introduced rent regulation. Though operating within very different frameworks, both the MBR and rent stabilization systems provide for periodic increases in maximum rent ceilings that are tied to changes in operating costs. Whether these increases have been large enough to offset the full effects of inflation and to preserve the real value of rental housing capital remains an open ques-

---

*See Appendix A-1 for an updated analysis of actual mix of lease terms in effect in 1981.

**The first fuel adjustment, a 2.5 percent, 2.0 percent and 0.5 percent addition to 1-, 2- and 3-year leases respectively, became effective in March 1979 for new leases entered into in the year beginning July 1, 1978. Effective January 1, 1980, an additional $12 a month was ordered for these leases, reduced to $8 a month in July 1980. A fuel adjustment of $8 per month per apartment was added to all leases signed between January 1, 1979 and June 30, 1980 to take effect upon the first anniversary of the lease. These adjustments were and are temporary and expire with the lease.

*† Where electricity is included in rent, maximum increases are 14 percent for one-year renewals, 17 percent for 2-year and 20 percent for 3-year renewals. If the tenant pays for fuel, the schedule is 6.5 percent, 9.5 percent, 12.5 percent for 1-, 2- and 3-year lease renewals.

tion. To help shed further light on this issue, the following section analyzes recent operating cost experiences in the New York City rental housing market.

Operating Costs in the Rent Stabilized Stock

This section concentrates on operating costs to help understand whether the City's present rent regulation system contributes to a cost-revenue squeeze that reportedly plagues the rental housing industry in New York. To do this, it is useful to examine the rate at which operating costs for rent stabilized apartments in New York City have changed over the past 15 years, the magnitude of changes in particular components of cost and the effects of these changes on operating expense ratios for pre- and post-'47 stabilized apartments. The primary source of data for this analysis has been the annual survey of price changes for operating costs in post-'47 rent stabilized apartments the Bureau of Labor Statistics (BLS) carried out for New York City.[34]

The BLS Index of Operating Costs. Every year the BLS survey prices the same quantity and quality of a variety of goods and services which, together with taxes and fees, span the full range of operating expenditures for rental housing. By repeating the same survey each year, the BLS can determine the rate at which overall operating costs and individual cost components for post-'47 buildings change from year to year. By converting current prices into 1967 dollars and setting the price index for that year at 100, it is possible to determine how operating conditions have changed.

The BLS price index of operating costs for post-'47 rent stabilized apartments has more than tripled since 1967 (Table 2-4). Another way of interpreting a price index change is in terms of changes in purchasing power. Thus, a given market basket of rental housing components that would have cost a landlord $100 to purchase in 1967 would cost more than $300 today. This is to be compared to an overall increase in the cost of living in New York of 156 percent.

Year-to-year increases in the price index reached double digits four times between 1967 and 1981. The highest single-year increase occurred around the time of the Arab oil embargo in 1973-1974, when the operating cost index soared 19 percent. The remaining three peaks, each in the 13 percent range, occurred in the periods 1970-71, 1979-80 and 1980-81. The lowest single-year increase recorded by BLS was in 1977-78, when the index inched up just .5 percent. After this brief respite, however, the overall price of operating costs rose 39 percent between 1978 and 1981.

In 1967, the base year, the largest single operating cost component was real estate taxes. Together with related fees, these accounted for 46 percent of the operating and maintenance items priced by BLS (Table 2-5). Direct labor costs were a distant second at 16 percent, while fuel and utilities costs were third at 13 percent. The relative importance of the individual components has changed considerably. Increasingly, energy-related costs dominate the operating cost index. From a low of 13 percent of the typical operating and maintenance budget in 1967, the price of fuel and utilities has increased steadily to nearly 25 percent of the cost of the BLS market basket in 1974, 26 percent in 1979 and 36 percent in 1981. While 46

TABLE 2-2: PERMITTED RENT INCREASES FOR RENT STABILIZED BUILDINGS NEW YORK CITY, 1971-1981

Period	Percentage Rent Increase	Rent Index
7/1/70-6/30/71	--	100.00
7/1/71-6/30/72	5.4	105.40
7/1/72-6/30/73	5.4	111.09
7/1/73-6/30/74	5.6	117.36
7/1/74-6/30/75	5.6	123.96
7/1/75-6/30/76	5.3	130.57
7/1/76-6/30/77	5.5	137.74
7/1/77-6/30/78	4.2	143.57
7/1/78-6/30/79	7.7	154.67
7/1/79-6/30/80	10.3	170.57
7/1/80-9/30/81	11.9	190.92

SOURCE: Table XVI Explanatory Statement and Findings of the Rent Guidelines Board in Relation to 1981-82 Lease Increase Allowances for Apartments Under the Jurisdiction of the Rent Stabilization Law, July 31, 1981, p. 17.

EXHIBIT 2-3. PERMITTED RENT INCREASES IN RENT CONTROLLED AND RENT STABILIZED APARTMENTS, NEW YORK CITY, 1970-1981

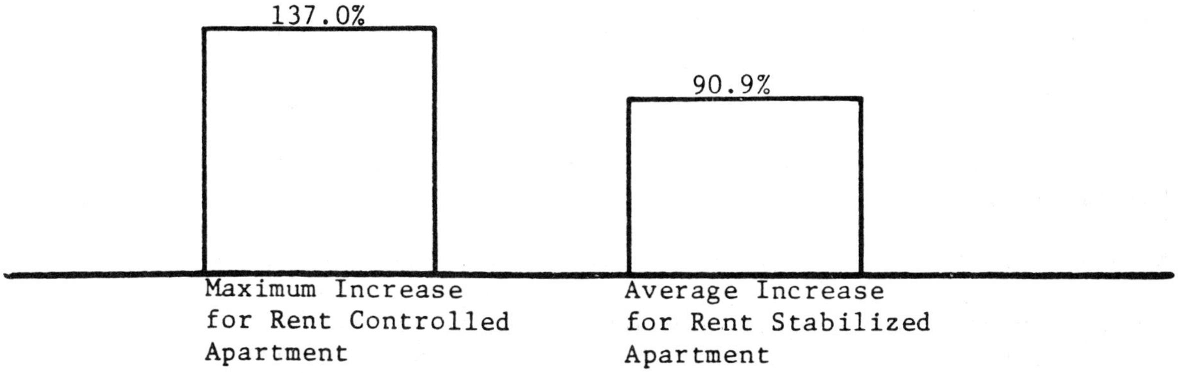

SOURCES: Tables 2-1 and 2-2.

TABLE 2-3. MAXIMUM RENT INCREASES FOR LEASES ENTERED INTO BETWEEN OCTOBER 1, 1981, AND SEPTEMBER 30, 1982, ALL RENT STABILIZED APARTMENTS, NEW YORK CITY

	Lease Term		
	1 year	2 years	3 years
Lease renewal	10.0%	13.0%	16.0%
Lease renewal (electricity included)	14.0%	17.0%	20.0%
Lease renewal (fuel excluded)	6.5%	9.5%	12.5%
New lease	25.0%	28.0%	31.0%

SOURCE: "Explanatory Statement and Findings of the Rent Guidelines Board in Relation to 1981-82 Lease Increase Allowances for Apartments Under the Jurisdiction of the Rent Stabilization Law" (p.1), July 31, 1981.

EXHIBIT 2-4. MAXIMUM RENT INCREASES FOR LEASES ENTERED INTO BETWEEN OCTOBER 1, 1981, AND SEPTEMBER 30, 1982, ALL RENT STABILIZED APARTMENTS, NEW YORK CITY

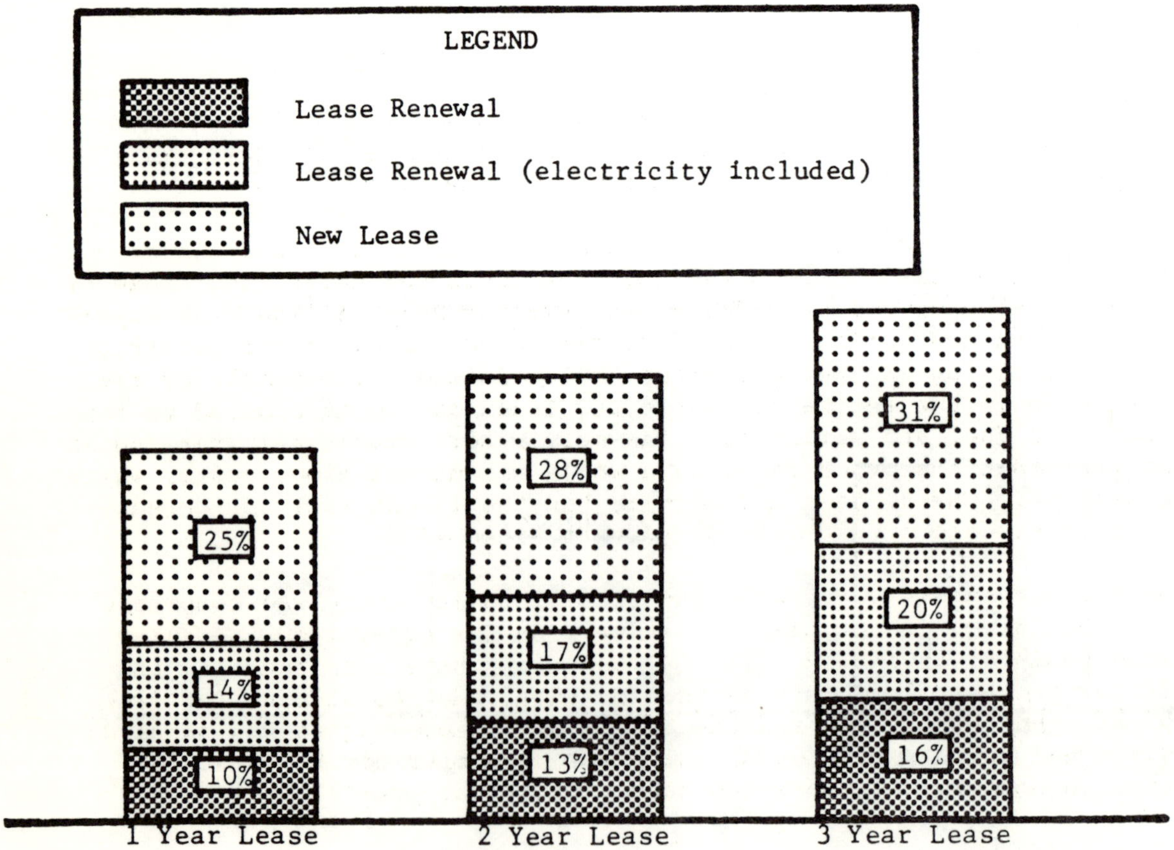

SOURCE: Table 2-3

TABLE 2-4. PRICE INDEX OF OPERATING COSTS FOR RENT STABILIZED APARTMENT HOUSES, NEW YORK CITY, APRIL 1967-1981

Year	Index	Percent Change
1967	100.0	-
1968	103.5	3.5
1969	107.6	4.0
1970	116.6	8.4
1971	132.2	13.4
1972	139.7	5.7
1973	150.8	7.9
1974	179.7	19.2
1975	191.3	6.5
1976	203.5	6.4
1977	219.5	7.9
1978	220.5	0.5
1979	238.6	8.2
1980	270.3	13.3
1981	305.7	13.1

SOURCE: 1981 Price Index of Operating Costs for Rent Stabilized Apartments in New York City, Regional Report 70, U.S. Department of Labor, Bureau of Labor Statistics, June 1981. Table 2, p.4.

cents of every operating dollar went for taxes, and only 13 cents for fuel and utilities in 1969, 36 cents of every operating and maintenance dollar went for energy costs and only 26 cents for taxes by 1981.

Given that the index affects a fixed market basket of goods and services, the variation in long-term inflation rates is the underlying cause of their shifting relative weights (Table 2-6; Exhibit 2-5). As would be expected from the above discussion, energy-related price increases far outstripped all others, rising 722 percent since 1967. Indeed, almost half of the 15 year increase in the entire composite BLS index can be attributed to the soaring costs of fuel and utilities. The only other component increasing at a greater rate than the price index as a whole was direct labor costs, which rose 214 percent. Taxes, fees and permits had the lowest rate of increase of any major cost category, a mere 74 percent since 1967.

The BLS survey was begun when the stabilized inventory was comprised entirely of buildings constructed after 1947, so its price index pertains only to the post-'47 inventory. Pre-'47 buildings have been entering the stabilization program since 1974 because of ETPA, and now account for two-thirds of all rent stabilized apartments. A series of weights can be used to translate BLS price survey data, which was developed for the post-'47 stock, into changes in the operating cost picture for pre-'47 buildings.[35]

TABLE 2-5. THE RELATIVE IMPORTANCE OF COMPONENTS OF OPERATING COSTS OF POST-1947 STABILIZED APARTMENT HOUSES, NEW YORK CITY, SELECTED YEARS

	1967	1974	1979	1981
Total	100.0%	100.0%	100.0%	100.0%
Taxes, fees & permits	46.1	37.1	33.0	26.2
Labor	15.6	16.4	17.7	16.0
Fuel and Utilities	13.3	24.8	26.3	35.7
Contractor Services	11.1	10.3	10.6	10.3
Administrative	8.3	6.2	6.3	6.0
All other*	5.6	5.2	6.1	5.8

*Includes insurance, parts and supplies and replacement costs.

SOURCE: 1981 Price Index of Operating Costs For Rent Stabilized Apartment Houses in New York City, Regional Report 70, U.S. Department of Labor, Bureau of Labor Statistics, June 1981, Chart 5, p.11.

The relative importance of various operating components varies significantly between older and newer buildings (Table 2-7). Although pre-'47 stabilized apartment buildings might be expected to be less energy-efficient than post-'47 ones, City studies have found fuel expenditures to be about the same for both categories, while all other operating outlays were lower for older units. Consequently, the proportion of pre-'47 operating and maintenance budgets attributable to fuel costs is around 1.5 times as great as for post-'47 buildings. In contrast, direct labor costs are only about 60 percent as important in older buildings as in newer ones, and taxes account for 50 percent less of operating and maintenance budgets in pre-'47 than in post-'47 apartments.

Taking account of the differences in the relative weights of the cost elements for pre- and post-'47 buildings results in different rates of change in operating costs for these two components of the stabilized inventory. For the period April 1980 to April 1981 the Guidelines Board estimates that the costs of operating post-'47 stabilized apartments rose by 12 percent, while the rate was 16 percent for pre-'47 buildings.

Operating and Maintenance Ratios. The operating and maintenance (O&M) ratio is the percentage of rent that owners allocate to operating and maintenance costs. It is an important indicator of the economic state of the rental housing industry because the higher the ratio, the lower the percentage of the rent roll that is available to cover vacancy losses and rent arrears, mortgage costs and profits. High O&M ratios present very difficult operating choices to owners of rental housing, especially during periods of rising interest rates, when financing for multi-family housing, and older properties in particular, is hard to come by or available only at very high rates and for very short terms. The Rent Guidelines Board uses the O&M ratio to assess the reasonableness of the allowed rent adjustments for new leases in stabilized apartments.

TABLE 2-6. PRICE INCREASES FOR OPERATING COST COMPONENTS OF RENT STABILIZED APARTMENT HOUSES, NEW YORK CITY, 1967-1981

	Percent Increase 1967-1981	Percent of Index Increase Accounted For
Total Index	205.7%	--
Taxes, fees and permits	74.2	16.6%
Labor	213.6	16.1
Fuel and Utilities	721.5	46.6
Contract Services	183.5	9.9
Administrative	120.1	4.9
All other*	219.0	5.9

*Includes insurance, parts and supplies, and replacement costs.

SOURCE: 1981 Price Index of Operating Costs For Rent Stabilized Apartment Houses in New York City, Regional Report 70, U.S. Department of Labor, Bureau of Labor Statistics, June 1981, Chart 4, p.9.

EXHIBIT 2-5. PRICE INCREASES FOR OPERATING COST COMPONENTS OF RENT STABILIZED APARTMENT HOUSES, NEW YORK CITY, 1967-1981

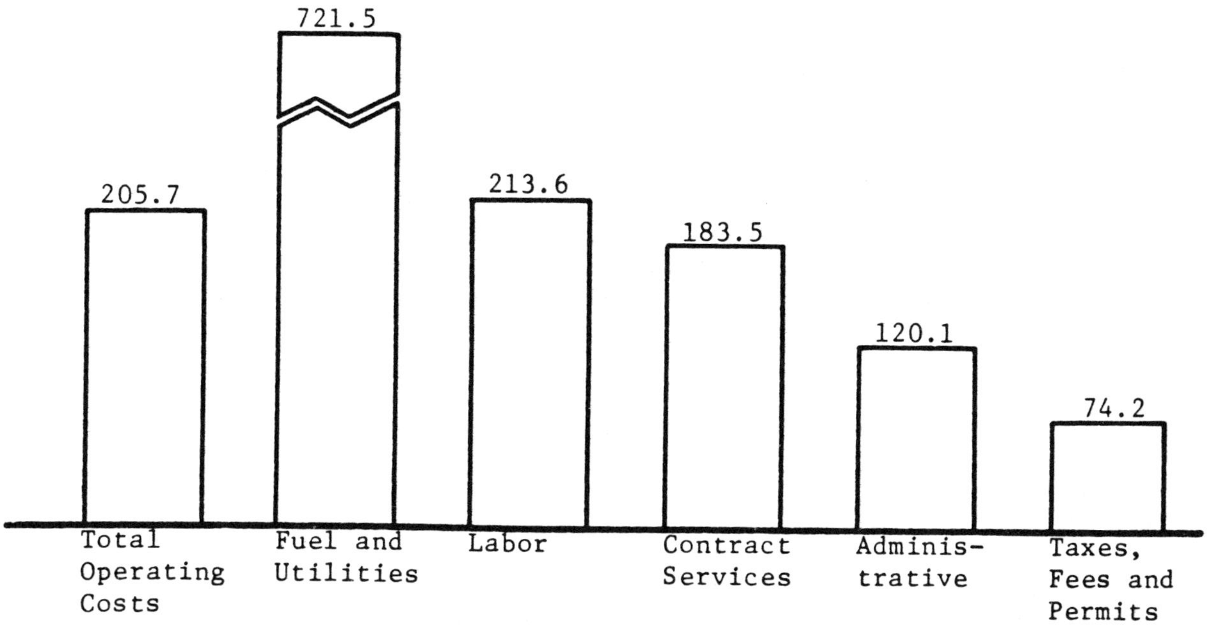

SOURCE: Table 2-6.

TABLE 2-7. COMPARISON OF 1980-1981 CHANGES IN SELECTED COMPONENTS OF THE PRICE INDEX OF OPERATING COSTS FOR PRE-'47 AND POST-'47 BUILDINGS*, NEW YORK CITY

	1980-1981 Weighted Percentage Increase	
	Pre-'47	Post-'47
Total Operating Costs	16.0	12.1
Taxes, fees, permits	0.4	0.8
Labor cost	0.7	1.3
Fuels	9.2	5.1
Utilities	2.5	2.4
Administrative Costs	0.9	0.6
Insurance	0.6	0.4

*Includes the Rent Guidelines Board's 10 percent reduction in fuel consumption for 1979-1980 that reflects the Board's belief that spiraling fuel costs have encouraged owners to take energy conservation measures.

SOURCE: Explanatory Statement and Findings of Rent Guidelines Board in Relation to 1981-82 Lease Increase Allowances for Apartments Under the Jurisdiction of the Rent Stabilization Law, July 31, 1981, Tables IV and V, p. 9.

According to the Board, average O&M ratios have increased by around 27 percent, from 55 percent in 1971 to 70 percent in 1981 and by 11 percent between 1978 and 1981 alone (Table 2-8). This recent jump can be compared to the more gradual 15 percent climb in the index over the first seven years of the rent stabilization program, during which time operating costs were far less inflationary than now. The 11-year increase in O&M costs means that, holding constant the quality of building operations, the proportion of the rent dollar available to cover vacancy losses, pay debt service and return a profit has declined from 45 to just 30 percent. In assessing the significance of this steady rise in the O&M burden, the Board noted in 1980 that as long as the rent increases it grants generally reflect the magnitude of actual increases in O&M costs, owners' net incomes will remain constant while their O&M ratios will rise.[36] While it is true that a pass-through of all O&M cost increases will maintain a constant cash flow, the profitability of a building will decline in real terms with a continued rise in the O&M ratio, because the owner's returns to equity are not being adjusted for inflation and the shrinking value of the dollar. The Guidelines Board's 1981 rent order does acknowledge this.[37]

The argument over whether the Guidelines Board rent increases have covered increases in O&M costs, while important and subject to some debate, may not be as critical as the demonstrated spiral in the O&M ratio. Continued high rates of inflation will ultimately lead to further erosion of equity values unless allowable rent increases are high enough to eventually lower O&M ratios.

TABLE 2-8. OPERATING AND MAINTENANCE COST-TO-RENT RATIO FOR RENT STABILIZED BUILDINGS, NEW YORK CITY, 1972-1982

Period*	O & M:Rent Ratio
1971	0.55
1972	.55
1973	.56
1974	.62
1975	.62
1976	.64
1977	.65
1978	.63
1979	.64
1980	.68
1981	.70

*Periods run from July 1 thru June 30.

SOURCE: Explanatory Statement and Findings of the Rent Guidelines Board in Relation to 1981-82 Lease Increase Allowances for Apartments Under the Jurisdiction of the Rent Stabilization Law, July 31, 1981, p. 17, Table XVI.

APPENDIX

THE DISTRIBUTION OF LEASE TERMS IN THE RENT STABILIZED SECTOR

Knowing the actual distribution of one-, two- and three-year lease terms in effect in the stabilized sector is important for several reasons. First, the rent increase orders issued by the Guidelines Board vary with the lease term and allow higher rent increases for multi-year than for one-year renewals. Second, because increases permitted in multi-year renewal leases are based upon the Board's projection of future inflation rates, the market impacts of an error in its estimate of the inflation rate will depend on the proportion of multi-year leases signed during the period covered by a particular rent order. Third, to provide an overview of the effects of its actions on revenue, the Board computes a weighted average rent increase for the stabilized sector, which it updates annually. Because allowable rent increases vary with lease terms, the accuracy of the weighted average rent increase depends on the correctness of the Board's assumptions about the actual distribution of single- and multi-year leases.

Based on a field study done in 1976, the Guidelines Board assumes a 25, 20 and 55 percent distribution of one-, two- and three-year leases respectively in the stabilized sector.[38] The Rent Stabilization Association has challenged the continued use of this assumption, alleging that because of rising inflation more tenants in stabilized units now choose three-year leases than did so in 1976. The Rent Stabilization Association asserts that because the Guidelines Board has underestimated inflation rates, its projection of future operating costs have been low as well, resulting in more modest allowable rent increases for multi-year as opposed to one-year leases. It also claims that rent increases allowed for recent multi-year leases would be greater if the Board had estimated inflation rates more accurately. Recognizing the importance of precise information on lease terms, the Census Bureau was asked, for the first time, to collect data on lease terms as part of the 1981 Housing and Vacancy Survey.

The actual distribution of lease terms in effect in the stabilized sector varies from the Guidelines Board's 1976-based estimates, but the differences tend to offset each other (Table A2-1). While it is true that the actual proportion of one-year stabilized leases currently in effect is approximately one quarter less than the Board had estimated, the 1981 proportion of three-year leases in effect is also one-quarter lower than the Board's 1976 estimate suggests. The result of these errors is to produce almost equivalent average lease terms throughout the stabilized sector, regardless of whether the Board's assumed lease mix or the 1981 mix reported in the Housing and Vacancy Survey is used. The Housing and Vacancy Survey reported an average lease term of 2.2 years for all rent stabilized units; the average lease term using the Board's estimate is 2.3 years.

TABLE A2-1. DISTRIBUTION OF LEASE TERMS FOR RENT STABILIZED UNITS WITH LEASES, NEW YORK CITY, 1981

Lease Terms (Years)	Pre-'47	Post-'47	Total Rent Stabilized	Distribution Assumed by Rent Guidelines Board
1	23%	13%	19%	25%
2	47%	24%	39%	20%
3	30%	63%	42%	55%
Average lease term*	2.1	2.5	2.2	2.3

*Average lease terms were calculated using a weighted average. Weights used were each sector's respective proportion of the stabilized inventory with leases (pre-'47 weighted .628 and post-'47 weighted .372).

SOURCE: U.S. Bureau of the Census, 1981 New York City Housing and Vacancy Survey.

It is important to point out that the above data on actual lease distributions refer only to those renter-occupied units which have leases (Table A2-2). Nearly eight out of 10 rent controlled units are rented without written leases, since neither maximum allowable rent increases under the MBR system nor security of tenure depends on them. Surprisingly, 13 percent of all stabilized apartments are currently rented without written leases.

TABLE A2-2. PERCENTAGE OF RENTER HOUSEHOLDS WITHOUT LEASES, BY CONTROL STATUS, NEW YORK CITY, 1981

Control Status	Percent Without Leases
Total Renters	35
Controlled	79
Decontrolled	65
Total Stabilized	15
Pre-'47 Stabilized	17
Post-'47 Stabiized	5
Other	34
Number Reporting	1,774,848*

*Excludes "not reported" and "don't know" categories.

SOURCE: U.S. Bureau of the Census, 1981 New York City Housing and Vacancy Survey.

NOTES

1. Paul L. Niebanck, Rent Control and the Rental Housing Market: New York City, 1968, (New York: New York Housing and Development Administration, 1970), p. 20.

2. Richard O. Davies, Housing Reform During the Truman Administration, (Columbia, Missouri: University of Missouri Press, 1966), p. 40.

3. Ibid., p. 41.

4. Ibid.

5. Niebanck, p. 21.

6. Frank S. Kristof, "The Effects of Rent Control and Rent Stabilization in New York City," Chapter 6 in Rent Control: Myths and Realities, The Fraser Institute, 1981, p. 127.

7. Ibid., p. 130.

8. Ibid., p. 128.

9. Niebanck, p. 21.

10. Kristof, p. 133.

11. Housing Development Administration and the Department of Consumer Affairs, Report to the Mayor On An Investigation Into Rental Increases in the Non-Controlled Housing Market, 19 February, 1969, New York City.

12. New York City Conciliation and Appeals Board, Tenants and Owners' Rights and Duties Under the Rent Stabilization Law, no date; pp. 2-3.

13. See, for example, "1981 Price Index of Operating Costs For Rent Stabilized Apartment Houses in New York City," Regional Report 70, Bureau of Labor Statistics, Department of Labor, June 1981.

14. New York City Rent Guidelines Board, Order Number 12, Rent Levels July 1, 1980 through September 30, 1981, July 28, 1980, p. 9.

15. New York City Housing and Development Administration, The Maximum Base Rents Formula: A Cost Index Approach to Controlled Rents, no date, p. 3.

16. Ibid., p. 9.

17. Ibid., p. 10.

18. Kristof, p. 134.

19. See, for example, F. A. Hayek et al., Rent Control, A Popular Paradox: Evidence on the Economic Effects of Rent Control, The Fraser Institute, Vancouver, B.C., Canada, 1975; Walter Block and Edgar Olsen, editors,

Rent Control: Myths and Realities, The Fraser Institute, Vancouver, B.C., Canada, 1981; C. Peter Rydell, C. Lance Barnett, Carol E. Hillestad, Michael P. Murray, Kevin Neels, and Robert H. Sims, "The Impact of Rent Control on the Los Angeles Housing Market," N-1747-LA, The Rand Corporation, August 1981.

20. See, for example, U.S. Comptroller General, Report to the Congress: Evaluation of Alternatives for Financing Low and Moderate Income Rental Housing, PAD 80-13, General Accounting Office, Sept. 30, 1980, Chapter 4; C. Duncan MacRae and Margery Austin Turner, "Developer Supply, Investor Demands and Multifamily Housing Production: A Pilot Study," Working Paper No. 1290-03, The Urban Institute, 1980; James E. Wallace, "Federal Income Tax Incentives in Low- and Moderate-Income Rental Housing," The Economics of Federal Subsidy Programs, Joint Economic Committee, 92nd Congress, Oct. 1972, pp. 676-705.

21. See, for example, George Sternlieb, The Tenement Landlord, New Brunswick, Center for Urban Policy Research, Rutgers University, 1966, Chapter V; Michael A. Stegman, Housing Investment in the Inner City: The Dynamics of Decline, Cambridge, The MIT Press, 1972, pp. 94, 95; Michael A. Stegman and Howard J. Sumka, "Nonmetropolitan and Inner City Housing Investment Markets, Journal of the American Real Estate and Urban Economics Association, vol. 2, Fall 1974, pp. 81-100.

22. Peter Rydell, et al, p. vii.

23. See, for example, George Sternlieb and James W. Hughes, The Future of Rental Housing (New Brunswick: The Center for Urban Policy Research, Rutgers University, 1981), p. 93.

24. George Sternlieb and Bernard Indik, The Ecology of Welfare Housing (New Brunswick: Transaction Books, 1972).

25. George Sternlieb, The Urban Housing Dilemma (New Brunswick: Center for Urban Policy Research, Rutgers University, 1972), Chapter 9.

26. Frank S. Kristof, "The Nation's Rental Housing Inventory; Does it Have a Future?" New York City Rent Stabilization Association, January 26, 1981 (mimeo); Frank S. Kristof, "The Effects of Rent Control and Rent Stabilization in New York City," in Block and Olsen, editors Rent Control: Myth and Realities, pp. 125-147.

27. John Gilderbloom, Moderate Rent Controls: The Experiences of U.S. Cities (Washington, DC: Conference on Alternative State and Local Policies, May 1980), p. iii.

28. Communication with New York City Rent Control Division, Department of Housing Preservation and Development.

29. Communication with New York City Rent Control Division, Department of Housing Preservation and Development.

30. Communication with New York City Rent Control Division, Department of Housing Preservation and Devlopment.

31. The Maximum Base Rents Formula: A Cost Index Approach to Controlled Rents, New York City Housing and Development Administration, no date, p. 8.

32. New York City Department of Housing Preservation and Development, "Schedule of Typical Rent Control Increases 1970-1981," August 20, 1981.

33. New York City Rent Guidelines Board, Explanatory Statement and Findings of the Rent Guidelines Board in Relation to 1981-1982 Lease Increase Allowances for Apartments Under the Jurisdiction of the Rent Stabilization Law, July 1981, p. 2.

34. Bureau of Labor Statistics, 1981 Price Index of Operating Costs for Rent Stabilized Apartment Houses in New York City, Regional Report 70 (New York: U.S. Department of Labor, Bureau of Labor Statistics, June, 1981).

35. Explanatory Statement, p. 5

36. Ibid., p. 11.

37. Ibid., p. 23.

38. Ibid., p. 21.

CHAPTER 3

POPULATION AND HOUSING IN NEW YORK CITY

Major demographic changes occurred in New York City during the 1970s. These changes are presented here based on population and housing data from the 1980 Decennial Census. Although the primary source of data for this report is the 1981 Housing and Vacancy Survey, the Census data provide a national and regional context in which to view New York's changes. Differences between the 1980 Census and the 1981 Housing and Vacancy Survey are described in an appendix to the chapter.

Nationwide Population Shifts

During the 1970s, two major trends in population movement were identified. One was the movement from the Northeast and North Central regions of the country to the South and West. The other was the shift from large cities and metropolitan areas to smaller cities and nonmetropolitan areas. Between 1970 and 1980, the population in the 50 largest metropolitan areas in the country grew by 7 percent, while the growth rate for all metropolitan areas was 9 percent.[1] These gains pale next to the 15 percent population increase in nonmetropolitan areas. With respect to regional changes in population, "each day during the past decade, the South gained 3,433 people; the West gained 2,280. Together they netted nearly nine times as many new residents as the Northeast and North Central states, capturing fully 90 percent of the decade's population increases"[2] (Table 3-1). The 17 largest metropolitan areas in the South gained 4.2 million people during the decade while the 10 largest SMSAs in the Northeast lost 1.4 million people.[3] In the Northeast, the biggest loss was found in New York City, where the metropolitan population declined by nearly 900,000 people.[4]

Population and Housing in New York City

Although New York City's population loss was the largest in the Northeast, the City held its own compared to other Frostbelt cities. With a 1980 population count of just over seven million people, New York's 10 year population loss equalled 10.4 percent, virtually matching the 10.8 percent loss in Chicago.* Philadelphia, Baltimore and Washington, D.C. had loss rates approximately one-third to one-half greater than New York City's while Detroit, Cleveland and St. Louis lost people at twice New York's rate.

---

*The 1970 Census of Population and the Census of Population and Housing, as well as the Advance Reports of the 1980 Census of Population and Housing and the Supplementary Reports of the 1980 Census of Population, provided much of the data on which this chapter is based. Although the Advance and Supplementary Reports present final Census figures, current litigation in progress between the City of New York and the Bureau of the Census may result in changes to these figures at a later date.

TABLE 3-1. CHANGES IN POPULATION AND HOUSING UNITS IN SELECTED FROSTBELT AND SUNBELT CITIES, 1970-1980

	Percent Change 1970-1980	
	Population	Housing Units
New York	-10.4	+ 0.7
St. Louis	-27.2	-15.3
Cleveland	-23.6	- 9.3
Detroit	-20.5	-11.1
Philadelphia	-13.4	+ 1.7
Baltimore	-13.1	- 0.9
Washington, D.C.	-15.7	- 0.6
Chicago	-10.8	- 2.9
Phoenix	+35.2	+54.2
Houston	+29.2	+58.3
San Diego	+25.5	+41.6
San Antonio	+20.1	+36.6
Tulsa	+ 9.3	+28.8
Dallas	+ 7.1	+28.7
Los Angeles	+ 5.5	+10.7

SOURCE: 1980 Census of Population and Housing, PHC80-V, Advance Reports, Final Population Counts, U.S. Department of Commerce, Bureau of the Census.

While the population was declining in New York City, the number of households remained reasonably constant, falling less than 2 percent. This disparity between population and household loss rates resulted primarily from a continued decline in the size of households. In 1970, the average New York City household consisted of 2.76 persons.[5] By 1980, the average household size had declined 9.8 percent to under 2.5 persons.

The size of the City's housing stock remained relatively constant over the decade. Despite persisting problems of housing abandonment, net additions to the stock exceeded losses by almost 22,000 units. Although the 1950s and 1960s witnessed a greater increase than was seen during the 1970s (Table 3-2), New York City fared well in comparison to other Frostbelt cities. Chicago's housing stock declined by nearly 3 percent and Cleveland's by close to 10 percent. In St. Louis and Detroit net housing losses for the decade were 15 and 11 percent respectively.

Population and Housing Shifts Among Boroughs

These citywide statistics obscure some dramatic differences among the boroughs in terms of both population and households (Table 3-3). Population loss was quite unevenly distributed across the City. Over the decade the Bronx lost 20 percent and Brooklyn 14 percent of their 1970 populations. Together, their loss of almost 700,000 residents accounted for 82 percent of the City's net population decline. In Manhattan and Queens, the declines were more modest at 7 and 5 percent respectively. Only Richmond's popula-

TABLE 3-2. NEW HOUSING UNIT CHANGE, NEW YORK CITY, 1950-1980

Years	Number	Percent
1950-1960	+250,000	+10.0
1960-1970	+180,000	+ 6.6
1970-1980	+22,000	+ 0.7

SOURCE: 1950-1970 data from George Sternlieb, Housing and People in New York City, New York Housing and Development Administration, 1973, p. 31; 1980 data from 1980 Census of Population and Housing, PHC80-V-34.

tion grew between 1970 and 1980. Because of its small population base, however, Richmond's 19 percent growth rate translates into an actual increase of around 57,000 people over the decade.

The change in the number of households also varied substantially among the boroughs. Both the Bronx and Brooklyn experienced household declines between 1970 and 1980, though at lower rates than in the case of their populations. In the other three boroughs the number of households actually increased. Most notably, despite a 7 percent population decline in Manhattan, the number of households actually grew by a modest 2.5 percent over the decade. Similarly, Queens' 5 percent population loss was more than offset by a 3 percent increase in its household count. Finally, Richmond's 33 percent household increase is fully half again as great as its population growth rate.

Although four boroughs lost population, only two lost housing units. The Bronx and Brooklyn together accounted for all of the City's gross housing losses of almost 79,000 units, which were offset by housing gains in the other three boroughs. The number of units in Manhattan and Queens increased 6 and 5 percent respectively, while the housing stock in Richmond expanded by 32 percent. Thus, what at first appears to be a rather stable housing picture is not one at all. The modest 10-year increase of 22,000 units in the City is the net effect of sizeable housing losses in the Bronx, more modest declines in Brooklyn, moderate growth in Manhattan and Queens, and high growth in Richmond.

The Racial and Ethnic Composition of New York

The changes in the racial and ethnic composition of New York City's population over the last decade are dramatic (Table 3-4). Estimating the true extent of some of those changes is complicated by differences in the way people of Hispanic ancestry were classified in the 1970 and 1980 Censuses. Nonetheless, it is possible to gauge the relative magnitudes of population change by adjusting for these methodological variations (Exhibit 3-1).

TABLE 3-3. POPULATION AND HOUSING CHARACTERISTICS BY BOROUGH, NEW YORK CITY, 1970-1980

Borough	Population			Housing Units			Households			Persons per Household		
	1970	1980	% change	1970	1980	% change	1970	1980	% change	1970	1980	% change
New York City Total	7,894,862	7,071,030	-10.4	2,924,281	2,946,098	+ 0.7	2,836,872	2,788,221	-1.7	2.76**	2.49	-9.8
Bronx	1,471,701	1,169,115	-20.6	508,789	451,053	-11.3	497,222	429,191	-13.7	2.91	2.66	-8.6
Brooklyn	2,602,012	2,230,936	-14.3	902,622	881,367	- 2.4	876,119	828,257	- 5.5	2.94	2.67	-9.2
Manhattan	1,539,233	1,427,533	- 7.3	714,593	754,549	+ 5.6	687,283	704,259	+ 2.5	2.17	1.96	-9.7
Queens	1,986,473*	1,891,325	- 4.8	708,316	740,129	+ 4.5	690,056	711,940	+ 3.2	2.85	2.63	-7.7
Richmond	295,443	352,121	+19.2	89,961	119,000	+32.3	86,192	114,574	+32.9	3.3	3.00	-9.1

*There is a discrepancy concerning the 1970 population of Queens. The 1970 General Population Characteristics reports that the population was 1,986,473; the 1980 Census of Population and Housing reports that the 1970 population was 1,987,174, a difference of 701 persons. Where Census data is used in this report, the figure reported in the 1970 General Population Characteristics will be used.

**The 1970 persons per household figure is reported by Bloomberg, p.48; the 1980 figure was estimated based on a weighted average of the individual borough household sizes as reported by the Census.

SOURCE: Table 2, Advance Reports, 1980 Census of Population and Housing, PHC80-V-34; Supplementary Reports, 1980 Census of Population, PC80-S1-2: Table 33, General Characteristics for County Subdivisions, Volume 34, 1970 General Population Characteristics.

TABLE 3-4. CHANGES IN THE RACIAL AND ETHNIC COMPOSITION OF NEW YORK CITY, 1970-1980

Racial and Ethnic Group	1970	1980	Difference	Percent Change
Total	7,894,862	7,071,030	- 823,832	-10.4
White	4,846,560	3,637,620	-1,208,940	-24.9
Black	1,668,115	1,784,124	+ 116,009	+ 7.0
Hispanic	1,202,281	1,405,957	+ 203,676	+16.9
Other	177,906	243,329	+ 65,423	+36.8

NOTE: Population figures are adjusted as indicated in Exhibit 3-1.

SOURCE: Black and Hispanic population figures for 1980 are from Table 2, PHC80-V-34, Advance Reports, 1980 Census of Population and Housing. 1970 data on Black and Hispanic population counts are from "Census Shows Major Shift in Region's Demographics," The New York Times, April 12, 1981.

The most striking change in New York's profile is the continuing decline in the White population. New York lost an estimated one-quarter of its White residents between 1970 and 1980 -- a decline of more than 1.2 million people. In contrast, the City's Black and Hispanic populations grew. They now comprise 45 percent of the City's seven million residents. The Black population increased by almost 7 percent, while the Hispanic population grew 17 percent.*

Racial and Ethnic Composition by Borough. Like the size of their populations, the racial and ethnic makeup of the City's boroughs vary substantially. Whites outnumber other racial and ethnic groups in Queens by two to one and in Richmond by more than five to one. In contrast, the Bronx has roughly equal numbers of Whites, Blacks and Hispanics, while in Brooklyn, the number of Whites is 91,000 lower than the combined minority population, but the ratio is still nearly one to one (Table 3-5).

These and other differences in racial and ethnic makeup are the results of substantial redistributions since 1970 (Table 3-6). The Bronx experienced an estimated 45 percent loss of Whites; in Brooklyn the White decline was 30 percent. Coupled with Manhattan's 11 percent loss of Whites, the 1980 Census marks the first time that Whites have ever accounted for less than 50 percent of the populations of three different boroughs in New York City.

Despite an overall decline in the total population of the Bronx over the decade, the Black and Hispanic populations there grew slightly. Brooklyn

---

*For data on changes in the racial and ethnic composition between 1978 and 1981, see Table A1-4.

EXHIBIT 3-1. ADJUSTMENT OF THE 1970 AND 1980 CENSUS POPULATION CLASSIFICATIONS

The Decennial Census classifies people according to their race: White, Black, Other, etc. Hispanic is an ethnic rather than a racial classification; consequently, for the Census, Hispanics identify themselves both by race and by ethnic origin. Because the Census Bureau reports that Hispanics primarily identified themselves as White in 1970 and as "Other" in 1980, adjustments to the Census-reported racial counts had to be made to improve the consistency between the 1970 and 1980 enumerations.

Census Classifications 1970

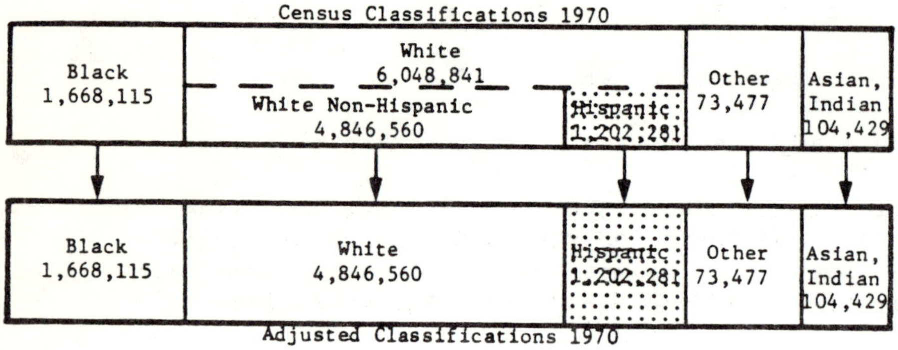

Adjusted Classifications 1970

The racial counts for 1970 were adjusted by subtracting the total reported Hispanic population from the total White population to derive separate White and Hispanic population totals. To the extent that a small number of Hispanics were classified as Black or "Other", this adjustment somewhat underestimates the White population not of Hispanic origin.

Census Classifications 1980

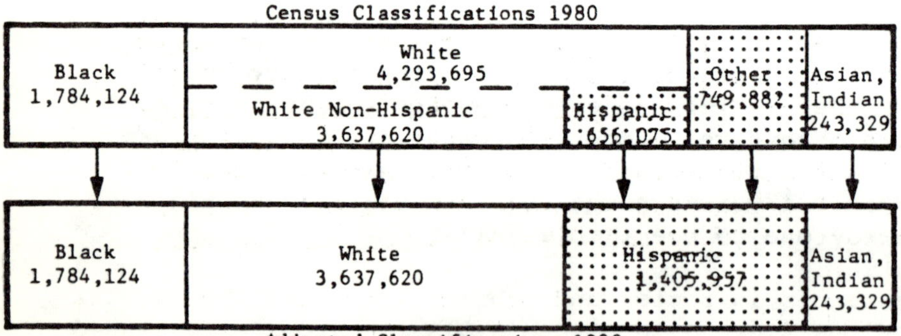

Adjusted Classifications 1980

In 1980, the Census Bureau reported that the "Other" racial category included primarily Hispanics. It was assumed for this report that Hispanics not classified as "Other" were classified as White. The number of Hispanics who classified themselves as White was estimated as the difference between the "Other" category and the total reported Hispanic population. This difference was subtracted from the total White population to form the adjusted White population total. Again, to the extent that Hispanics classified themselves as Black, this adjustment underestimates the White, nonHispanic population count.

TABLE 3-5. RACIAL AND ETHNIC COMPOSITION OF NEW YORK CITY BY BOROUGH, 1980

	Total	White	Black	Hispanic	Other
Total	7,071,030	3,637,620	1,784,124	1,405,957	243,329
Bronx	1,169,115	382,941	371,870	396,730	17,574
Brooklyn	2,230,936	1,069,855	722,816	392,118	46,147
Manhattan	1,427,533	706,118	309,693	335,803	75,919
Queens	1,891,325	1,178,177	354,129	262,422	96,597
Richmond	352,121	300,529	25,616	18,884	7,092
		Percent Distribution			
Total	100.0%	51.4	25.2	19.9	3.4
Bronx	100.0%	32.8	31.8	33.9	1.5
Brooklyn	100.0%	48.0	32.4	17.6	2.1
Manhattan	100.0%	49.5	21.7	23.5	5.3
Queens	100.0%	62.3	18.7	13.9	5.1
Richmond	100.0%	85.3	7.3	5.4	2.0

NOTE: Population figures are adjusted as indicated in Exhibit 3-1.

SOURCE: Table 2, Advance Counts, 1980 Census of Population and Housing, PHC80-V-34.

also experienced a modest 4 percent growth of Hispanics and a more sizable 10 percent increase of Blacks. Manhattan's relatively substantial increase of Hispanics, however, stands in stark contrast to the surprisingly high 19 percent decline among Blacks. Indeed, Manhattan was the only borough to witness an absolute decline in its Black population during the seventies. While Queens lost one-quarter of its 1970 White inhabitants, its Hispanic population doubled. Richmond also gained minority residents over the decade. Because of the small base from which its minority growth rates are calculated, however, the net gain of almost 10,000 Blacks translates to a large 62 percent growth rate, while a similarly sized increase of Hispanics amounts to a 97 percent rate of growth for them over the decade. Unlike the other boroughs, however, minority growth in Richmond was concurrent with an increase in the White population.

TABLE 3-6. CHANGES IN THE RACIAL AND ETHNIC COMPOSITION OF NEW YORK CITY BY BOROUGH, 1970-1980

	Total		White		Black		Hispanic		Other	
	Persons	Percent	Persons	Percent	Persons	Percent	Persons	Percent	Persons	Percent
Total	-823,832	-10.4	-1,208,940	-24.9	+116,009	+ 7.0	+203,676	+ 16.9	+65,423	+ 36.8
Bronx	-302,586	-20.6	- 311,324	-44.8	+ 14,189	+ 4.0	+ 10,136	+ 2.6	-15,587	- 47.0
Brooklyn	-371,076	-14.3	- 458,164	-30.0	+ 66,622	+10.2	+ 14,349	+ 3.8	+ 6,117	+ 15.3
Manhattan	-111,700	- 7.3	- 86,050	-10.9	- 70,749	-18.6	+ 38,669	+ 13.0	+ 6,430	+ 9.3
Queens	- 95,148	- 4.8	- 385,926	-24.7	+ 96,123	+37.3	+131,237	+100.0	+63,418	+191.1
Richmond	+ 56,678	+19.2	+ 32,524	+12.1	+ 9,824	+62.2	+ 9,285	+ 96.7	+ 5,045	+246.5

SOURCE: Black and Hispanic population figures for 1980 are from Table 2, PHC80-V-34, Advance Reports, 1980 Census of Population and Housing. 1970 data on Black and Hispanic population counts are from "Census Shows Major Shift in Regions Demographics," The New York Times, April 12, 1981. 1970 and 1980 data for White and "others" were derived as explained in Exhibit 3-1.

APPENDIX

DIFFERENCES BETWEEN THE 1980 CENSUS OF POPULATION AND THE 1981 HOUSING AND VACANCY SURVEY

The 1980 Census of Population and the 1981 Housing and Vacancy Survey were completed about a year apart. This, however, does not fully account for the differences in their respective population counts and racial and ethnic distributions. Rather, the principal causes of these differences are statistical factors and variations in enumeration policies.

The difference in the two population counts is 75,430 people.* There are two causes for this although it is impossible to determine how much of the difference is caused by each. The first factor is time. The Housing and Vacancy Survey was completed approximately 10 months after the 1980 Census; some of the disparity in population count is due to this alone. The other contributing factor concerns households in "special places." Although both counts measure only population in households, the Census enumerated households located in "special places" such as transient hotels, penitentiaries and dormitories, while the Housing and Vacancy Survey did not. The Census Bureau estimates that in 1981 there were 35,000 households in "special places" that were not counted in the Housing and Vacancy Survey. If these households were the same size as the median New York City household, households in "special places" alone would account for more than three-quarters of the population difference in the two counts.

In addition to the different population counts, the 1980 Census and the Housing and Vacancy Survey contain different household counts.** In March 1981, the Housing and Vacancy Survey estimated that there were 108,222 fewer households in New York City than had been counted by the Census in April 1980. Although the time-lag between the enumerations and the different treatment of households in "special places" account for some of this difference, two statistical factors also contribute to the variance in household count. These factors are sampling and nonsampling error. Sampling error does not apply to the 1980 Census because the Census is a complete enumeration of every household, and not a sample survey. However, the Housing and Vacancy Survey counts are estimates derived from a sample, and are therefore

---

	1981 Housing and Vacancy Survey	1980 Census	Difference
*Population in households	6,872,294	6,947,723	-75,430
**Number of households	2,679,999	2,788,221	-108,222

susceptible to sampling error.* In March 1981, the Housing and Vacancy Survey estimated that there were 2,680,000 households in New York City. The standard error corresponding to this estimate is approximately 17,900 households. If, as is the case 95 times out of 100, the true value of a sample estimate will lie within plus or minus two standard errors of that estimate, then the actual household count in New York City in 1981 was between 2,644,000 and 2,716,000. Thus, depending upon where the true value lies within this interval, the actual difference between the Housing and Vacancy Survey estimate and the 1980 Census could range between 72,000 and 144,000 households.**

The nonsampling error affecting the household count is a result of basing part of the sample frame on an incomplete universe of all possible households. The sample for the Housing and Vacancy Survey was selected from four sample frames, the first of which consisted of all housing units included in the 1970 Census.*** Since it is likely that the 1970 enumeration undercounted households, especially minority households, the base from which the 1981 Housing and Vacancy Survey sample frame was drawn was not the universe of all housing units, and hence injects some degree of bias into the survey results.

In addition to their small differences in population and household counts, the two enumerations vary in their respective distributions of the population into the major racial and ethnic groups (Table A1-1). The Housing and Vacancy Survey identifies only individuals of "Puerto Rican birth or parentage," while the Census of Population identifies "Hispanic" individuals. The latter includes individuals of Mexican, Mexican-American, Chicano, Puerto Rican, or Cuban origins or ancestry, in addition to those whose origins or ancestry are in South or Central America, Spain, the Canary Islands, the Dominican Republic, and certain other places.[6]

---

*Sampling error reflects the fact that the estimates derived from the Survey sample are apt to differ from the actual values being estimated. The standard error is an estimate of a statistical sampling error.

**To obtain the range of difference between the 1980 Census and the 1981 Housing and Vacancy Survey, the upper limit of the interval containing the number of households estimated by the 1981 Housing and Vacancy Survey (2,716,000), and the lower limit (2,644,000) are subtracted from the 1980 Census count (2,788,000).

***The second frame consisted of all housing units constructed since the 1970 Census, while the third was a list of units built since 1970 under the supervision of the New York State Urban Development Corporation. The final frame was a list of addresses involved in New York City's J-51 tax-exemption and tax-abatement program. These addresses were of two types. One list included commercial-use structures with upper floors rented for residential use. The second list was for special places at the time of the 1970 Census that were residential at the time of the 1980 Housing and Vacancy Survey. (See 1981 <u>New York Housing and Vacancy Survey, Sample Design, Estimation Procedure and Reliability Statement</u>.)

TABLE A3-1. COMPARISON OF THE ADJUSTED 1980 CENSUS OF POPULATION AND THE 1981 HOUSING AND VACANCY SURVEY RACIAL AND ETHNIC POPULATIONS, NEW YORK CITY

1980 Census of Population			1981 Housing and Vacancy Survey		
Racial/Ethnic Group	Persons	Percent	Racial/Ethnic Group	Persons	Percent
Total	7,071,030	100.0	TOTAL	6,872,294	100.0
White	3,637,620	51.4	White	3,642,487	57.2
Black	1,784,124	25.2	Black	1,526,718	24.0
Hispanic	1,405,957	19.9	Puerto Rican	764,634	12.0
Other	243,329	3.4	Other	429,692	6.8
			Not reported	508,763	--

NOTE: The 1980 Census of Population includes racial/ethnic data for persons in both "special places" and households; the Housing and Vacancy Survey includes only persons in households.

SOURCE: 1980 Census of Population adjusted as described in Exhibit 3-1; U.S. Bureau of the Census, 1981 New York City Housing and Vacancy Survey.

The differences between the Hispanic and Puerto Rican counts in the two enumerations cannot be fully explained because the reports currently available from the 1980 Census do not separate individuals of Puerto Rican birth or parentage from those of "other Hispanic" origins. The 1981 Housing and Vacancy Survey provides no informaton on whether those Hispanics who are not Puerto Rican were classified in the White or Black racial categories.

The 1981 Housing and Vacancy Survey does, however, provide a separate breakout of Puerto Rican and "Other Spanish" households from all other households. These data show that for every two Puerto Rican households in New York City there is one Spanish, non-Puerto Rican, household (Table A3-2). By applying the same relationship to the Housing and Vacancy Survey population count (Table A3-1), and adjusting the White count downward by the same amount that the Hispanic count is increased by, the compatibility between the two enumerations is increased (Table A3-3).

Besides the difference in the racial and ethnic classifications used in the two enumerations, three other factors affect the compatibility of the racial and ethnic data. The high number of persons and households not reporting race and ethnic origin in the Housing and Vacancy Survey, the inclusion of racial and ethnic data from "special places" and group quarters* in the Census but not in the Housing and Vacancy Survey, and the fact that the Housing and Vacancy Survey data are derived from a sample population while the 1980 Census tried to obtain information from each

*At the time this was written, 1980 Census data on race and ethnic origin were available only for the total population which included persons in "special places" as well as group quarters.

individual help to explain the variation between the Census and the Survey.

TABLE A3-2. ETHNIC ORIGIN OF HOUSEHOLDER, NEW YORK CITY, 1981

Ethnic Origin	Households	Percent
Total	2,679,999	100.0
Puerto Rican	258,889	9.9
Other Spanish	132,829	5.1
All other	2,213,152	85.0
Not reported	75,129	--

SOURCE: U.S. Bureau of the Census, 1981 New York City Housing and Vacancy Survey.

TABLE A3-3. COMPARISON OF THE ADJUSTED 1980 CENSUS OF POPULATION AND THE ADJUSTED 1981 HOUSING AND VACANCY SURVEY RACIAL AND ETHNIC POPULATIONS, NEW YORK CITY

1980 Census of Population			1981 Housing and Vacancy Survey		
Racial/Ethnic Group	Persons	Percent	Racial/Ethnic Origin	Persons	Percent
Total	7,071,030	100.0	Total	6,872,294	100.0
White	3,637,620	51.4	White	3,387,609	53.2
Black	1,784,124	25.2	Black	1,526,718	24.0
Hispanic	1,405,957	19.9	Hispanic	1,019,512	16.0
Other	243,329	3.4	Puerto Rican	764,634	12.0
			Other Spanish	254,878	4.0
			Other	429,692	6.8
			Not reported	508,763	--

SOURCE: 1980 Census of Population adjusted as described in Exhibit 3-1; U.S. Bureau of the Census, 1981 New York City Housing and Vacancy Survey, adjusted as explained in the text.

TABLE A3-4. CHANGES IN THE RACIAL AND ETHNIC COMPOSITION OF NEW YORK CITY, 1978-1981

	1978	1981	Percent Change 1978 - 1981
Total	6,947,986	6,872,294	- 1.1
White	3,804,861	3,642,487	- 4.3
Black	1,547,468	1,526,718	- 1.3
Puerto Rican	804,084	764,634	- 4.9
Other	336,147	429,692	+27.8
Not reported	445,425	508,763	N.A.

SOURCE: U.S. Bureau of the Census, 1978 and 1981 New York City Housing and Vacancy Surveys.

NOTES

1. Cheryl Russell, "A Tale of Fifty Cities," American Demographics, May 1981, p. 24.

2. Cheryl Russell and Bryant Robey, "Follow the Sun: Census Shifts Explained," American Demographics, March 1981, p. 18.

3. Russell, "A Tale of Fifty Cities," p. 24.

4. *Ibid.*, p. 24.

5. Lawrence N. Bloomberg, The Rental Housing Situation in New York City, New York City Housing and Development Administration, January 1976, p. 48.

6. U.S. Department of Commerce, Bureau of the Census, Questionnaire Reference Book: 20th Decennial Census -- 1980; D-561, pp. 22-23.

CHAPTER 4

AN OVERVIEW OF THE HOUSING MARKET IN NEW YORK CITY

Introduction

New York City's occupied housing inventory has grown by 22,800 units since 1978 (Table 4-1). More than 80 percent of these recent net additions are occupied by owners, and the remainder by tenants. Though very small (3,857 units), the increase in New York's occupied rental stock in the past three years is encouraging (Table 4-2). In contrast to the occupied stock, the total housing inventory has gained only 9,500 units since 1978, and the number of available rental vacancies has declined by 16,500. The far larger growth of the occupied than of the total stock cannot be entirely attributed to the reduction in the number of rental vacancies because some losses to the stock since 1978 originated in the occupied sector (see Chapter 9). Chapter 9 presents an analysis of rental housing market dynamics and components of inventory change in New York. The present chapter provides an overview of housing in the City and focuses on the structural characteristics of the stock by location, class and occupancy. A discussion of the nature and condition of the ownership market can be found here, alongside the analysis of the rental sector.

Structure Size and Occupancy Patterns

Three distinguishing features of New York City's housing market are its high proportion of large multi-family buildings, a correspondingly high rate of rental occupancy and the dramatic extent to which occupancy patterns vary across the City. New York has almost four times more occupied units in structures of at least five dwelling units than does the nation as a whole (62 percent versus 16 percent).[1] Half of the City's housing stock is in buildings with 21 or more units, and more than one-third is in buildings of at least 50 dwelling units. According to the 1979 Annual Housing Survey, two out of every three households across the country own their homes, but less than three in 10 New Yorkers do (Table 4-3). Not surprisingly, a far higher share of the City's homeowners live in cooperatives or condominiums than is the case nationally. In New York more than one in five homeowners live in cooperatives or condominiums* while the national rate is just 2.5 percent.[2]

---

*Although the Housing and Vacancy Survey combines cooperative and condominium units into one ownership class, other data indicate that cooperatives are the overwhelming form of multi-family homeownership in New York City. For both convenience and relative accuracy, therefore, references to cooperative/condominium ownership will hereafter be shortened to cooperative ownership. See, The Conversion of Rental Housing to Condominiums and Cooperatives, Appendix 1 Field Report, "Conversion Activity in the New York City and Nassau-Suffolk, New York SMSAs," U.S. Department of Housing and Urban Development, 1980, pp. 215 and 222.

TABLE 4-1. THE SIZE AND COMPOSITION OF THE HOUSING INVENTORY IN NEW YORK CITY, 1975, 1978 AND 1981

	1975	1978	1981	Change 1978-1981 Number	Change 1978-1981 Percent
Total housing units	2,838,731	2,782,835	2,792,339	+ 9,504	+ 0.3
Total owner units	726,283	734,881	754,745	+19,864	+ 2.7
Owner-occupied	719,750	727,206	746,112	+18,906	+ 2.6
Vacant for sale	6,533	7,675	8,633	+ 958	+12.5
Total rental units	2,056,005	1,988,712	1,976,044	-12,668	- 0.6
Renter-occupied	1,999,037	1,930,030	1,933,887	+ 3,857	+ 0.2
Vacant for rent	56,968	58,682	42,157	-16,525	-28.2
Total vacant units not available for sale or rent	56,443	59,242	61,550	+2,308	+ 3.9
Dilapidated	22,878	13,723	15,504	+1,781	+13.0
Seasonal	1,052	1,957	3,081	+1,124	+57.4
Sold, not yet occupied	1,791	2,765	1,427	-1,338	-48.4
Rented, not yet occupied	10,388	11,506	10,823	- 683	- 5.9
Held for occasional use	1,819	2,614	3,294	+ 680	+26.0
Held for other reasons	18,515	26,677	27,421	+ 744	+ 2.8

SOURCES: 1975 data from Bloomberg, pp. 170 and 213, and from 1975 New York City Housing and Vacancy Survey; 1978 data from Peter Marcuse, Rental Housing in the City of New York, January 1979, pp. 104-105, and from 1978 New York City Housing and Vacancy Survey; 1981 data from U.S. Bureau of the Census, 1981 New York City Housing and Vacancy Survey.

TABLE 4-2. OCCUPANCY STATUS OF OCCUPIED HOUSING UNITS, NEW YORK CITY, SELECTED YEARS

	1970		1975		1978		1981	
	Number*	Percent	Number	Percent	Number	Percent	Number	Percent
Total occupied	2,786,000	100.0	2,718,787	100.0	2,657,236	100.0	2,679,999	100.0
Renter-occupied	2,118,000	76.0	1,999,037	73.5	1,930,030	72.6	1,933,887	72.2
Owner-occupied	668,000	24.0	719,750	26.5	727,206	27.4	746,112	27.8

*1970 numbers are rounded to nearest thousand. Percentages are based on rounded numbers.

SOURCES: 1970 data from Marcuse, p. 77; 1975 data from 1975 New York City Housing and Vacancy Survey; 1978 data from 1978 New York City Housing and Vacancy Survey; 1981 data from U.S. Bureau of the Census, 1981 New York City Housing and Vacancy Survey.

TABLE 4-3. SELECTED CHARACTERISTICS OF THE OCCUPIED HOUSING STOCK, NEW YORK CITY, 1981

	Number	Percent	Median Number of Units in Structure
All Occupied Units	2,679,999	100.0	20.5
Renter-occupied units	1,933,887	72.2	36.7
Owner-occupied units	746,112	27.8	1.9
In structures with 1-5 units	1,008,206	37.9	1.8
In structures with 6 or more units	1,652,230	62.1	60.5
In structures with 50 more more units	905,186	34.0	128.8
Owner-occupied units that are in cooperatives or condominiums	165,010	22.1	137.1

SOURCE: U.S. Bureau of the Census, 1981 New York City Housing and Vacancy Survey.

Differences By Borough. The unequal distribution of large structures and widely differing owner occupancy rates in each of the boroughs clearly illustrate the City's varied housing pattern. Half of the rented units in Manhattan are in buildings with 60 apartments or more, while almost 40 percent are in buildings with at least 100 apartments. At the other extreme, half of all renter-occupied units in Richmond are in one- and two-family structures, while just one in nine are in buildings containing 100 or more apartments (Table 4-4). Variation in homeownership rates parallels this pattern. While just 11 percent of all households in Manhattan own either cooperatives or houses, the homeownership rate is close to two-thirds in Richmond (Table 4-5). Queens is less homogeneous than Richmond in terms of both structure size and tenure. More than two in five Queens households own their homes, and almost one in five of its renters live in buildings of at least 100 units. The 25 percent of Queens' renters who live in one- or two-family units is much lower than Richmond's percentage but exceeds the rates in the remaining three boroughs by a substantial amount.

Even within the homeownership sector, the City's five boroughs are distinctly different. For one thing, the relative distributions of ownership of conventional homes and cooperatives vary greatly across the City. Also, each borough's share of state or city assisted versus private cooperatives differs (Table 4-6). Queens contains more than 40 percent of all conventionally owned homes but a substantially smaller share of the City's

TABLE 4-4. SIZE DISTRIBUTION OF BUILDINGS IN NEW YORK CITY, BY BOROUGH, 1981

Borough	Median Number of Units in Renter Occupied Buildings	Percent of Renters in Buildings with 100 or more units	Percent of Renters in Buildings with 1 or 2 units
Total	36.7	23.2	13.0
Bronx	46.5	22.6	7.5
Brooklyn	14.6	12.4	17.8
Manhattan	60.2	37.7	0.6
Queens	22.5	19.4	24.9
Richmond	2.6	11.5	49.8

SOURCE: U.S. Bureau of the Census, 1981 New York City Housing and Vacancy Survey.

TABLE 4-5. HOMEOWNERSHIP RATES IN NEW YORK CITY, BY BOROUGH, 1981

	Total*	Conventionally Owned Houses	Cooperatives	Renters
Total	27.8%	21.7%	6.1%	72.2%
Bronx	21.3	14.0	7.2	78.7
Brooklyn	27.4	24.4	3.0	73.6
Manhattan	11.4	1.4	10.1	88.6
Queens	42.2	36.2	6.0	57.8
Richmond	63.6	61.1	2.5	36.4

*Includes both conventionally owned houses and cooperatives.

SOURCE: U.S. Bureau of the Census, 1981 New York City Housing and Vacancy Survey.

cooperatives. In the Bronx, however, large state-assisted developments like Coop-City give that borough a 40 percent share of all assisted cooperatives compared to 10 percent of conventionally owned homes. Manhattan has more than half the City's private cooperatives and less than 2 percent of its conventionally owned homes.

TABLE 4-6. LOCATION OF OWNER-OCCUPIED HOUSING IN NEW YORK CITY, BY BOROUGH, 1981

	Conventionally Owned Houses	Cooperatives: City/State Assisted	Cooperatives: Private
	Percent Distribution		
Total	100.0	100.0	100.0
Bronx	10.0	39.9	6.1
Brooklyn	33.6	24.2	9.0
Manhattan	1.5	17.1	53.6
Queens	43.2	18.7	28.7
Richmond	11.6	--	2.6

SOURCE: U.S. Bureau of the Census, 1981 New York City Housing and Vacancy Survey.

The Age of the Stock

Older buildings predominate even within the cooperative sector. More than 60 percent of all private cooperatives were built at least 20 years ago, which indicates that this is a traditional form of ownership in New York, and that a large share of this stock has been converted from rental housing rather than having been built for multiple ownership (Table 4-7).* Only 10 percent of private cooperatives have been built since 1970. The assisted ownership market reflects the high level of construction during the 1960s under the Mitchell-Lama program. Sixty percent of all state or city assisted cooperatives were built between 1960 and 1969, while less than one-quarter were built between 1970 and 1977. Both the conventional owner-occupied and renter-occupied housing inventories are very old. Over 67 percent of the former and 62 percent of the latter were built at least 35 years ago. In contrast, less than 5 percent of conventionally owned and 9 percent of renter occupied dwellings were built after 1970.**

---

*HUD's national study of conversions estimated that approximately 12,000 rental units in New York City were converted to cooperatives between 1970 and 1979. See, The Conversion of Rental Housing to Condominiums and Cooperatives: A National Study of Scope, Causes and Impacts, Department of Housing and Urban Development, 1980, p. IV-7 (percentage converted to absolute number).

**While data for comparable years are not available for other cities, the following data show the percentage of owner- and renter-occupied housing which were built before 1950 in selected Frostbelt cities.

[continued]

TABLE 4-7. YEAR STRUCTURE BUILT BY OWNERSHIP STATUS, NEW YORK CITY, 1981

	Renter-Occupied	Conventionally Owned Homes	Cooperatives State/City Assisted	Cooperatives Private
	Percent Distribution			
Total	100.0	100.0	100.0	100.0
1978 or later	1.0	0.6	--	2.2
1970-1977	7.1	3.7	24.4	7.6
1960-1969	12.8	11.3	60.1	28.0
1947-1959	16.8	16.7	14.5	30.8
1946 or earlier	62.3	67.7	0.9	31.5

SOURCE: U.S. Bureau of the Census, 1981 New York City Housing and Vacancy Survey.

Seriously Substandard Housing

The condition of New York City's rental housing stock will be dealt with in considerable detail in Chapter 6. Suffice it to say here, however, that the incidence of seriously substandard housing in New York City is not very great, although it varies significantly by ownership status (Table 4-8). Overall, approximately 3 percent of the occupied stock was judged by Census enumerators to be dilapidated in the first quarter of 1981. The rental stock has a dilapidation rate almost four times higher than the owner-occupied stock.† A similar pattern exists with respect to the proximity of the City's occupied housing to boarded-up and other vacant structures. While one out of every five occupied dwellings in New York is located on a street containing boarded-up structures, the rate for owner-occupied structures is just 11 percent and for renter units it is 23 percent.†

An Overview of Vacancies

The supply of available vacant units for rent or sale in New York City is very small. Among all owner units, the net vacancy rate is just over one percent (Table 4-9). Of the three homeownership sectors, the lowest net vacancy rate is for conventionally owned houses and is well below 1 percent. For state assisted cooperatives, the net vacancy rate is 2.63 percent and for private cooperatives it is 3.33 percent. The net vacancy

---

[**continued]	New York	St. Louis	Cleveland	Philadelphia	Washington, DC
Owner-occupied	17.4	38.8	38.9	47.1	27.1
Renter-occupied	52.4	45.8	44.8	28.7	42.2

†Each time this symbol appears in the chapter, the probability is 95 percent that differences between the values referred to are not due to chance.

TABLE 4-8. INCIDENCE OF DILAPIDATED HOUSING IN THE OCCUPIED HOUSING STOCK AND THE PRESENCE OF BOARDED-UP STRUCTURES ON THE STREET, NEW YORK CITY, 1981

	Total Reported	Occupied, Dilapidated	Percent
All occupied units	2,638,161	87,329	3.3
Owner-occupied	733,889	8,043	1.1
Renter-occupied	1,904,272	79,287	4.2

	Total Reported	Occupied Units With Boarded-up Structures on Street	Percent
All occupied units	2,652,704	522,668	19.7
Owner-occupied	738,616	77,281	10.5
Renter-occupied	1,914,088	445,388	23.3

NOTE: The "total reported" entries are different because the number of households reporting on other boarded-up structures on their street was greater than the number of households reporting on dilapidation.

SOURCE: U.S. Bureau of the Census, 1981 New York City Housing and Vacancy Survey.

TABLE 4-9. NET VACANCY RATES IN THE RENTER AND OWNER HOUSING STOCKS, NEW YORK CITY, 1981

	Net Vacancy Rate
All renter housing	2.13%
All owner housing	1.14
Conventionally owned homes	0.58
Private cooperatives	3.33
State/City assisted cooperatives	2.63

SOURCE: U.S. Bureau of the Census, 1981 New York City Housing and Vacancy Survey.

rate for rental units is 2.13 percent, a decline of 28 percent from the 2.95 percent rental vacancy rate documented in the 1978 Housing and Vacancy Survey. A detailed discussion of rental vacancies can be found in Chapter 5.

Homeownership, Incomes and Carrying Charges

Homeownership rates vary not only by location in the City, but also by race and other household characteristics. Overall, 28 percent of New York

TABLE 4-10. HOMEOWNERSHIP RATES, BY RACE AND ETHNIC GROUPS AND BY INCOME, NEW YORK CITY, 1981

Race and Ethnic Group	Homeownership Rate
All households	27.8%
White	34.0
Black	23.3
Puerto Rican	8.6
Other	20.6
Income Group	
<$4,000	10.3%
4,000-7,999	15.5
8,000-14,999	22.8
15,000-24,999	35.3
25,000 or more	46.7

SOURCE: U.S. Bureau of the Census, 1981 New York City Housing and Vacancy Survey.

TABLE 4-11. MEDIAN INCOMES OF RENTERS AND HOMEOWNERS AND THE INCIDENCE OF POVERTY IN NEW YORK CITY, 1981

	Median Household Income	Percent Below Federal Poverty Level
All households	$12,687	20.3%
All renters	11,001	25.3
All owners	20,333	7.7
Conventionally owned homes	20,705	7.9
City or State assisted cooperatives	15,129	8.3
Private cooperatives	24,177	5.4

SOURCE: U.S. Bureau of the Census, 1981 New York City Housing and Vacancy Survey.

households own their homes, but the rate among Whites is 34 percent, among Blacks 23 percent, and among Puerto Ricans 9 percent (Table 4-10). Ownership rates also vary significantly by income, although the differences among income groups might not be as great as in other communities where the overall ownership rate is much higher.† Ownership rates average around 16 percent in the $4,000-7,999 income range. The curve is relatively flat as incomes increase, peaking at 47 percent for households with incomes above $25,000. Nevertheless, income differences between owners and renters are still substantial. In 1980, the median income of renters in New York City was 54 percent that of homeowners, i.e., $11,001 compared to $20,333 (Table 4-11).† Among owners, those living in privately sponsored cooperatives had a median income 19 percent higher than that of homeowners as a group, while occupants of assisted cooperatives had a median income one-quarter below that of all owners. There is a much higher rate of poverty among renters than owners, and even within the ownership sector more poor households live in conventionally owned houses and assisted cooperatives than in private cooperatives.

Monthly carrying charges for cooperatives are influenced by the presence or absence of public subsidies (Table 4-12). The median monthly charge for all cooperatives is $290, or 9 percent more than the median citywide rent of $265. State or city assisted cooperatives have a median monthly carrying charge of $267, and private ones are substantially more expensive at $321 per month.† While 14 percent of these unassisted developments cost less than $200 a month, 17 percent cost at least $750.

TABLE 4-12. MONTHLY CARRYING CHARGES FOR COOPERATIVES IN NEW YORK CITY, 1981

Monthly Carrying Charge	All Cooperatives	City/State Assisted Cooperatives	Private Cooperatives
Total	100.0%	100.0%	100.0%
Less than $200	13.6	12.3	14.3
$200-399	63.2	79.9	53.3
$400-749	12.7	7.8	15.7
$750 or more	10.5	--	16.7
Median	$290	$267	$321

SOURCE: U.S. Bureau of the Census, 1981 New York City Housing and Vacancy Survey.

The Rental Stock

Losses in the Controlled Sector. As discussed in Chapter 2, under current regulations the size of the rent controlled inventory is bound to decrease. No new buildings are subject to rent control and controlled units in buildings of fewer than six apartments are decontrolled upon vacancy, while those in larger buildings come under rent stabilization. Conversions to

TABLE 4-13. CONTROL STATUS OF RENTER-OCCUPIED HOUSING UNITS, NEW YORK CITY, 1975, 1978, AND 1981

	Number of Units			Change 1978-1981	
	1975*	1978	1981	Number	Percent
Total	1,999,000	1,930,030	1,933,887	+ 3,857	+ 0.2
Controlled	642,000	402,361	285,733	-116,628	-29.0
Decontrolled	251,000	268,112	282,084	+ 13,972	+ 5.2
Stabilized total	770,000	871,697	928,355	+ 56,658	+ 6.5
Pre-'47	467,000	551,779	615,497	+ 63,718	+11.5
Post-'47	303,000	319,918	312,858	- 7,060	- 2.2
Public housing	165,000	164,765	166,123	+ 1,358	+ 0.8
Other	171,000	223,095	271,593	+ 48,497	+21.7

*Rounded to the nearest thousand.

SOURCES: 1975 data from Bloomberg, p. 72; 1978 data from Marcuse, p. 194; 1981 data from U.S. Bureau of the Census, 1981 New York City Housing and Vacancy Survey.

cooperatives and condominiums or to nonresidential use, along with mergers, city foreclosure for back taxes, and other forms of landlord abandonment, are all ancillary causes of the decline in the rent controlled sector. Since 1978, the controlled inventory has declined 29 percent, there are 116,600 fewer controlled apartments now than three years ago (Table 4-13). The number of rent controlled apartments dropped 37 percent, 239,600 units, between 1975 and 1978.

Additions to the Decontrolled and Pre-'47 Sectors. If all vacated controlled apartments were to remain in the private residential inventory as separate rental units, and if no decontrolled or pre-'47 stabilized apartments were to change use or drop out of the private market, these two sectors would gain the same number of units as the controlled inventory loses. Obviously, neither of these presumptions holds. The rate at which previously controlled units increase the size of the decontrolled and pre-'47 stabilized inventories has risen between 1978 and 1981 compared to 1975-1978. Between 1978 and 1981, the decontrolled and pre-'47 stabilized inventories grew by 77,700 units, or by two-thirds the number of apartments by which the rent controlled stock declined. This contrasts with the period 1975-1978, when the net increase in decontrolled and pre-'47 stabilized stocks equalled 43 percent of the decline in the number of rent controlled apartments. Although nothing definitive can be said about these relative rates of change, the lower loss rate in the more recent period is consistent with a tighter rental market and fewer withdrawals than in the earlier period (more will be said about this in the discussion of losses in Chapter 9). This is particularly so since the number of vacant available apartments declined by 16,500 between 1978 and 1981.

The Post-'47 Stock. On the surface at least, the above analysis seems to be contradicted by the slight decline in the size of the post-'47 stabilized sector over the past three years. The 2 percent decline, which translates into a loss of 7,100 units after accounting for gross additions through new construction, net conversions, etc., does not imply a vigorous market for newer, higher quality housing in the City, especially since this sector actually grew by 16,900 units between 1975 and 1978. The net decline in post-'47 stabilized apartments since 1978 should not necessarily be interpreted as a rise in the abandonment rate, or as a softness in this market, because conversions to cooperatives are increasingly frequent in New York and are concentrated in the newer rental stock. Between 1978 and 1981 the owner-occupied stock grew by 13,200 more units than would be expected from the level of new construction in the City.* This supports the view that the net decline in the post-'47 stabilized inventory since 1978 is partly due to conversion (to cooperatives) and reflects a tightening market and not a decline in the demand for high quality rental housing.

Proportional Representation of Market Sectors. Rent controlled units now account for only 15 percent of the City's occupied rental stock, the same proportion as decontrolled apartments. The largest sector, pre-'47 stabilized apartments, makes up 32 percent of the occupied inventory, twice the proportion represented by post-'47 stabilized housing. In other words, 66 percent of all occupied rent stabilized housing in New York City is pre-'47, versus 63 percent three years ago. Low-rent public housing has remained virtually constant at 166,100 units since 1978, and accounts for nearly 9 percent of the rental stock. The miscellaneous category "other" makes up the last 14 percent. Included in "other" are apartments which have never been regulated, single room occupancy units, federally assisted housing not subject to the rent regulation system, and city-owned *in rem* housing, nearly 34,000 units of which are occupied (see Chapter 10). Indeed, it is likely that much of the 22 percent net increase in "other" housing since 1978 comes from an expansion of the occupied *in rem* inventory.

Location. Manhattan and Brooklyn together account for more than 65 percent of all rent controlled apartments, followed by Queens and then the Bronx (Table 4-14). Virtually none of Richmond's 40,400 occupied rental units are controlled, which is not surprising given its relatively recent development. Similarly, precisely because so much of its housing stock is in one- and two-family structures, a relatively large proportion of Richmond's rental stock falls into the decontrolled category. The vast majority of decontrolled units, however, are in Brooklyn and Queens, with Brooklyn's share being a disproportionately high 54 percent of the City's total. Nearly two-thirds of all pre-'47 stabilized units are in Brooklyn and Manhattan; Manhattan and Queens account for 70 percent of the post-'47 stabilized inventory in the City.

Relative changes in the spatial concentration of the different market sectors are due to variations in additions and withdrawals throughout the boroughs as well as to mobility rates within the controlled inventory.

---

*The expected number of owner-occupied units was 732,927 based on the number of owner-occupied units in 1978 (727,206) plus the number of owner-occupied units built between 1978 and 1981 (5,721).

Since 1978, for example, the Bronx's proportion of the City's total rent controlled inventory has fallen from 18 to 15 percent of the total, while its share of the pre-'47 stabilized stock has decreased by 1.5 percentage points. On the other hand, Manhattan's relative share of the controlled market has grown slightly since 1978, from 35 to 37 percent of the total. Finally, Brooklyn accounts for 11,600 of the City's 14,000 unit increase in the decontrolled stock, so that its share of that inventory grew slightly over the past three years.

Structure Class

Tenements. One striking feature of the City's rental market is the continued importance of the tenement, which was the first form of multi-family structure in New York. In the 1850s, the typical Old Law tenement on the Lower East Side of Manhattan consisted of "a 25-by-25 foot front house, four or five stories high, with dark interior stairs, having 2 lines of rooms on each floor with dark bedrooms in the center, and a similar 25-by-25 foot rear house at the end of the lot leaving a 25-foot square internal court."[3] Some time later, larger, more modern working class houses which had more interior light and air, fireproof shafts and staircase halls, separate waterclosets for each family and less lot coverage were built. These New Law buildings became known by the city legislation that institutionalized their form: the Tenement House Act of 1901.[4]

Apartments in tenement buildings still number more than 737,600, or 40 percent of the occupied rental stock. Although New Law tenements continue to outnumber Old Law units by almost three to one, there are still nearly 185,000 occupied Old Law tenements in New York. Moreover, the rate of decline in the number of tenements has slowed considerably (Table 4-15). In the seven years between 1968 and 1975, the number of occupied Old Law tenements declined by 15 percent, and by another 15 percent between 1975 and 1978. Between 1978 and 1981, however, the total has hardly changed. New Law apartments exhibit a different loss pattern, mainly because they are heavily concentrated in the Bronx, but here too, the most recent three-year period shows a loss rate one-third as great as the previous three-year period. The number of occupied New Law tenements fell by 4 percent or 22,100 units between 1978 and 1981, compared to 12 percent, or 74,928 units, between 1975 and 1978.

Old and New Law tenements were supplemented later by the still larger, more modern multi-family structures that we know today. It was the Multiple Dwelling Law of 1929 which officially made the New Law tenement an unacceptable building form in New York City. Since all multiple dwelling structures built after 1929 must conform to the basic standards first codified in that law, the portion of the City's occupied rental stock classified as post-'29 dwellings continues to grow. In 1968, nearly 600,000 units, or 29 percent of the City's occupied rental stock, was in post-'29 multiple dwellings. By 1981 the number had risen to 716,800 -- 39 percent of the rental inventory.

Control Status of Tenements

Over 60 percent of the City's occupied tenements are subject to rent stabilization and slightly more than one-quarter are still under rent

TABLE 4-14. CONTROL STATUS OF RENTER-OCCUPIED HOUSING UNITS, BY BOROUGH, NEW YORK CITY, 1978 AND 1981

		Total	Bronx	Brooklyn	Manhattan	Queens	Richmond
All Renter Units	1978	1,930,030	328,735	581,746	581,020	402,390	36,139
	1981	1,933,887	325,874	581,207	584,912	401,533	40,361
Controlled	1978	402,361	70,256	117,276	141,558	72,477	794
	1981	285,733	43,838	82,189	104,854	54,483	368
Decontrolled	1978	268,111	24,959	141,660	7,882	84,357	9,253
	1981	282,084	25,639	153,287	9,915	83,235	10,008
Pre-'47 Stabilized	1978	551,779	125,482	157,588	206,186	62,321	201
	1981	615,497	130,375	170,116	237,496	77,329	182
Post-'47 Stabilized	1978	319,198	29,653	53,894	126,880	104,518	4,973
	1981	312,858	32,328	55,779	117,195	101,502	6,054
Public Housing	1978	164,765	38,475	55,320	48,795	17,018	5,156
	1981	166,123	40,147	55,823	46,897	18,303	4,953
Other*	1978	223,096	39,909	56,007	49,719	61,697	15,762
	1981	271,593	53,548	64,103	68,554	66,682	18,796
				Percent Distribution			
All Renter Units	1978	100.0	17.0	30.1	30.1	20.8	1.9
	1981	100.0	16.9	30.1	30.2	20.8	2.1
Controlled	1978	100.0	17.5	29.1	35.2	18.0	0.2
	1981	100.0	15.3	28.8	36.7	19.1	0.1
Decontrolled	1978	100.0	9.3	52.8	2.9	31.5	3.5
	1981	100.0	9.1	54.3	3.5	29.5	3.5
Pre-'47 Stabilized	1978	100.0	22.7	28.6	37.4	11.3	--
	1981	100.0	21.2	27.6	38.6	12.6	--
Post-'47 Stabilized	1978	100.0	9.3	16.8	39.7	32.7	1.6
	1981	100.0	10.3	17.8	37.5	32.4	1.9
Public Housing	1978	100.0	23.4	33.6	29.6	10.3	3.1
	1981	100.0	24.2	33.6	28.2	11.0	3.0
Other*	1978	100.0	17.9	25.1	22.3	27.7	7.1
	1981	100.0	19.7	23.6	25.2	24.6	6.9

*For 1978, "Other" includes never-regulated and publicly aided and 1,2 rooms lacking facilities. For 1981, "Other" includes state or city assisted and all other rental housing.

SOURCE: U.S. Bureau of the Census, 1978 and 1981 New York City Housing and Vacancy Surveys.

TABLE 4-15. STRUCTURE CLASSIFICATION OF RENTER-OCCUPIED HOUSING UNITS, NEW YORK CITY, SELECTED YEARS

	1968**	1975**	1978	1981	Change 1978-1981
Total reported	2,046,000	1,935,000	1,863,871	1,839,142	-24,729
Old Law tenements	258,000	219,000	186,115	184,629	- 1,486
New Law tenements	720,000	650,000	575,072	552,928	-22,144
Multiple built after 1929	591,000	675,000	712,479	716,793	+ 4,314
1-2 Family houses converted to apts.	153,000	101,000	97,427	108,421	+10,994
All other structures*	324,000	289,000	292,778	276,372	-16,406
			Percent Distribution		
Total reported	100.0	100.0	100.0	100.0	- 1.3
Old Law tenements	12.6	11.3	10.0	10.0	- 0.8
New Law tenements	35.2	33.6	30.9	30.1	- 3.9
Multiple built After 1929	28.9	34.9	38.2	39.0	+ 0.6
1-2 Family houses converted to apts.	7.5	5.2	5.2	5.9	+11.3
All other structures*	15.9	15.0	15.7	15.0	- 5.6

*1968 and 1975 includes other multiple dwellings and 1-2 family houses. 1978 and 1981 includes tenements used for single room occupancy, 1-2 family houses converted to rooming houses; miscellaneous class B structures, apartment hotels built before 1929 and 1-2 family houses.

**1968 and 1975 numbers rounded to nearest thousand.

SOURCE: 1968 data from Niebanck, p. 105, 1975 data from Bloomburg, p. 236; 1978 data from Marcuse, p. 281; 1981 data from U.S. Bureau of the Census, 1981 New York City Housing and Vacancy Survey.

(wide)

control (Table 4-16). Due to the larger size of New Law tenements however, apartments in them are much less likely than Old Law units to become decontrolled upon vacancy. Twelve percent of occupied Old Law and 5 percent of occupied New Law units are decontrolled. Post-'29 multiple dwellings are predominantly in the post-'47 stabilized sector (61 percent), although nearly one-fifth are classified as pre-'47 stabilized units and 12 percent are still subject to rent control.

New Law tenements, then, dominate the controlled and pre-'47 stabilized sectors, accounting for 57 and 58 percent of their respective inventories (Table 4-17). Apartments in post-'29 buildings make up 92 percent of all

TABLE 4-16. STRUCTURE CLASSIFICATION BY CONTROL STATUS OF RENTER-OCCUPIED HOUSING UNITS, NEW YORK CITY, 1981

	Total		Con-	Decon-	Stabilized		State/ City
	Number	Percent	trolled	trolled	Pre-'47	Post-'47	Assisted
Total*	1,537,565	100.0%	18.6	18.3	40.0	20.3	2.7
Old Law tenement	175,268	100.0%	24.6	11.5	62.7	1.1**	--
New Law tenement	532,065	100.0%	28.4	5.0	65.7	0.8**	--
Multiple built after 1929	469,212	100.0%	12.0	0.1	19.2	60.5	8.3
Apt. hotel built before 1929	7,794	100.0%	20.6	--	74.7	--	4.7
1-2 Family house converted to apartments	103,018	100.0%	13.6	34.3	34.9	16.7	0.5
All other structures***	188,550	100.0%	6.8	87.3	5.0	0.4	0.5
Not reported, not found, data not available	61,660	100.0%	10.6	56.8	23.9	7.5	1.2

*Does not include public housing or "other rental housing."

**By definition, Old and New Law Tenements were built before 1929. The percentages indicated here result from nonsampling error.

***Includes tenements used for single room occupancy, 1-2 family houses converted to rooming houses, miscellaneous class B structures, and 1-2 family houses.

SOURCE: U.S. Bureau of the Census, 1981 New York City Housing and Vacancy Survey.

TABLE 4-17. CONTROL STATUS BY STRUCTURE CLASSIFICATION OF RENTER-OCCUPIED HOUSING UNITS, NEW YORK CITY, 1981

	Total	Con- trolled	Decon- trolled	Stabilized Pre-1947	Stabilized Post-1947**
			Percent Distribution		
Total Multi-unit buildings	100.0	100.0	100.0	100.0	100.0
Old Law tenement	11.6	16.1	24.0	18.3	0.6
New Law tenement	34.8	56.6	31.8	58.3	1.5
Multiple built after 1929	45.1	21.0	0.4	15.0	92.2
Apartment hotel built pre-1929	0.5	0.6	--	1.0	--
1-2 Family houses converted to apartments	6.8	5.2	42.1	6.0	5.6
Other*	1.2	0.4	1.6	1.4	0.2

*"Other" includes tenements used for single room occupancy; 1-2 family houses converted to rooming houses; miscellaneous class B structures.

**By definition, all post-'47 stabilized units are in multiple unit build--ings constructed after 1929. Other structure classifications represented in the post-'47 stabilized distribution are the result of nonsampling error.

NOTE: "--" signifies less than 0.05%.

SOURCE: U.S. Bureau of the Census, 1981 New York City Housing and Vacancy Survey.

post-'47 stabilized units, 21 percent of controlled and just 15 percent of pre-'47 stabilized dwellings. Decontrolled apartments are more likely to be in one- and two-family houses that have been converted to apartments (42 percent) than in any other kind of structure, although nearly 33 percent are in New Law and 25 percent are in Old Law tenements. These latter proportions might seem high, given that decontrolled apartments are all in buildings with fewer than six units, but 15 percent of all Old Law and 6 percent of all New Law tenements are in small buildings (Table 4-18). Six percent of New Law units might appear to be inconsequential; however, it amounts to more than 32,200 apartments.

Since the economics of residential real estate in New York City favor high density development, each period's additions to the inventory are larger than the previous one's (Table 4-19). The median unit constructed between 1947 and 1959 is in a building containing 58 apartments; in the sixties the median new apartment was in a building with more than 124 apartments. The trend toward larger buildings has continued into the seventies and does not seem likely to change in the foreseeable future. Between 1970

TABLE 4-18. NUMBER OF UNITS IN STRUCTURE BY STRUCTURE CLASSIFICATION FOR RENTER-OCCUPIED HOUSING UNITS, NEW YORK CITY, 1981

	Old Law Tenement	New Law Tenement	Multiple Built After 1929*
	Percent Distribution		
Total	100.0	100.0	100.0
1-5	14.5	5.9	1.5
6-9	23.2	10.8	1.7
10-19	29.2	9.2	2.4
20-49	29.2	44.3	15.8
50-99	3.1	23.2	26.5
100 or more	0.8	6.6	52.2
Median	13.1	35.8	106.9

*Includes public housing.

SOURCE: U.S. Bureau of the Census, 1981 New York City Housing and Vacancy Survey.

TABLE 4-19. MEDIAN NUMBER OF UNITS IN STRUCTURE, BY YEAR STRUCTURE BUILT, FOR RENTER-OCCUPIED HOUSING UNITS, NEW YORK CITY, 1981

		Year Structure Built				
	All Units	1946 or earlier	1947-1959	1960-1969	1970-1977	1978-1981
Median number of units	36.7	22.9	58.1	124.2	190.6	199.5+

SOURCE: U.S. Bureau of the Census, 1981 New York City Housing and Vacancy Survey.

and 1977, newly constructed buildings in New York City contained a median of 191 apartments. Additions since then contain a median of more than 200 units.

After a decade of no change, the median number of rooms in the City's rental stock has begun to decline again. The typical New York apartment will probably continue to shrink in the near future. There are several reasons for this: tenements, especially New Law ones, contain larger apartments than later buildings and will drop out of the inventory at higher rates than the latter; rental housing construction in the City is very expensive; demand for housing is strong; and household size is likely to remain small (Table 4-20). Today the median apartment in the City has 3.5 rooms. Fourteen percent of all apartments contain one or two rooms and 21 percent have at least five. Three-room apartments make up 36 percent of the

TABLE 4-20. SIZE OF RENTER-OCCUPIED HOUSING UNITS, NEW YORK CITY, SELECTED YEARS

Number of Rooms	1968	1975	1978	1981
Total	100.0%	100.0%	100.0%	100.0%
1	5.5	3.9	4.9	5.8
2	9.0	8.9	9.0	8.6
3	32.5	34.3	34.7	35.5
4	30.6	31.2	29.8	29.2
5	14.5	14.4	14.1	14.0
6 or more	7.7	7.3	7.5	6.9
Median	3.6	3.6	3.6	3.5

SOURCE: 1968, 1975 and 1978 data from Marcuse, p. 89; 1981 data from U.S. Bureau of the Census, 1981 New York City Housing and Vacancy Survey.

total inventory, compared to 33 percent in 1968. All other room counts remained the same or declined by small amounts.

Much of the unsubsidized recent new residential development in New York has been in Manhattan, where land and development costs are the highest in the City, household size the smallest, and effective market demand the strongest. These factors contribute further to the tendency toward smaller apartments. Sixty-five percent of all one-room and half of all two-room apartments in the City are in Manhattan (Table 4-21).

TABLE 4-21. SIZE OF RENTER-OCCUPIED HOUSING UNITS, BY BOROUGH, NEW YORK CITY, 1981

Number of Rooms	Total	Bronx	Brooklyn	Manhattan	Queens	Richmond
1	100.0%	6.4	13.9	64.9	14.0	0.8
2	100.0%	9.0	22.2	49.8	18.1	0.9
3	100.0%	18.9	26.6	29.4	23.0	2.1
4	100.0%	18.7	33.1	25.5	20.1	2.6
5	100.0%	19.9	32.2	23.5	22.4	2.0
6 or more	100.0%	12.8	39.1	21.4	23.4	3.3
Median	3.5	3.6	3.7	3.2	3.5	3.8

The Demand Side of the Market

Household Size and Composition. Size and composition of households are crucial aspects of market demand in New York. Half of all New York households contain one or two people (Table 4-22). Median household size for homeowners is slightly lower than 2.5, while for renters it is 1.9. Indeed, almost 70 percent of New York renter households contain one or two people (Table 4-22). This represents a 17 percent increase since 1965. At the same time, the proportion of renter households with at least six persons has dropped from 5 percent in 1965 to just 3 percent in 1981.

TABLE 4-22. SIZE OF HOUSEHOLD IN RENTER-OCCUPIED UNITS, NEW YORK CITY, SELECTED YEARS

Persons in Household	1965	1975	1978	1981
Total	100.0%	100.0%	100.0%	100.0%
1	26.9	33.7	37.2	38.9
2	31.4	30.5	29.7	29.3
3	16.7	15.1	14.5	14.6
4	13.6	11.4	10.4	9.9
5	6.4	5.0	4.7	4.5
6 or more	5.0	4.3	3.3	2.8
Median number of persons	2.2	2.0	1.9	1.9

SOURCE: 1968, 1975 and 1978 data from Marcuse, p. 21; 1981 data from U.S. Bureau of the Census, 1981 New York City Housing and Vacancy Survey.

Single person households account for 39 percent of all renters and are disproportionately White, while Blacks and Puerto Ricans are represented in large households at about twice their representation in the overall stock

TABLE 4-23. HOUSEHOLD SIZE BY RACE AND ETHNIC GROUP, ALL RENTER HOUSEHOLDS, NEW YORK CITY, 1981

	Median Household Size	All Renters	Single Person Households	Households With At Least 6 Members
Total	1.9	100.0%	100.0%	100.0%
White	1.7	57.1	67.1	25.3
Black	2.2	23.4	20.5	42.9
Puerto Rican	2.6	13.1	8.0	22.4
Other	2.4	6.4	4.4	9.3

SOURCE: U.S. Bureau of the Census, 1981 New York City Housing and Vacancy Survey.

(Table 4-23). These basic differences are reflected in median household sizes: 1.7 people for Whites, 2.2 for Blacks and 2.6 for Puerto Ricans.

Borough. Living patterns vary in the City and show differences in household size and composition (Table 4-24). The Bronx has the largest median household, consistent with its large minority population, but the median household there is still only 2.2 people. Brooklyn, which also has a very high concentration of minority residents and relatively spacious apartments, is the only other borough where the median household size exceeds two. On the other hand, half of all renter households in Manhattan are single people (Table 4-25).

TABLE 4-24. HOUSEHOLD SIZE BY BOROUGH, ALL RENTER HOUSEHOLDS, NEW YORK CITY, SELECTED YEARS

	Median Persons				
	1965	1968	1975	1978	1981
Total	2.2	2.2	2.0	1.9	1.9
Bronx	2.5	2.4	2.3	2.2	2.2
Brooklyn	2.4	2.4	2.2	2.2	2.1
Manhattan	1.8	1.7	1.6	1.5	1.5
Queens	2.3	2.3	2.1	2.0	1.9
Richmond	3.0	2.6	2.2	2.1	2.0

NOTE: When computing median values, the U.S. Bureau of the Census defines each household size class in such a way that a whole number is the midpoint of each class. Thus, the one-person size class ranges from 0.5 to 1.5, the 2-person class from 1.5 to 2.5, etc. This procedure tends to overestimate the median household size by 0.5. Re-estimating the above medians from raw data, where each size class is defined as 1 person, 2 persons, 3 persons, etc., produces the following results which we think give a more accurate representation of differences in household size among boroughs:

	1978	1981
Total	1.4	1.4
Bronx	1.7	1.7
Brooklyn	1.7	1.5
Manhattan	1.0	1.0
Queens	1.5	1.4
Richmond	1.6	1.5

SOURCE: 1965-1978 data from Marcuse, p. 61; 1981 data from U.S. Bureau of the Census, 1981 New York City Housing and Vacancy Survey.

Small size is a natural corollary of households consisting only of adults. Seven out of 10 occupied units in New York house no children under 18. The absence of young children in the City is even more dramatic. Fully 87 percent of all households include no children under age six, and owners are less likely than renters to have small children (Table 4-26). Consistent with their smaller household size and, as subsequent analyses will indicate, their more advanced age, White households are less likely than others to include children. Within the rental sector, 80 percent of White households have no members under 18, compared to 57 percent of Black and 48 percent of Puerto Rican renter households.

TABLE 4-25. SINGLE-PERSON HOUSEHOLDS BY BOROUGH, ALL RENTER HOUSEHOLDS, NEW YORK CITY, SELECTED YEARS

	Total	1965	1968	1975	1978	1981	Percent Change 1965-1981
	Percent Distribution						
Bronx	100.0	19.2	22.3	26.3	29.7	30.9	+ 60.9
Brooklyn	100.0	22.0	22.7	27.2	31.3	34.0	+ 54.5
Manhattan	100.0	40.4	42.8	48.4	50.5	50.4	+ 24.8
Queens	100.0	21.2	23.3	29.9	32.9	35.9	+ 69.3
Richmond	100.0	16.7	19.2	26.6	33.1	35.3	+111.4

SOURCE: 1965 data from Niebanck, p. 76; 1968, 1975 and 1978 data from Marcuse, p. 50; 1981 data from U.S. Bureau of the Census, 1981 New York City Housing and Vacancy Survey.

TABLE 4-26. HOUSEHOLDS WITHOUT CHILDREN, ALL HOUSEHOLDS, NEW YORK CITY, 1981

	All Occupied	Owner-Occupied	Renter-Occupied
Households with no members under 18 yrs.	70%	67%	72%
Households with no children under 6 yrs.	87%	89%	86%

SOURCE: U.S. Bureau of the Census, 1981 New York City Housing and Vacancy Survey.

Age and Sex of Householders

Half of all household heads in New York are older than 47. For owners the median age is 55, and for renters it is 43. The age difference among racial and ethnic groups in the rental sector is clear.* At the median, White households are 10 years older than Black households and 13 years older than Puerto Rican ones. This indicates a higher incidence of elderly households among Whites than among other racial and ethnic groups. Twenty-seven percent of all White renter household heads are over 65, versus 12 percent of Blacks and 8 percent of Puerto Ricans.

TABLE 4-27. AGE OF HOUSEHOLD HEAD, BY RACE AND ETHNIC GROUP, ALL RENTER HOUSEHOLDS, NEW YORK CITY, 1981

	Total	White	Black	Puerto Rican	Other
Median age	43.4	47.7	37.2	34.6	35.1
Percent 65 or older	19.3%	26.7%	11.6%	8.2%	10.2%

SOURCE: U.S. Bureau of the Census, 1981 New York City Housing and Vacancy Survey.

Sixty percent of all New York renters over the age of 65 live alone, while another 34 percent live with one other person (Table 4-28). Older people are still disproportionately housed in rent controlled apartments. The median age of household heads in controlled apartments is 64 years, compared to 43 for all renters and 39 for occupants of stabilized apartments (Table 4-29). Indeed, one-fifth of all current tenants in controlled units

TABLE 4-28. HOUSEHOLD COMPOSITION OF ELDERLY RENTER HOUSEHOLDS, NEW YORK CITY, 1975, 1978 AND 1981

	Percent Distribution		
Household Composition	1975	1978	1981
Total	100.0%	100.0%	100.0%
One person	52.2	55.3	59.5
Two persons	40.2	37.4	34.2
Three or more persons	7.5	7.3	6.4

SOURCE: 1975 and 1978 data from Marcuse, p. 44; U.S. Bureau of the Census, 1981 New York City Housing and Vacancy Survey.

---

*Data are not available for owners.

TABLE 4-29. AGE OF HOUSEHOLD HEAD BY CONTROL STATUS, ALL RENTER HOUSEHOLDS, NEW YORK CITY, 1981

	All Renters	Controlled	Decontrolled	All Stabilized
Median age	43.4	63.8	41.2	39.3
Percent 65 or older	19.3%	47.5%	14.4%	12.4%

SOURCE: U.S. Bureau of the Census, 1981 New York City Housing and Vacancy Survey.

are at least 75 years old. No more than 14 percent of the tenants in any other market sector are as old.

Small household size and older age are also consistent with a high incidence of female-headed households. Although some changes in the Census definition of household head might exaggerate the recent increase in the number of female households, there is little doubt that this growth is real (Table 4-30).* The Census Bureau reports that the proportion of female owner households has grown from 20 to 26 percent in the conventional sector since 1978, and from 32 to 39 percent in cooperatives. Female-headed renter households reportedly increased from 42 to 47 percent of the total sector between 1978 and 1981 (Table 4-30).

TABLE 4-30. THE INCIDENCE OF FEMALE-HEADED HOUSEHOLDS AMONG OWNERS AND RENTERS, NEW YORK CITY, 1978 AND 1981

	Conventional Owners		Cooperative Owners		Renters	
	1978	1981	1978	1981	1978	1981
Percent of female householders	20.2	25.7	32.1	38.9	42.1	47.0

SOURCE: 1978 data from Marcuse, p. 82; 1981 data from U.S. Bureau of the Census, 1981 New York City Housing and Vacancy Survey.

Regardless of household size, more female than male heads of households are 65 or over (23 versus 16 percent)(Table 4-31). Among single-person households, however, the difference is much more dramatic. Forty percent of all female renters living alone are at least 65, compared to just 16 percent of all male renters living alone. Conversely, one-third of all female renters living alone are under 45, compared to 57 percent of all male

*See Chapter 8 for discussions of definition problem.

renters living alone. Thus, despite the fact that more women are entering the professions, setting up independent households and making their demands known in the housing market, one out of five female householders are over 65 and living alone, compared to just one out of 22 males. Chapter 8 explores this issue further through an examination of the differences in household incomes of men and women.

Public Assistance

Household Characteristics of the Welfare Population. The federally supported program of public assistance is an important part of the City's housing picture because of the large number of families it supports, and the more than 350 million dollars it funnels into New York's rental market each year.[5] The small increase (from 11 to 13 percent) in the number of City renter households who received public assistance in 1980 as opposed to 1970 is substantially less than the increase in poverty during the decade. More than one in five New York renters lived in poverty in 1970, compared to one in four in 1981.* Household characteristics determine dependency on welfare. Few older households receive public assistance, regardless of household size. The data show that less than 1 percent of all renters aged 65 or more are now on welfare, versus 2 percent in 1970. The institution of the Supplemental Security Income (SSI) program, which replaced the Old Age Assistance program and is not considered welfare, probably accounts for this decline (Table 4-32). In no household size class do more than 1.2 percent

TABLE 4-31. AGE AND SEX OF HOUSEHOLD HEAD, FOR SINGLE PERSON AND ALL RENTER HOUSEHOLDS, NEW YORK CITY, 1978 AND 1981

Age of Household Head	Single Person Households: Male	Single Person Households: Female	All Renter Households: Male	All Renter Households: Female
	Percent Distribution			
Total	100.0	100.0	100.0	100.0
Under 45 years	56.5	33.9	54.3	52.0
45 to 61 years	24.6	20.9	26.2	21.1
62 to 64 years	3.4	5.3	3.7	3.6
65 years and over	15.5	39.9	15.8	23.3

SOURCE: U.S. Bureau of the Census, 1981 New York City Housing and Vacancy Survey.

---

*17.8 percent of all renter households were below the poverty level in 1970; Sternlieb, p. 167.

TABLE 4-32. HOUSEHOLD SIZE OF RENTER HOUSEHOLDS RECEIVING PUBLIC ASSISTANCE, NEW YORK CITY, 1970 AND 1981

Number of Persons in Household

	Total		One		Two		Three		Four		Five		Six or More		Median	
	1970	1981	1970	1981	1970	1981	1970	1981	1970	1981	1970	1981	1970	1981	1970	1981
Total households	100.0%	100.0%	100.0%	100.0%	100.0%	100.0%	100.0%	100.0%	100.0%	100.0%	100.0%	100.0%	100.0%	100.0%	2.1*	1.9
Households receiving public assistance	11.0	13.3	8.8	4.9	7.9	10.1	12.0	22.3	11.6	24.6	17.3	29.6	27.9	40.3	3.2	3.1
With head over 65	2.2	0.8	4.1	1.2	2.1	0.7	1.0	0.5	1.0	0.3	0.8	0.2	0.2	0.3	1.8	1.4

*Median calculated from rounded figures.

SOURCES: 1970 data from Sternlieb, pp. 160 and 218; 1981 data from U.S. Bureau of the Census, New York City Housing and Vacancy Survey.

of older households receive welfare. For all households, however, the incidence of public assistance increases directly with household size from 5 percent of all single-person households to 40 percent of households with six or more members. The housing difficulties of large New York families are thus compounded by low income and the fact that for nearly half of them, the principal source of their income -- i.e., public assistance -- makes them undesirable tenants to many landlords.[6] It is nevertheless important to recognize that large families do not predominate in the welfare population. More than 60 percent of all welfare households include no more than three people, including 36 percent with just one or two people (Table 4-33).

TABLE 4-33. HOUSEHOLD SIZE OF RENTER HOUSEHOLDS RECEIVING PUBLIC ASSISTANCE, NEW YORK CITY, 1981

Number of Persons in Household	Households Receiving Public Assistance: Total	Households Receiving Public Assistance: With Head Over 65	Households Not Receiving Public Assistance
	Percent Distribution		
Total	100.0	100.0	100.0
1	13.9	56.9	41.3
2	22.1	27.3	30.3
3	25.1	8.8	13.4
4	19.4	4.3	9.1
5	10.4	1.4	3.8
6 or more	9.2	1.2	2.1

SOURCE: U.S. Bureau of the Census, 1981 New York City Housing and Vacancy Survey.

Female and minority households are far more likely than others to receive public aid. Just 2 percent of all nonelderly male-headed households are on welfare, compared to 10 percent of all nonelderly female-headed households (Table 4-34).*† Similarly, only 4 percent of all White renters receive public assistance while the rates of Black and Puerto Rican welfare dependency are, respectively, five and nine times as high (Table 4-35).† Twenty-three percent of all Black and 38 percent of all Puerto Rican renter households in New York City currently receive welfare. In other words, public assistance recipients in New York are overwhelmingly likely to belong to racial and ethnic minority groups (Table 4-36).† Thirty-nine percent of all welfare households are Black, 37 percent are Puerto Rican and 6 percent are "other," most of these being of Asian origin. Fewer than one out of five welfare families are now White, although in 1970 nearly one out of three welfare households was. Although this dramatic change in the composition of

*64.4 percent of all public assistance recipients are minority female householders.

TABLE 4-34. PERCENT OF RENTER HOUSEHOLD HEADS RECEIVING PUBLIC ASSISTANCE, BY AGE AND SEX, NEW YORK CITY, 1977 AND 1981

	1978	1981
	Percent Distribution	
Total	100.0	100.0
Households receiving public assistance	13.4	13.3
Under 65	12.4	12.2
Male headed	3.0	2.2
Female headed	9.4	10.0
Over 65	0.8	0.8
Age or sex of household head not reported	0.2	0.3

SOURCE: U.S. Bureau of the Census, 1978 and 1981 New York City Housing and Vacancy Survey.

TABLE 4-35. RACE AND ETHNIC ORIGIN OF RENTER HOUSEHOLDS RECEIVING PUBLIC ASSISTANCE, NEW YORK CITY, 1981

	Total	White	Black	Puerto Rican	Other
		Percent Distribution			
All renter reported	100.0	100.0	100.0	100.0	100.0
Receiving public assistance	13.3	4.4	23.3	38.0	13.4

SOURCE: U.S. Bureau of the Census, 1981 New York City Housing and Vacancy Survey.

the welfare population is largely due to a change in the definition of welfare, which no longer includes Supplemental Security Income, several socio-economic changes also contribute. Characteristics of the White population in New York have changed since 1970. White households are smaller and less likely to include children, their median age is higher and the size of the White population has declined. This, as well as the substantial increase in the number of low-income Black and Puerto Rican households is reflected in the composition of the 1981 welfare population.

TABLE 4-36. RACE AND ETHNIC ORIGIN OF RENTER HOUSEHOLDS RECEIVING PUBLIC ASSISTANCE, NEW YORK CITY, 1970 AND 1981

		Total	White	Black	Puerto Rican	Other
				Percent Distribution		
All renter households	1970	100.0	64.6	19.1	8.5	7.8
	1981	100.0	57.1	23.4	13.1	6.4
Households receiving public assistance	1970	100.0	32.3	39.7	25.5	2.5
	1981	100.0	18.5	38.8	36.5	6.2
With head over 65	1970	100.0	56.5	29.1	11.4	3.0
	1981	100.0	43.7	39.6	12.8	3.9

SOURCES: 1970 data from Sternlieb, p. 215; 1981 data from U.S. Bureau of the Census, 1981 New York City Housing and Vacancy Survey.

TABLE 4-37. MAINTENANCE AND HEATING DEFICIENCIES IN RENTER HOUSEHOLDS RECEIVING PUBLIC ASSISTANCE, NEW YORK CITY, 1981

	All Renter Households	Households Receiving Public Assistance	Households Not Receiving Public Assistance
		Percent Distribution	
Number of maintenance deficiencies:			
Total	100.0	100.0	100.0
None	44.6	20.2	47.5
1 or more	55.4	79.8	52.5
3 or more	20.6	46.4	17.2
Heating breakdown:			
Total	100.0	100.0	100.0
Yes	31.5	47.1	29.7
1 time	7.2	7.0	7.4
4 or more times	14.1	28.1	12.3
Additional heat needed:			
Total	100.0	100.0	100.0
Yes	29.9	52.3	27.0

SOURCE: U.S. Bureau of the Census, 1981 New York City Housing and Vacancy Survey.

Maintenance Deficiencies in Welfare Recipient Housing. Since welfare households are larger, are disproportionately minority, and are headed by women, it is not surprising that they are nearly three times likelier than others to live in housing with multiple maintenance deficiencies (Table 4-37).† Twenty-eight percent of them live in apartments which have repeated heating system failures, and 52 percent require supplemental heating assistance during the winter versus 12 and 27 percent of other households, respectively.

By Control Status. Given their age distribution and household composition, it is not surprising to find a very small percentage of welfare families living in rent controlled apartments. Six percent of all households receiving public assistance live in controlled apartments, 44 percent occupy pre-'47 stabilized units, 18 percent live in decontrolled units and another 20 percent live in public housing (Table 4-38).

TABLE 4-38. RENTER HOUSEHOLDS RECEIVING PUBLIC ASSISTANCE, BY CONTROL STATUS, NEW YORK CITY, 1981

Households	Total	Con-trolled	Decon-trolled	Stabilized Pre-'47	Stabilized Post-'47	Other*
			Percent Distribution			
All renters	100.0	100.0	100.0	100.0	100.0	100.0
Receiving public assistance	13.3	5.0	16.1	18.4	2.6	17.3
			Percent Distribution			
All renters	100.0	14.8	14.6	31.8	16.2	22.6
Receiving public assistance	100.0	5.5	17.7	43.9	3.1	29.9

*"Other" includes state or city assisted, public housing and all other rental housing not represented in the table.

SOURCE: U.S. Bureau of the Census, 1981 New York City Housing and Vacancy Survey.

The post-'47 stabilized sector has the lowest concentration of welfare households (3 percent); the controlled sector is next with 5 percent. Sixteen percent of the decontrolled and 18 percent of the pre-'47 stabilized sectors' tenants receive public assistance, as do 29 percent of all public housing tenants.

Gross Rents of Welfare Recipients. The median gross rent paid by households on welfare is 15 percent lower than the citywide median: $224 compared to $265 (Table 4-39). Furthermore, although the increase in the median rent for welfare families lagged behind the citywide increase of 143 percent between 1970 and 1981, the rents paid by welfare households have increased 133 percent during this time, from $96 to $224 a month.

TABLE 4-39. MEDIAN GROSS RENT BY PUBLIC ASSISTANCE STATUS, ALL RENTER-OCCUPIED UNITS, NEW YORK CITY, 1970 AND 1981

	Gross Rent		Percent Change
	1970	1981	1970-1981
All renter households	$109	$265	+143.1
Households receiving public assistance	96	224	+133.3
Households not receiving public assistance	112	273	+143.8

NOTE: Rents rounded to nearest dollar; percent change computed from rounded figures.

SOURCE: 1970 data from Sternlieb, pp. 107 and 230; 1981 data from U.S. Bureau of the Census, 1981 New York City Housing and Vacancy Survey.

TABLE 4-40. RENT-INCOME RATIOS FOR RENTER HOUSEHOLDS RECEIVING PUBLIC ASSISTANCE, NEW YORK CITY, 1981

	Gross Rent-Income Ratios						
	Total	<15%	15-19%	20-24%	25-29%	30-39%	40% or more
	Percent Distribution						
All renters	100.0	13.9	15.0	14.5	11.0	15.1	30.5
Households receiving public assistance	100.0	1.8	3.2	4.7	5.0	12.8	72.4
Households not receiving public assistance	100.0	15.9	17.1	16.1	12.0	15.5	23.5

SOURCE: U.S. Bureau of the Census, 1981 New York City Housing and Vacancy Survey.

Rent Burdens. Because rents in New York City have increased more rapidly than the shelter allocation for welfare recipients, the relative housing expense burdens of most public assistance households are high. Unlike nonwelfare recipients, 49 percent of whom spend less than 25 percent of their incomes for rent, fewer than 10 percent of all welfare households have rent-income ratios of less than 25 percent (Table 4-40). Similarly, while just 24 percent of nonwelfare households pay rents of 40 percent or more of their incomes, 72 percent of all welfare households do so. This rate is over twice that of all renters and three times as high as that of nonwelfare households.

NOTES

1. U.S. Department of Commerce, Bureau of the Census, Annual Housing Survey 1978, Current Housing Report Series H-150-78, Part A, U.S. and Regions, General Housing Characteristics, 1980, Table A-1.

2. U.S. Department of Commerce, Bureau of the Census, Annual Housing Survey 1979, Current Housing Report, Series H-150-79, Part A, General Housing Characteristics, U.S. and Regions, 1981, Table A-1.

3. Anthony Jackson, A Place Called Home (Cambridge), The MIT Press, 1976, p. 17.

4. Ibid., p. 122.

5. "An Examination of Payments Made to Private Landlords by New York City Public Assistance Recipients," New York State Department of Audit and Control, Office of the Welfare Inspector General, February 1, 1977.

6. See, for example, George Sternlieb and Bernard P. Indik, The Ecology of Welfare Housing (New Brunswick), Center for Urban Policy Research, Rutgers University,1973.

CHAPTER 5

VACANCIES

The vacancy rate for rental housing in New York City in the first quarter of 1981 was an extremely low 2.13 percent. This represents an almost 30 percent decline since the first quarter of 1978, when the vacancy rate was 2.95 percent (Table 5-1). The number of vacant housing units that are both available for rent and in habitable condition has declined by 28 percent since 1978, from 58,682 to 42,157. At the same time, the number of vacant, dilapidated apartments which are considered to be unsuitable for occupancy has increased by 13 percent since 1978, from approximately 13,700 to 15,500 (Table 5-2).

TABLE 5-1. VACANT AVAILABLE AND OCCUPIED RENTAL UNITS AND NET VACANCY RATES IN NEW YORK CITY, SELECTED YEARS

Year	Total	Occupied	Vacant Available	Net Rental Vacancy Rate
1981	1,976,044	1,933,887	42,157	2.13%
1978	1,988,712	1,930,030	58,682	2.95
1975	2,056,005	1,999,037	56,968	2.77
1970	2,200,100	2,167,100	33,000	1.50
1968	2,122,093	2,096,058	26,035	1.23
1965	2,145,454	2,077,031	68,423	3.19
1960	2,116,300	2,078,000	38,300	1.81

SOURCES: U.S. Bureau of the Census, 1965, 1968, 1975, 1978, 1981 New York City Housing and Vacancy Surveys; U.S. Bureau of the Census, Special Tabulations for New York City from 1970 Census of Population and Housing; 1960 data from Dr. Frank S. Kristof, "People, Housing and Rent Control in New York City," June 1964.

In general, rental vacancies are distributed across the City in rough proportion to each borough's share of the occupied rental stock. While the vacancy rate does differ somewhat by contract rent and structure type, the market significance of these variations is overwhelmed by the scarcity of vacancies throughout the market. A 2 percent vacancy rate is so low as to suggest serious restrictions on market choices and mobility, and increasingly upward pressures on rents. This chapter describes the vacancies in the City's rental stock in considerable detail, referring where appropriate to changes in occupancy conditions. The vacancy analysis here is more straightforward than in the two most recent reports in this series because the trend since 1975 has been a decline. Given the City's recent modest decline in the number of

TABLE 5-2. COMPOSITION OF ALL HOUSING VACANCIES IN NEW YORK CITY, 1978 AND 1981

	1978	1981
Total Vacant Units	125,599	112,340
Vacant Available Units		
Total	66,357	50,790
Available for rent	58,682	42,157
Available for sale	7,675	8,633
Temporarily Vacant Units		
Total	14,271	12,250
Rented, not yet occupied	11,506	10,823
Sold, not yet occupied	2,765	1,427
Vacant Units Not Available for Sale or Rent		
Total	44,971	49,300
Dilapidated	13,723	15,504
Seasonal	1,957	3,081
Held for occasional use	2,614	3,294
Held for other reasons	26,677	27,421

SOURCES: 1978 data from Marcuse, p. 105; 1981 data from U.S. Bureau of the Census, 1981 New York City Housing and Vacancy Survey.

dwellings and the substantial reduction in vacancies, New York's rental market is as tight now as has been documented in at least six years.

Estimating the Vacancy Rate

The Emergency Tenant Protection Act (ETPA), like its earlier rent control counterparts, defines a housing shortage in terms of a vacancy rate threshold of 5 percent. The law permits the City to declare an emergency in one or more classes of housing when the vacancy rates do not exceed 5 percent, or in the community as a whole if marketwide vacancies are below 5 percent. Like Local Law 30 of 1962, which embodies the City's rent control authority, ETPA requires the City to declare an end to the housing emergency once the vacancy rate rises above 5 percent. Because of the importance of this rate, both in terms of the proper administration of the rent regulation laws and as a key indicator of market conditions, it is necessary that there be both a broad understanding of how the vacancy rate is defined and confidence in the statistical accuracy of the estimated vacancy rates, as measured by the Bureau of the Census.

As used here, and in all previous reports in this series, the term vacancy rate is really a "net" rate because it includes only those vacant nondilapidated units that are available for rent:

$$\text{Net Rental Vacancy Rate} = \frac{\text{Vacant, Available for Rent}}{\text{Vacant, Available and Renter-Occupied}}$$

Dilapidated housing, though vacant and ostensibly available for rent, is not counted in the vacancy rate because it does not meet minimum standards of habitability. If this vacant housing were included, the rate in New York City would increase from a net of 2.13 percent to a gross rate of 2.90 percent. Comparable adjustments for 1978 would have increased the net rental vacancy rate of 2.95 percent to a gross rate of 3.49 percent.*

The net rental vacancy rate also excludes vacant seasonal housing, regardless of condition, since it does not provide year-round housing. Vacant apartments, even if in sound physical condition and not seasonal, are excluded from the net vacancy count if they are held off the market or are considered available only for occasional use. Finally, new rental housing that has never been occupied is considered available for rent as soon as the City has issued it a Certificate of Occupancy. This contrasts with the practice of the Annual Housing Survey and the decennial Census, which classify new housing that has all exterior windows and doors installed and final usable floors in place as vacant, available for rent, regardless of whether it has been granted a Certificate of Occupancy.**

Two kinds of errors are possible in the Census Bureau's statistical estimate of the net rental vacancy rate. The first is referred to as nonsampling error, such as the misclassification of a vacant unit as occupied, or vice versa. While explicit measures of nonsampling error are unavailable, the Census tries to keep them to an absolute minimum by sending a second enumerator to all sampled dwellings originally reported as vacant.

The second source of error in the vacancy estimate is sampling error, which results from the fact that the actual sample used in the 1981 Housing and Vacancy Survey is one of a large number of all possible samples of the sample size that could have been selected. Vacancy estimates derived from the different samples would differ from each other. While the exact sampling error, or the extent to which any particular sampling result differs from the average of all possible results, is unknown, the standard error of the estimate is a statistical measure that is commonly used to approximate sampling error. Because of the relevance of the vacancy rate to City housing policy, a high standard of accuracy is required of the Survey. It calls for the standard error of the estimate of the net rental vacancy rate to be no more than one-fourth of 1 percent if the actual net vacancy rate is 3 percent.

---

*Keeping in mind that the difference between net and gross vacancy rates is the exclusion of dilapidated units from the former, the overall gross vacancy rate in New York City, including owner and rental housing, is 2.41 percent. The net owner vacancy rate is 1.14 percent, virtually identical to the gross owner vacancy rate, since there are very few year-round dilapidated housing units for sale. The net vacancy threshold for owner housing needed to provide reasonable choice to housing consumers without untoward demand-induced upward price pressures is 1.5 percent, compared to 5 percent in the rental sector. The City's owner market does not seem to be as tight as the rental market.

**The 1980 Census of Population and Housing estimates owner and renter vacancy rates to be 1.27 and 3.32 percent respectively. See U.S. Bureau of the Census, 1980 Census of Housing, Supplementary Reports, HC80-S1-1, Selected Housing Characteristics by States and Counties: 1980.

In fact, the results of the Census survey show that the accuracy of the estimate is .17 percent.*

Vacancy Rates Across the City

As indicated above, the City's available vacancies are distributed throughout the boroughs in pretty much the same fashion as the occupied rental stock, except that Manhattan is underrepresented and the Bronx is somewhat overrepresented (Table 5-3). Nevertheless, net rental vacancy rates for the boroughs cluster tightly around the citywide average. Individual rates vary from a low of 1.90 percent in Manhattan, down 17 percent since 1978, to a high of 2.64 percent in Richmond. Most interesting of all, perhaps, is that the net vacancy rate in the Bronx was just 2.40 percent during the first quarter of 1981, down by more than half its 1978 rate. Clearly, such a dramatic decline in a borough as physically and economically distressed as the Bronx is not due to a sudden upward shift in demand. On the contrary, the total number of housing units in the Bronx fell by 13,000 since 1978, while the number of occupied rental units declined by 3,000. The cause is in the decline in the number of vacant available units from approximately 18,000 in 1978 to 8,000 in 1981.† Instead of these 10,000 physically habitable dwellings being absorbed

TABLE 5-3. VACANT AVAILABLE AND OCCUPIED RENTAL UNITS AND NET RENTAL VACANCY RATES, BY BOROUGH, NEW YORK CITY, 1978 AND 1981

Borough	Rental Units (thousands): Occupied		Vacant Available		Net Vacancy Rate	
	1978	1981	1978	1981	1978	1981
Total	1,930	1,934	59	42	2.95%	2.13%
Bronx	329	326	18	8	5.18	2.40
Brooklyn	582	581	18	13	3.07	2.11
Manhattan	581	585	14	11	2.29	1.90
Queens	402	402	8	9	1.88	2.23
Richmond	36	40	1	1	2.57	2.64

NOTE: Vacancy rates calculated based on unrounded data.

SOURCES: 1978 data from Marcuse, p. 102; 1981 data from U.S. Bureau of the Census, 1981 New York City Housing and Vacancy Survey.

---

*Statistically, the chances are that, 95 times out of 100, if a census of every housing unit in the City had been taken, the net vacancy rate would vary from the sample estimate by no more than .34 percent. That is, given the Census estimate of a net rental vacancy rate of 2.13 percent, the chances are 95 out of 100 that the true vacancy rate is neither less than 1.79 percent nor greater than 2.47 percent.

†The probability is .95 that differences between the values mentioned are not due to chance.

into the occupied rental stock, most of them have probably fallen into a vacant, dilapidated state, thereby dropping out of the net rental vacancy rate computation altogether, or have been demolished.

Vacancy Duration

Information on the length of time available apartments remain unrented is as telling as the vacancy rate, particularly in slowly growing or declining population centers. Simply put, if both the rental vacancy rate and the demand for housing are low, and housing opportunities are limited, market frictions will be less than would be the case if demand were high. If low vacancy rates are accompanied by extended vacancy durations not caused by the low quality or undesirable locations of available apartments, the tightness of the market might be of less concern than if vacancies are more quickly absorbed (Table 5-4).

TABLE 5-4. DURATION OF VACANCIES, ALL RENTER UNITS, BY BOROUGH, NEW YORK CITY, 1981

	Total	Bronx	Brooklyn	Manhattan	Queens	Richmond
			Percent Distribution			
Total	100.0	100.0	100.0	100.0	100.0	100.0
Less than 1 month	32.4	26.1	28.9	29.1	49.9	15.7
1-2 months	19.5	14.9	23.7	18.9	16.7	32.4
2-3 months	15.3	27.6	14.2	12.8	10.7	--
3-6 months	14.3	13.5	18.8	11.1	12.4	16.5
More than 6 months	18.6	17.9	14.4	28.1	10.3	35.4
Median months vacant in 1981	1.9	2.3	1.9	2.2	1.0	3.3
Median months vacant in 1978	2.3	1.7	2.4	3.6	2.6	1.7

SOURCE: U.S. Bureau of the Census, 1981 New York City Housing and Vacancy Survey.

With this in mind, it is noteworthy that vacancy durations were generally lower in early 1981 than in 1978. In several boroughs a substantially higher fraction of vacancies has been on the market a very short time than was the case three years ago (Table 5-4). The median rental vacancy duration in New York City is 1.9 months, a 17 percent decline since 1978 when it was 2.3 months. Around one-third of all available vacancies have been on the market for less than a month, and another fifth for between one and two months. Another indication that the City's low vacancy rate signals real market tightness is the decline in the percentage of vacancies that have been on the market for six months or more. In contrast to 1978, when 30 percent of all vacancies exceeded the six month duration, only 19 percent did so in 1981.

As with any composite, the citywide median rate blurs important differences across the City. Just about half of the available vacancies in Queens have been on the market for less than one month, which indicates very strong market demand, and only 10 percent of available vacancies in Queens have been on the market for six months or more.

Virtually identical fractions of available vacancies in Manhattan have been on the market for either less than one month (29 percent) or for more than six months (28 percent), which reflects the dual character of its rental stock. Although Manhattan contains 83 percent of the City's luxury rental stock (i.e., renting for more than $500 a month), it also has more than one-third of New York's remaining owner-occupied Old and New Law tenements. These include much of the City's poorest quality housing, and one-quarter of all the apartments classified by the Census as "other." "Other" includes city-owned housing taken for back taxes, one- and two-family rental houses, and federally assisted low and moderate income projects such as those developed under Section 221(d)(3) and Section 236 of the National Housing Act, as amended. Save for the one- and two-family houses of which Manhattan has very few, the borough's extended vacancies are concentrated in its tenement, city-owned, and federally assisted inventories. While Housing and Vacancy Survey data indicate that 11 and 22 percent respectively of all Old and New Law vacant units have been unoccupied for at least six months (Table 5-5), no data are available for the City's assisted stock. Nevertheless, it is reasonable to assume that some of the extended vacancies in Manhattan and elsewhere are concentrated in assisted projects, in view of the fact that project failure rates have been very high nationally, exceeding one-third for non-profit-sponsored new construction projects for families and 60 percent for rehabilitation projects for families.[1]

Thirty-five percent of Richmond's vacant available housing has been on the market for at least six months; this is the highest percentage in the City. Unlike Manhattan, however, Richmond contains no Old or New Law tenements. Nearly half the vacancies in Richmond are in buildings classified as "other" rental. The extended vacancies are most likely concentrated within Richmond's small inventory of old one- and two-family rentals and in its relatively large number of federally assisted projects. Because Richmond's rental stock and number of vacancies are small, very few extended vacancies can appear to show that Richmond is experiencing a general rental market problem rather than one localized in a small sector or several projects. Despite Richmond's experience, however, median vacancy durations are down in all boroughs but the Bronx, where it is up by one-third in the past three years. In Queens, the median number of months a vacancy has been on the market is down by 60 percent, in Manhattan by 40 percent and in Brooklyn by more than 17 percent since 1978, to less than two months.

Age and Type of Structure

The vacancy rate for newly built housing is higher than for others because of the time needed to rent all units (Table 5-6). For buildings first available for occupancy in 1978 or later, the net rental vacancy rate is 4.42 percent. This relatively high rate -- twice the citywide average -- stands in stark contrast to the 10 percent vacancy rate for newly built buildings at the time of the 1978 study. Net rental vacancy rates are under 2 percent for buildings built between 1947 and 1977, and when all post-'47 buildings are

TABLE 5-5. DURATION OF VACANCY BY STRUCURE CLASSIFICATION, ALL VACANT FOR RENT UNITS, NEW YORK CITY, 1981

	Total Reported	Total Multi-Unit Structures Reported	Tenements: Old Law	Tenements: New Law	Post-1929 Multi-Unit Structure	1-2 Family House Converted to Apartments	Other Multi-Unit Dwellings	1-2 Family House
			Percent Distribution					
Total	100.0	100.0	100.0	100.0	100.0	100.0	100.0	100.0
Less than 1 mo.	32.4	32.1	31.8	28.6	51.0	22.9	22.1	35.0
1 to 2 months	19.5	18.6	20.1	18.3	20.1	15.3	10.5	26.3
2 to 3 months	15.3	15.4	16.1	18.2	13.7	24.1	5.1	15.0
3 to 6 months	14.3	15.1	21.5	13.4	15.3	15.6	15.7	7.7
6 mos. or more	18.6	18.9	10.5	21.5	--	22.1	46.6	16.1

SOURCE: U.S. Bureau of the Census, 1981 New York City Housing and Vacancy Survey.

TABLE 5-6. NET RENTAL VACANCY RATES BY YEAR STRUCTURE BUILT, NEW YORK CITY, 1981

Year Structure Built	Available Vacancies	Net Vacancy Rate
Total	42,156	2.13%
Post-1947	11,930	1.63
1978-1981	902	4.42
1970-1977	1,779	1.30
1960-1969	3,222	1.30
1947-1959	6,027	1.84
Pre-1947	29,353	2.41
Not Reported	873	3.39

SOURCE: U.S. Bureau of the Census, 1981 New York City Housing and Vacancy Survey.

taken together, the net vacancy rate is just 1.63 percent. Regardless of rent control status, the vacancy rate for all pre-'47 buildings is 2.41 percent.

Vacancy rates do not vary significantly with structure type (Table 5-7), Except that multiple dwelling buildings classified as "other" by the Census, which include such special categories as rooming houses, tenements used for single-room-occupancy and other special purpose buildings too few in number to break out in the sample, have a vacancy rate of 12 percent. This reflects the generally poor condition and undesirability of this small and diverse housing stock. While New Law tenements have higher vacancy rates than Old Law tenements, there is no practical importance to the difference between a 1.8 and a 2.8 percent rate.

Contract Rent

The most interesting aspect of the pattern of vacancies arrayed by contract, or asking, rent is the flatness of the distribution (Table 5-8). Except for the most expensive apartments in New York, for which the net vacancy rate is less than 4 percent, vacancy rates range from less than 1 percent to 3 percent for all other rent classes. In virtually every rent class, including the highest, vacancy rates were lower in 1981 than three years ago.

Control Status

No vacancy rate can be computed for the controlled inventory because controlled apartments that are vacated become either decontrolled or stabilized, depending on building size. A vacancy rate for rent stabilized units can be computed in either of two ways: by ignoring or not ignoring the fact that the occupied rent controlled stock represents a potential pool of pre-'47 vacancies. By ignoring controlled apartments and replicating the procedures used thus far, the 19,700 pre-'47 stabilized available vacancies

TABLE 5-7. VACANT AVAILABLE RENTAL UNITS AND NET VACANCY RATES, BY STRUCTURE CLASSIFICATION, NEW YORK CITY, 1978 AND 1981

Structure Classification	Vacant Available Units, 1981	Net Rental Vacancy Rate 1978	Net Rental Vacancy Rate 1981
Multi-unit buildings	37,298	3.05%	2.17%
Old Law tenements	3,414	3.97	1.82
New Law tenements	15,826	3.99	2.78
Multiple dwellings built after 1929	8,510	1.65	1.17
1-2 Family houses converted to apartments	2,330	4.03	2.10
Other multiple dwellings*	3,631	8.05	12.02
Not reported, not found or not available	3,587	3.17	3.65
1-2 Family houses	4,860	2.29	1.91

*Includes apartment hotels built before 1929, tenements used for single-room-occupancy, one- to two-family houses converted to rooming houses, and miscellaneous class B structures.

SOURCES: 1978 data from Marcuse, p. 135; 1981 data from U.S. Bureau of the Census, 1981 New York City Housing and Vacancy Survey.

TABLE 5-8. VACANT AVAILABLE RENTAL UNITS AND NET VACANCY RATES, BY MONTHLY CONTRACT RENT, NEW YORK CITY, 1981

Monthly Contract Rent	Number of Vacant Available Units	Net Rental Vacancy Rate
Total	42,157	2.13%
Less than $100	923	0.87
$100-124	526	0.67
125-149	1,240	0.99
150-174	3,946	2.25
174-199	3,623	1.95
200-249	7,440	1.86
250-299	6,402	2.08
300-399	6,209	2.17
400-499	1,792	1.57
500-749	1,428	1.58
750-999	713	2.97
$1,000 or more	536	3.74
No cash rent or not reported	7,378	--

SOURCE: U.S. Bureau of the Census, 1981 New York City Housing and Vacancy Survey.

produce a net vacancy rate of 3.10 percent. Similarly, the 7,800 post-'47 stabilized available vacancies produce a net vacancy rate of 2.43 percent. When the vacancies in the pre- and post-'47 inventories are aggregated, a total stabilized net rental vacancy rate of 2.87 percent can be computed (Table 5-9).

TABLE 5-9. VACANCY RATE BY SELECTED CONTROL STATUS, NEW YORK CITY, 1981

	Number of Vacant Available Units	Net Vacancy Rate	Adjusted Net Vacancy Rate*
Controlled	N.A.	N.A.	N.A.
Decontrolled	6,261	2.17%	1.94%
All Stabilized	27,477	2.87	2.27
Pre-'47 Stabilized	19,693	3.10	2.22
Post-'47 Stabilized	7,784	2.43	2.43

*The vacancy rate for decontrolled and pre-'47 stabilized units is recalculated to reflect the fact that vacant units in these inventories can come from the controlled stock. Pre-'47 stabilized vacant units are drawn from both the pre-'47 stabilized stock and from rent controlled units which become vacant and are located in buildings with six or more units. Thus, controlled units located in structures with six or more apartments are included in the denominator when calculating the adjusted net vacancy rate. Similarly, controlled units in buildings with fewer than six units are included in the base for calculating the decontrolled adjusted net vacancy rate.

SOURCE: U.S. Bureau of the Census, 1981 New York City Housing and Vacancy Survey.

Inasmuch as rent controlled apartments in buildings containing six or more units become part of the stabilized inventory as soon as they are vacated, the alternative estimating procedure is to include all occupied controlled apartments in these buildings in the denominator of the vacancy equation. Doing so, of course, lowers the pre-'47 net vacancy rate from 3.10 to 2.22 percent and the total stabilized net vacancy rate from 2.87 to 2.27 percent. The post-'47 vacancy rate remains unchanged at 2.43 percent.

To be consistent, the net vacancy rate in the decontrolled sector should also be adjusted to account for the currently occupied stock of rent controlled apartments in buildings with fewer than six units. Including these controlled apartments in the equation lowers the decontrolled net vacancy rate from 2.17 to 1.94 percent.

Vacancies and Neighborhood Considerations

A full discussion of rental housing conditions can be found in Chapter 6. Here we simply describe the association between available vacancies and the presence of boarded-up structures nearby (Table 5-10). In general, the data indicate little net change in the degree of association between rental vacancies and boarded-up, burned-out buildings and the like. Overall, 45 percent of all available vacant units are located on blocks with boarded-up structures, an increase of 1 percent since 1978. In terms of control status, the greatest increase in this association has been in the decontrolled category. In 1981, 49 percent of all vacant decontrolled units were on blocks with derelict structures, an 11 percent increase since 1978.

TABLE 5-10. DISTRIBUTION OF OCCUPIED AND VACANT RENTAL UNITS BY PRESENCE OF BOARDED-UP STRUCTURES ON BLOCK (INTERVIEWER OBSERVATION), NEW YORK CITY, 1978 AND 1981

	Occupied			Vacant		
	1978	1981	Percent Change 1978-1981	1978	1981	Percent Change 1978-1981
Total	25.4%	23.3%	- 8.3%	44.7%	45.0%	+ 0.7%
Controlled	25.3	20.4	-19.4	N.A.	N.A.	N.A.
Decontrolled	28.3	27.9	- 1.4	43.6	48.6	+11.5
Pre-'47 Stabilized	34.1	30.8	- 9.7	54.9	48.9	-10.9
Post-'47 Stabilized	8.6	8.4	- 2.3	29.4	23.8	-19.0

SOURCES: 1978 data from Marcuse, p. 137; 1981 data from U.S. Bureau of the Census, 1981 New York City Housing and Vacancy Survey.

Pre-'47 stabilized vacant units are now as likely as vacant decontrolled units to be near boarded-up buildings. After a 19 percent, three-year decline, 24 percent of all post-'47 stabilized vacancies are also on blocks with boarded-up buildings.

NOTE

1. General Accounting Office, Evaluation of Alternatives for Financing Low and Moderate Income Rental Housing, PAO-80-13, September 30, 1980, p. 50.

CHAPTER 6

THE CONDITION OF RENTAL HOUSING

Introduction

This chapter describes the condition of the occupied rental stock in New York City, and identifies the significant changes that have occurred since 1978.* Two principal measures of physical housing conditions have been used -- dilapidation and maintenance deficiencies. Dwellings that are judged by Census enumerators to be in such poor condition as to pose a serious threat to the health and well-being of their occupants are classified as "dilapidated." Dilapidated and other occupied apartments receive varied maintenance and repairs. To gauge the magnitude of maintenance problems, the Housing and Vacancy Survey asked households a series of maintenance-related questions. Because the concept of dilapidation is subject to different operational definitions and inconsistent field application from one dwelling to another, and different households have different perceptions and expectations regarding maintenance, analysis of housing conditions based on these criteria is not conclusive. An assessment of changes in housing conditions in New York City using Housing and Vacancy Survey data must therefore be interpreted with care.

New York City and the Nation

Recognizing these data limitations, the results of the 1981 Housing and Vacancy Survey suggest that the condition of the City's occupied rental stock has deteriorated since 1978. This appears to be the case both in terms of dilapidation and increases in a wide range of maintenance problems. To help interpret the data on housing quality and to provide a frame of reference for this analysis, the chapter begins with a comparison of the frequency of various maintenance problems in New York and other American cities. Although there is no up-to-date survey of national housing conditions directly comparable to the 1981 New York Housing and Vacancy Survey, the Census Bureau has published national and regional housing condition data for the years 1978 and 1979.

Comparison of the Housing and Vacancy Survey data with these Census reports indicates that New York's occupied rental stock suffers higher rates of maintenance deficiencies than either the rental inventories of all central cities collectively or the inventories of all central cities in the Northeast (Table 6-1). This holds true for such physical housing

---

*See Marcuse for a detailed discussion of problems of definition and measurement of housing condition; pp. 145-149; see Glossary in this report for definitions of terms used in this chapter.

Table 6-1. DEFICIENCIES IN MAINTENANCE AND EQUIPMENT IN OCCUPIED RENTAL UNITS, FOR ALL CENTRAL CITIES, CENTRAL CITIES IN THE NORTHEAST AND NEW YORK CITY, 1978, 1979 AND 1981 (by percent in each category)

Maintenance and Equipment Deficiencies	New York City, 1981	All Central Cities 1979	All Central Cities in Northeast, '78 or '79
Additional heating needed	29.9	--	--
At least 1 heating breakdown	31.5	--	18.8
At least 4 heating breakdowns	14.1	--	--
Open cracks in ceiling or walls	22.2	14.0	--
Holes in floor	9.4	4.2	5.4
Broken plaster/peeling paint	16.9	9.0	13.2
Rodent infestation	24.3	--	20.1*
1 or more of above deficiencies	55.4	--	--
3 or more of above deficiencies	20.6	--	--
Boarded-up buildings on street	27.4 (R)** 23.3 (0)**	--	18.3
Overall Opinion of Neighborhood:			
Excellent	14.2	--	13.7*
Good or Fair	74.4	--	74.0*
Poor	11.4	--	12.3*

*Signifies 1978 data.

**(R) signifies respondent; (0) signifies observation.

NOTE: "All Central Cities" and "All Central Cities in Northeast" includes many cities with populations under 100,000.

SOURCES: 1979 data from Annual Housing Survey 1979, Current Housing Report Series H-150-79 Part A, General Housing Characteristics U.S. and Regions, Bureau of the Census, 1981, Tables A1 and B1; 1978 data from Annual Housing Survey 1978, Current Housing Report Series H-150-78, Part B, Indicators of Housing and Neighborhood Quality by Financial Characteristics, Bureau of the Census, 1980, Table B1; 1981 data from U.S. Bureau of the Census, 1981 New York City Housing and Vacancy Survey.

inadequacies as open cracks in interior walls and ceilings, as well as for more neighborhood-oriented problems reflected in numbers of boarded-up structures. Despite differences in deficiencies, however, renter households in New York and in other Northeastern cities rate the quality of their neighborhoods about the same.

Dilapidated Housing

As indicated earlier, the term "dilapidated" is intended to connote a serious degree of housing inadequacy due either to substandard original construction or to one or more less serious deficiencies which, when taken together, prevent the housing from providing habitable shelter. Over the past 10 years, the incidence of dilapidation in the City's occupied rental housing declined from around 5 percent to slightly more than 4 percent -- a 20 percent decline (Table 6-2). Although this modest decline may be an encouraging sign, the incidence of dilapidation has increased since 1978. In 1978, 3 percent of the housing stock was considered dilapidated. The estimated 17,000-unit increase in the number of occupied dilapidated apartments between 1978 and 1981 raised the citywide dilapidation rate from a low of 3 percent to its current 4 percent level.

TABLE 6-2. DILAPIDATED RENTER-OCCUPIED UNITS, NEW YORK CITY, SELECTED YEARS

	Number	Percent
1970	106,000	5.0
1975	110,000	5.7
1978	62,000	3.3
1981	79,000	4.2

SOURCES: 1970-78 data from Marcuse, p.150; 1981 data from U.S. Bureau of the Census, 1981 New York City Housing and Vacancy Survey.

Age of Building, Structure Class and Size. Factors other than building age, type and size determine whether rental units will or will not provide standard housing. Dilapidation rates do increase with age, for example, but the relationship is not overwhelming. While the likelihood that an apartment will be dilapidated is around six times as high in pre-'47 buildings as newer ones; only 6 percent of all pre-'47 buildings are dilapidated (Table 6-3). Similarly, Old Law tenements, all of which are at least 80 years old, are two-and-a-half times as likely to be dilapidated as New Law tenements; still, only 13 percent of all occupied Old Laws are dilapidated. While unit size seems to bear little relation to the incidence of dilapidation, building size does. In general, the very small and the very large buildings show the lowest rates of dilapidation, while the medium-size buildings are in the poorest condition. For buildings containing between 6 and

19 units, the incidence of dilapidation is 9 percent: more than twice the citywide average. This relationship is largely indirect, however, since this class includes more than half of the City's 184,000 occupied Old Law tenements.

TABLE 6-3. SELECTED STRUCTURE CHARACTERISTICS AND LOCATION OF DILAPIDATED UNITS IN NEW YORK CITY, 1981

	Number	Percent of All Renter-Occupied Units
Year Structure Built		
1970-1977	718	0.5
1960-1969	924	0.4
1947-1959	4,496	1.4
Pre-1947	72,622	6.2
Structure Class		
Old Law	24,034	13.3
New Law	29,085	5.3
Post-'29 apartments	4,677	0.7
Size of Unit		
1-2 rooms	11,007	4.1
3-4 rooms	50,297	4.1
5 rooms or more	16,721	4.3
Number of Units in Structure		
1-5	20,160	4.8
6-19	25,762	9.1
20-49	23,879	5.7
50 or more	9,312	1.2
Control Status		
Controlled	13,984	5.0
Decontrolled	15,783	5.7
Pre-'47 Stabilized	37,048	6.1
Post-'47 Stabilized	382	0.1
Borough		
Bronx	16,093	5.0
Brooklyn	27,922	4.9
Manhattan	27,661	4.8
Queens	6,720	1.7
Richmond	891	2.2

SOURCE: U.S. Bureau of the Census, 1981 New York City Housing and Vacancy Survey.

Control Status. The data indicate that the dilapidation rate is slightly lower for controlled than for either pre-'47 stabilized or decontrolled apartments. While the absolute differences in the rates are not very great across control categories, proponents of rent regulation are likely to interpret these data to mean that rent control per se does not cause dilapidation. Long-term occupancy and lack of turnover may prolong the nondilapidated state of some portion of the controlled stock. This might be true of apartments occupied by older tenants who are less likely than large families with unsupervised children, for example, to abuse their apartments, and who might also be less assertive about the provision of landlord-provided maintenance services. Alternatively, if poorer quality housing is more likely to have short-term tenancies than better housing, dilapidation levels in the pre-'47 stabilized stock would be higher than in controlled housing, with the differences between the two rates having no practical meaning in terms of the effects of rent control on housing conditions.

Deficiencies in Maintenance and Equipment

Poorly functioning building equipment systems and other maintenance deficiencies also impair the quality of housing. Because such a high percentage of New York City's rental stock is in relatively large, very durable buildings, it would be inappropriate to judge the City's housing condition entirely on the extent of dilapidation. For housing to be adequate, it must provide reliable housing services which require basic building systems to be sound and to operate reliably.

Over the years, the periodic Housing and Vacancy Surveys have reported on several maintenance-related dimensions of rental housing which seem to be highly correlated with overall housing conditions. The deficiencies are:

- additional heating required in the winter because the apartment's regular heating system does not keep the household warm
- at least one heating breakdown of six hours or more during the heating season
- open cracks in interior ceilings, walls or floors
- broken plaster and/or peeling paint on interior walls or ceilings
- the presence of rodents.

In contrast to the very low rate of dilapidation, the proportion of the rental stock failing on any one of these measures is quite high, frequently exceeding one out of five occupied dwellings. Moreover, more than half of the stock suffers from at least one deficiency and nearly 18 percent fail on three or more measures (Table 6-4).*

*Comparative data on these deficiencies in the total occupied versus the dilapidated occupied stock indicate much higher failure rates in the latter. The fact that the frequencies for dilapidated housing are not higher than

TABLE 6-4. DEFICIENCIES IN MAINTENANCE AND EQUIPMENT, ALL RENTER-OCCUPIED AND OCCUPIED DILAPIDATED UNITS, NEW YORK CITY, 1978 AND 1981 (by percent in each category)

	All Renter Occupied		Dilapidated Renter Occupied	
	1978	1981	1978	1981
Additional heating requiredd	25.4%	29.9%	55.1%	55.9%
Heating breakdowns				
1 or more times	31.3	31.5	57.9	60.1
4 or more times	12.2	14.1	32.8	38.1
Cracks in ceilings/ walls	20.8	22.2	64.5	61.5
Holes in floors	7.5	9.4	28.9	36.7
Broken plaster/ peeling paint	16.1	16.9	48.0	44.0
Rodents	21.1	24.3	66.3	56.5
Deficiencies				
1 or more	53.7	55.4	89.1	86.1
3 or more	17.8	20.6	62.9	57.3

NOTE: Calculations based on the number reporting for each deficiency.

SOURCES: 1978 data from Marcuse, pp. 160 and 163; 1981 data from U.S. Bureau of the Census, 1981 New York City Housing and Vacancy Survey.

Finally, and most importantly, in virtually every case the deficiency rate has increased over the last three years. While most of these increases are small percentages, they represent a relatively large number of units in which conditions may have worsened since 1978. Thus, for example, although the number of dwellings which have suffered at least four separate winter heating breakdowns was just 2 percentage points higher in 1981 than 1978, this means that almost 24,000 more households have heating problems now than three years ago. The same is true for the presence of rodents. The 3 percent higher average in 1981 indicates a rodent problem for approximately 47,000 additional renter households.† Finally, the nearly 3 percent rise in

*[continued] they are reflects either the unreliability of dilapidation as a measure of uninhabitability and/or that occupants of dilapidated housing have lower expectations of what constitutes "normal" maintenance (see Table 6-4).

†Each time this symbol appears in the chapter, the probability is .95 that differences between the values referred to are not due to chance.

the number of dwelling units with three or more separate problems translates into deteriorating housing conditions for around 34,000 more tenants in 1981 than in 1978.†

Structure Type, Rent and Location. The most interesting variation in deficiency rates occurred in tenements. Although both Old and New Law tenements have higher rates of maintenance problems than all rental units taken together, and rates for both sectors have risen since 1978, Old Laws have lower deficiency rates than New Laws and have not experienced as severe an increase in problems since 1978 (Table 6-5).

TABLE 6-5. DEFICIENCIES IN MAINTENANCE AND EQUIPMENT BY SELECTED STRUCTURE CLASS, ALL RENTER-OCCUPIED UNITS, NEW YORK CITY, 1978 AND 1981 (by percent in each category)

	Year	All Renter Occupied	Old Law	New Law	Multiples After 1929	1-2 Family Converted to Apartments
Additional heating required	1978	25.4	37.2	31.0	20.3	27.0
	1981	29.9	40.0	38.8	23.7	31.6
Heating breakdowns						
1 or more times	1978	31.3	43.5	43.8	24.0	30.2
	1981	31.5	39.9	47.7	24.2	24.8
4 or more times	1978	12.2	19.7	18.6	8.5	9.5
	1981	14.1	18.3	24.9	8.9	12.0
Cracks in ceiling/ walls	1978	20.8	33.3	34.1	10.8	19.0
	1981	22.2	34.1	37.2	12.1	18.6
Holes in floor	1978	7.5	13.8	13.3	2.1	9.3
	1981	9.4	15.4	17.1	3.0	9.1
Broken plaster/ peeling paint	1978	16.1	25.6	25.9	9.2	14.3
	1981	16.9	24.9	27.0	11.7	13.3
Rodent infestation	1978	21.1	34.2	35.0	11.2	13.0
	1981	24.3	35.4	40.5	13.5	17.4
Deficiencies						
1 or more	1978	53.7	72.9	69.2	43.4	54.5
	1981	55.4	71.2	72.5	46.4	50.7
3 or more	1978	17.8	31.4	31.2	8.1	13.7
	1981	20.6	32.5	36.5	10.5	15.5

SOURCES: 1978 data from Marcuse, p. 162; 1981 data from U.S. Bureau of the Census, 1981 New York City Housing and Vacancy Survey.

Old Law tenements are almost three times as likely as New Laws to be dilapidated, but the fact that just 2 percent of all Old Laws versus 28 percent of all New Laws in New York are in the Bronx and that more than 8,000 of the latter have been removed from the inventory since 1978 might partially explain their relatively low dilapidation rate compared to Old Laws. Dilapidated apartments in New Law tenements are more likely to be vacated, particularly in the Bronx, than are Old Law apartments in, say, Manhattan. Moreover, if the level of distress in the Bronx continues to grow, maintenance levels are bound to decline and the frequency of maintenance problems in New Laws will continue to rise relative to Old Laws.

The frequency of maintenance problems varies inversely with contract rent. The incidence of multiple problems ranges from a high of one out of four occupied units that rent for less than $30 per room, to around one out of 17 for apartments with a contract rent of more than $200 per room (Table 6-6).

TABLE 6-6. DEFICIENCIES IN MAINTENANCE AND EQUIPMENT BY CONTRACT RENT PER ROOM, ALL RENTER-OCCUPIED HOUSING UNITS, NEW YORK CITY, 1978 AND 1981 (by percent in each category)

			Contract Rent per Room					
Deficiencies	Year	Total	Less than $30	$30-49	$50-74	$75-99	$100-199	$200 or more
None	1978	46.3	38.8	41.0	44.1	51.2	58.0	67.4
	1981	44.6	38.0	35.1	38.9	48.1	53.2	67.6
3 or more	1978	17.8	24.8	22.8	18.3	11.4	8.7	4.1
	1981	20.6	27.3	29.4	25.3	15.5	11.9	6.1

NOTE: Percentages based on number reporting on all five deficiencies (need for additional heating; heating breakdowns; cracks in ceilings, walls or floors; broken plaster and peeling paint; rodents).

SOURCES: 1978 data from Marcuse, p. 161; 1981 data from U.S. Bureau of the Census, 1981 New York City Housing and Vacancy Survey.

In general, maintenance problems are fairly widespread throughout the stock and are not disproportionately concentrated in any single borough (Table 6-7). For example, while deficiency rates are typically higher in the Bronx than in Brooklyn, the differences are not very great. The ranking of condition from worst to best starts with the Bronx and ends with Richmond, as would be expected, but the frequencies of most problems in Manhattan and Queens are still quite high. The rates for multiple breakdowns in heating systems in Manhattan and Queens are 14 and 10 percent, respectively, while for rodents the rates are 20 and 15 percent, respectively.

TABLE 6-7. DEFICIENCIES IN MAINTENANCE AND EQUIPMENT IN RENTER-OCCUPIED UNITS, BY BOROUGH, NEW YORK CITY, 1978 AND 1981

	Year	Bronx	Brooklyn	Manhattan	Queens	Richmond
Additional	1978	31.8	25.2	25.6	20.7	17.7
heating req'd	1981	34.5	34.1	29.2	22.5	18.3
Heating breakdown						
1 or more times	1978	37.3	30.5	32.5	27.4	12.5
	1981	36.8	32.4	32.3	26.3	17.2
4 or more times	1978	16.6	11.9	12.7	8.8	4.4
	1981	18.5	14.9	14.1	10.4	7.0
Cracks in	1978	27.5	21.6	22.2	12.5	14.1
ceilings/walls	1981	27.2	25.0	23.3	13.8	13.4
Holes in floor	1978	9.9	8.9	7.6	3.5	4.6
	1981	11.7	11.1	9.9	4.9	2.7
Broken plaster/	1978	20.0	15.4	19.3	9.5	10.1
peeling paint	1981	21.1	17.1	20.0	9.9	8.8
Rodent	1978	29.8	25.4	18.7	11.9	8.9
infestation	1981*	34.3	29.9	20.9	14.9	8.3
Deficiencies						
1 or more	1978	62.1	54.8	54.3	45.6	36.8
	1981	63.5	59.7	54.9	46.3	31.3
3 or more	1978	26.3	18.5	18.6	9.3	8.0
	1981	26.8	24.2	21.1	11.4	9.4

*Calculated figures; percentages listed in Housing & Vacancy Survey not correct.

SOURCES: 1978 data from Marcuse, p. 165; 1981 data from U.S. Bureau of the Census, 1981 New York City Housing and Vacancy Survey.

Rent Control Status. Perhaps as important as any comparisons of maintenance conditions here are those pertaining to control status (Table 6-8). Consistent with the findings on dilapidation rates, controlled units are less likely than pre-'47 stabilized apartments to have maintenance deficiencies. One out of four controlled apartments had at least three maintenance problems, while the rate for pre-'47 stabilized units was closer to one in three.† As suggested earlier, while this could imply that stable occupancy and long-term tenure are conducive to operating economies, the data might just reflect higher turnover rates in the poorer quality stock.

TABLE 6-8. DEFICIENCIES IN MAINTENANCE AND EQUIPMENT IN RENTER-OCCUPIED UNITS, BY CONTROL STATUS, NEW YORK CITY, 1978 AND 1981 (by percent in each category)

	Year	Controlled	Decontrolled	Stabilized Pre-1947	Stabilized 1947 or later
Total (thousands)	1978	402	268	552	320
	1981	286	282	615	313
Additional heating required	1978	28.2%	20.6%	31.8%	15.8%
	1981	35.0	25.4	36.1	18.2
Heating breakdown 1 or more times	1978	39.8	18.4	45.2	22.0
	1981	39.6	19.6	43.8	24.1
4 or more times	1978	16.2	5.7	18.7	6.3
	1981	18.8	8.8	21.1	7.5
Cracks in ceilings/walls	1978	27.4	14.8	32.1	9.3
	1981	26.6	19.0	33.6	8.6
Holes in floors	1978	8.8	6.8	13.3	2.2
	1981	9.9	9.3	15.8	1.9
Broken plaster/ peeling paint	1978	22.0	10.9	24.0	6.7
	1981	20.5	10.6	25.3	7.2
Rodent infestation	1978	22.0	18.1	35.0	9.1
	1981	23.2	22.5	37.2	12.5
Deficiencies 1 or more	1978	61.9	41.4	70.3	37.6
	1981	61.7	45.6	69.8	41.6
3 or more	1978	23.2	12.0	30.1	5.8
	1981	25.1	15.5	32.5	7.6

SOURCES: 1978 data from Marcuse, p. 246; 1981 data from U.S. Bureau of the Census, 1981 New York City Housing and Vacancy Survey.

Because decontrolled housing is not subject to any form of rent regulation, there is a tendency to overlook its condition. Deficiencies in this market sector are lower than in either controlled or pre-'47 stabilized housing. Nevertheless, conditions in decontrolled housing have worsened more since 1978 than in the other sectors. This is the case for apartments having multiple heating system failures, and for such problems as holes in floors and open cracks in walls and ceilings.

Since the size of the decontrolled stock did increase by some 14,000 units since 1978, it could be that the higher incidence of maintenance problems is due to the inclusion in this sector of lower-than-average quality controlled housing that was vacated. While this may have happened, it does not fully explain the worsening condition of this stock. The net increase in the size of the decontrolled stock between 1978 and 1981 was only 5 percent, while most of the maintenance problems increased by substantially greater rates. In other words, the condition of housing already part of the decontrolled sector in 1978 has worsened since then.

Overcrowding and Under-Utilization of Space

Statistics on overcrowding, like those on high rent burdens, reflect a mismatch between households and their housing more than housing problems *per se*. Theoretically, at least, overcrowding can be reduced by reallocating the existing supply of living space without structurally altering the stock. This is not true with physical housing problems. The long-term decline in household size means that overcrowding now affects a small proportion of renter households. Using the traditional measure of overcrowding -- more than one person per room -- 7 percent of all renters in New York live in overcrowded conditions (Table 6-9). Although the rate has not changed since 1978, the present level of overcrowding is less than half of what it was in 1960 (14 percent) and 20 percent lower than it was in 1975 (8 percent). The rate of serious overcrowding -- i.e., more than 1.5 persons per room -- has also declined dramatically, from around 5 percent in 1960 to 2 percent in 1981.

TABLE 6-9. PERSONS PER ROOM, ALL RENTER-OCCUPIED UNITS, NEW YORK CITY, SELECTED YEARS

Persons per room	1960	1965	1970	1975	1978	1981
1.01 or more	292,000	227,000	233,000	160,000	125,000	123,000
(percent)	14.1	11.0	10.8	8.1	6.5	6.5
1.51 or more	99,000	68,000	64,000	38,000	29,000	31,000
(percent)	4.8	2.9	3.0	1.9	1.5	1.7

NOTE: All numbers have been rounded to the nearest thousand. All percentages are calculated from unrounded numbers.

SOURCES: 1960-1978 data from Marcuse, p. 182; 1981 data from U.S. Bureau of the Census, 1981 New York City Housing and Vacancy Survey.

Understandably, large families suffer overcrowding in disproportionately high numbers (Table 6-10). More than one-third of all renter households containing five people were overcrowded in 1981, while nearly one in 10 lived in seriously overcrowded apartments. Nearly two-thirds of all households of six or more were overcrowded and 14 percent were severely so.

TABLE 6-10. PERSONS PER ROOM BY HOUSEHOLD SIZE, FOR LARGE RENTER HOUSEHOLDS, NEW YORK CITY, 1978 AND 1981

	Persons Per Room			
	1978		1981	
Household Size	1.01+	1.51+	1.01+	1.51+
5 person households	36.5%	5.8%	34.7%	8.7%
6 persons or more	80.2%	16.5%	66.3%	14.4%

SOURCES: 1978 data from Marcuse, p. 184; 1981 data from U.S. Bureau of the Census, 1981 New York City Housing and Vacancy Survey.

In his 1968 report, Niebanck completed a sophisticated analysis of space use in which he defined a set of occupancy standards relating household size to living space.* His purpose was to test the hypothesis that rent control contributed to a misallocation of dwelling space by discouraging mobility and the adjustment of housing space to changes in household size. He determined that 20 percent of all renter households were overcrowded in 1965 and that 16 percent were "undercrowded," or living in apartments that, by his norms, were too large (Tables 6-11 and 6-12).

Replicating Niebanck's analysis with 1981 data indicates that overcrowding has declined from 20 to 14 percent, while undercrowding has increased from 16 to 20 percent of all households. In the controlled stock, undercrowding has increased from 19 percent of all households in 1965 to 27 percent in 1981, and in decontrolled apartments, from 26 to 38 percent.

Underutilization rates in both pre- and post-'47 stabilized sectors were 12 percent in 1981, or between one-half and one-third of what they were in controlled and decontrolled apartments. Using Niebanck's standards, these same two control sectors are least likely to be overcrowded. In the controlled stock, overcrowding fell from 17 percent of all households in 1965 to 7 percent in 1981, and in the decontrolled from 19 percent to 8 per-

---

*Niebanck defined the following occupancy standards:

Household Size	Number of Rooms for Overcrowding	Number of Rooms for Normal Occupancy	Number of Rooms for Underutilization
1 person	1	2-3	4 or more
2 persons	1	2-4	5 or more
3 persons	1-3	4	5 or more
4 persons	1-4	4-5	6 or more
5 persons	1-4	5-7	8 or more
6 or more persons	1-5	6 or more	indeterminate

See Niebanck, 1968, p. 131.

TABLE 6-11. OVERCROWDING IN RENTER-OCCUPIED HOUSING UNITS, BY SIZE OF HOUSEHOLD AND SELECTED CONTROL STATUS, NEW YORK CITY, 1965 AND 1981 (all numbers in thousands)

	All Renter-Occupied			Controlled			Decontrolled			Pre-'47 Stabilized		Post- '47 Stabilized	
	Total	1965	1981	Total	1965	1981	Total	1965	1981	Total	1981	Total	1981
All													
Households #		416	271		225	20		34	22		124		49
%	100%	20.2	14.3	100%	17.0	7.3	100%	18.5	8.1	100%	20.5	100%	16.1
Size of Household:													
1 person	100%	21.5	13.1	100%	9.4	4.8	100%	16.0	6.0	100%	15.2	100%	18.7
2 persons	100%	3.0	2.1	100%	1.6	0.6	100%	3.7	0.7	100%	3.3	100%	3.2
3 persons	100%	28.6	24.1	100%	30.6	22.8	100%	24.2	11.4	100%	40.6	100%	26.8
4 persons	100%	14.9	13.0	100%	17.9	15.2	100%	12.7	3.6	100%	26.0	100%	20.2
5 persons	100%	50.0	43.4	100%	54.2	56.9	100%	30.6	28.1	100%	57.7	100%	61.5
6 or more persons	100%	69.9	65.7	100%	74.0	55.4	100%	51.2	39.9	100%	85.4	100%	83.3

NOTES: 1. 1965 data available only for "All Renter-Occupied," "Controlled," and "Decontrolled," because there were no stabilized units at that time.
2. Definition of overcrowding obtained from Niebanck, p. 131.
3. Percentages for each year based on total number of households within each size category reporting for that year.

SOURCES: 1965 data from Niebanck, p. 133; 1981 data from U.S. Bureau of the Census, 1981 New York City Housing and Vacancy Survey.

TABLE 6-12. UNDERUTILIZATION OF HOUSING SPACE IN RENTER-OCCUPIED UNITS, BY HOUSEHOLD SIZE AND SELECTED CONTROL STATUS, NEW YORK CITY, 1965 AND 1981 (All numbers in thousands)

	All Renter-Occupied			Controlled			Decontrolled			Pre-'47 Stabilized		Post-'47 Stabilized	
	Total	1965	1981	Total	1965	1981	Total	1965	1981	Total	1981	Total	1981
All Households #		330	372		247	74		47	104		73		37
%	100%	16.0	19.7	100%	18.7	26.5	100%	25.5	38.3	100%	12.2	100%	12.1
Size of Household:													
1 person	100%	20.8	23.5	100%	27.5	31.6	100%	26.3	46.1	100%	16.0	100%	15.0
2 persons	100%	14.1	16.2	100%	15.6	21.6	100%	28.3	37.8	100%	8.8	100%	7.9
3 persons	100%	25.5	31.2	100%	27.1	31.5	100%	46.2	56.8	100%	18.8	100%	20.0
4 persons	100%	12.9	13.0	100%	12.4	15.2	100%	27.0	30.7	100%	4.2	100%	5.9

NOTES: 1. 1965 data available only for "All Renter-Occupied," "Controlled," and "Decontrolled," because there were no stabilized units at that time.

2. Definition of underutilization obtained from Niebanck, p.131.

3. For 5 or more person households it is impossible to determine underutilization with an open-ended "6 or more rooms" class in the Housing and Vacancy Survey.

4. Percentages for each year based on total number of households within each size category reporting for that year.

SOURCES: 1965 data from Niebanck, p. 135; 1981 data from U.S. Bureau of the Census, 1981 New York City Housing and Vacancy Survey.

cent. In contrast, 20 percent of all tenants in pre-'47 stabilized apartments and 16 percent of tenants in post-'47 stabilized apartments are overcrowded.

Who Lives in Inadequate Housing?

Race and Ethnic Origin. Although one out of every 25 renters in New York City live in dilapidated housing and one out of every five live in apartments that have at least three maintenance deficiencies, different population groups suffer from these probelms in vastly different proportions (Table 6-13). For example, less than 3 percent of all White renters occupy dilapidated housing, while the rate among Blacks is 6 percent.† More strikingly, 9 percent of all Puerto Rican renters live in some of the worst housing in the City.

TABLE 6-13. INADEQUATE RENTAL HOUSING BY SELECTED HOUSEHOLD CHARACTERISTICS, NEW YORK CITY, 1981

Selected Characteristics	Percent Who Occupy Dilapidated Housing	Percent Who Occupy Housing With Three or More Maintenance Deficiencies
All renters	4.2	20.6
White households	2.5	12.5
Black households	5.9	34.5
Puerto Rican households	9.4	38.1
One-person households	3.6	15.6
Five or more person households	6.1	34.1
Female-headed households	4.5	24.9
Household heads 65 years or older	2.4	14.1
Households below 100% of the federal poverty level	8.6	N.A.
Receiving Public Assistance	12.2	46.5
Households spending:		
at least 25% of income for rent	5.6*	26.6**
at least 40% of income for rent	6.8*	31.0**

*Gross rent.
**Contract rent; not available for gross rent.

SOURCE: U.S. Bureau of the Census, 1981 New York City Housing and Vacancy Survey.

This racial/ethnic pattern is repeated for the incidence of multiple maintenance problems, although the difference between Blacks and Puerto Ricans is smaller. Whites are about one-third as likely as either Blacks or Puerto Ricans to live in apartments with at least three maintenance problems. Larger fractions of all groups suffer from maintenance-related housing problems than from dilapidation.

Because of the very substantial income differences among the three population groups and the strong relationship between income and housing quality (see Chapter 8), the above data cannot be used in any conclusive way to test for racial or ethnic discrimination in the housing market. For example, the proportion of renter households with incomes below $4,000 who occupy dilapidated housing is almost triple that for households with incomes between $20,000 and $25,000 (8 percent as compared to 3 percent).† More than twice the percentage of renters with incomes below the poverty level live in dilapidated housing compared to the City as a whole, while for households receiving public assistance the dilapidation rate exceeds the citywide rate by three to one (12 percent versus 4 percent). Considering that the median income of Black renter households is only around two-thirds that of Whites, and that incomes of Puerto Rican households lag even further behind, it would be expected that even without discrimination Whites would be less likely than the others to occupy physically inadequate housing.

Other Socioeconomic Characteristics. Important differences in housing conditions also exist with respect to other household characteristics. The rate of housing inadequacies in one- and two-room apartments is lower than for larger ones. Single person households are consequently less likely than others to live in dilapidated dwellings or ones with multiple maintenance problems (Table 6-13). Large families are more than twice as likely as single individuals to occupy seriously deficient housing, while the elderly, a large proportion of whom live alone, are less likely than most other groups to live in the poorest quality housing in the City. Female-headed households, on the other hand, are relatively more likely to occupy inadequate housing. Finally, because poor housing in New York is relatively expensive and consumes a large share of poor people's incomes, even those who spend at least 40 percent of their incomes for rent are more likely than all renters to occupy inadequate housing. This is true both for dilapidated housing, where almost 7 percent of all households with rent-income ratios of at least 40 percent reside, and for maintenance-deficient housing which is occupied by 31 percent of all those with such excessive rent burdens. Finally, nearly half of all welfare families, most of whom also have high rent-income ratios, live in apartments with many maintenance problems.

Neighborhood Quality

In 1981, Census enumerators documented that 23 percent of occupied apartments are in buildings with boarded-up units or on blocks with boarded-up buildings, compared to the 25 percent rate found in 1978 (Table 5-10). In both 1978 and 1981, 45 percent of all available vacancies in the City were on streets with nearby boarded-up apartments and buildings.

Few implications can be drawn from these data without much more information on occupancy patterns and housing conditions at the block and neighborhood level (See Chapter 9). If, for example, normal market processes are driving vacancies to the most deteriorated buildings in the most distressed neighborhoods, with the worst housing dropping out of the market and the least desirable neighborhoods emptying out in response to lower levels of housing demand, the association of vacancies and boarded-up structures could be a positive sign. If, however, the presence of boarded-up or other derelict buildings on the street were to cause families in fully occupied buildings to flee, thus upsetting stable occupancy patterns and threatening the financial viability of marginally sound rental operations to the extent that physically sound housing is abandoned, then the tendency of vacant housing to cluster on blocks with boarded-up structures might actually reflect the self-perpetuating nature of the dynamics of decline and the premature destruction of neighborhood housing stocks.

Boarded-up Buildings and Control Status. Recognizing the limitations of the data, it is still useful to assess the locations of boarded-up buildings to see if control status seems to be an important part of the overall picture. Just as with dilapidation rates and the incidence of various maintenance problems, the probability that a rental unit will be in the same building or on the same block as boarded-up buildings varies with control status. Consistent with the earlier findings, apartments that are still under rent control are less likely to be near boarded-up buildings than are either decontrolled or pre-'47 stabilized units (Table 6-14). Decontrolled apartments are 37 percent more likely to be in buildings or on blocks with boarded-up structures than are controlled units.† Pre-'47 stabilized apartments are 50 percent more likely than controlled units to be near boarded-up buildings.†

TABLE 6-14. PRESENCE OF BOARDED-UP STRUCTURES ON STREET (INTERVIEW OBSERVATION), ALL RENTER-OCCUPIED AND VACANT AVAILABLE UNITS, BY CONTROL STATUS, NEW YORK CITY, 1981

	Controlled	Decontrolled	Stabilized Pre-1947	Stabilized Post-1947
Occupied				
Percent with board-ups on street	20.4	27.9	30.8	8.4
Vacant				
Percent with board-ups on street	N.A.	48.6	48.9	23.8

NOTE: Household responses to question of the presence of board-ups results in consistently higher rates: for controlled units the rate is 23.6 percent; decontrolled, 31.6 percent; pre-1947, 33.8 percent, and post-1947, 11.7 percent.

SOURCE: U.S. Bureau of the Census, 1981 New York City Housing and Vacancy Survey.

The analysis suggests that long-term tenancy may help maintain the economic viability of older buildings which may be unable to recover from either prolonged or frequent vacancies and the high costs of short-term tenancies. That nearly half of all decontrolled and pre-'47 stabilized vacancies are in buildings or on blocks with boarded-up buildings lends further support to the argument that stable tenancy is one of the keys to keeping financially afloat in the lower reaches of the City's rental market.

Adequacy of Neighborhood. Although it is difficult to interpret subjective measures having to do with neighborhood quality, both the 1978 and 1981 Housing and Vacancy Surveys asked renters to rate the adequacy of their neighborhoods (Table 6-15). What is most striking about the responses is that they have not changed in the three years. In both 1978 and 1981, approximately 14 percent of all renter households judged their neighborhoods to be excellent and approximately 11 percent judged them to be poor. The remaining three-quarters opted for either "good" or "fair" ratings.

TABLE 6-15. THE RELATIVE ADEQUACY OF NEIGHBORHOOD, ALL RENTER HOUSEHOLDS, NEW YORK CITY, 1978 AND 1981

	Adequacy of Neighborhood			
	Excellent	Good	Fair	Poor
1978	14.5%	41.7%	32.0%	11.9%
1981	14.2	41.7	32.7	11.4

SOURCE: 1978 data from Marcuse, p. 179; 1981 data from U.S. Bureau of the Census, 1981 New York City Housing and Vacancy Survey.

CHAPTER 7

THE LEVEL OF RENTS

Chapter 2 described the regulations that govern rent increases for controlled and stabilized apartments. That discussion indicated that, in contrast to the war-time system of rent control which allowed no increases, the newer program permits rent levels in the controlled and stabilized inventories to rise along with operating costs. Between 1970 and 1981, median gross rents for all occupied units in New York City more than doubled, from $109 a month to $265 (Table 7-1).* More importantly, rents increased at a faster rate than the cost of living, with the result that median rents rose by 12 percent in real terms over the eleven year period. Rents did not increase steadily however; between 1978 and 1981 real rents registered a 5 percent decline. During this time median rents rose by 26 percent, but the cost of living, as measured by the Consumer Price Index, increased by nearly one-third. The post-1970 squeeze on net operating income is, therefore, a relatively recent phenomenon. This chapter analyzes the level of rents in different market sectors, emphasizing changes in the past three years since the last comprehensive assessment of rental housing conditions in New York City.

Rent Inflation and Housing Quality

Before proceeding with the rent analysis, it should be noted that the recently released report of the President's Commission on Housing argues that average rent changes in the rental stock are an inappropriate measure of rent inflation because the characteristics of the supply change between the times the prices are measured.[1] The Commission cites Ira S. Lowry's analysis of national data and states that between 1950 and 1970, median rents across the country rose at twice the rate reflected in the rent component of the Consumer Price Index (CPI) for that period.[2] The CPI measures price changes for a constant quality dwelling.** With median rent increases still exceeding

---

*The Housing and Vacancy Survey provides data on both gross rent and contract rent. Gross rent includes utility costs, either paid as part of rent or by the tenant directly to the utility company. Contract rent is the asking rent for the unit and may or may not include utilities. Most analyses of housing costs in this chapter refer to occupied units and use gross rent because of the importance of utility costs in the housing picture. Analysis of asking rents for vacant units presented in Chapter 5 is in terms of contract rents. For comparative purposes it should be noted that contract rents have exhibited similar patterns to gross rents over the decade, increasing by 147 percent between 1970 and 1981 in current dollars, and by 15 percent in constant dollars. Similarly, between 1978 and 1981, median contract rents increased from $186 to $235, or by 26 percent, and declined by around 4 percent in real terms.

**The rent component of the Consumer Price Index for the New York-Northeastern New Jersey Metropolitan Area increased by 96 percent between April 1970 and April 1981 while actual rents rose by 143 percent.

changes in the CPI rent index by 20 percent during the 1970s, Lowry and the Commission conclude that a substantial portion of actual rent increases over the past 30 years has been due to improvements in average housing quality, rather than rent inflation. Thus, some of the resulting increase in the relative rent burden of households is a function of their consuming more and better housing today than in the 1950s.[3]

The overall changes in New York City rents noted above are not measured for constant quality housing units and may be affected either by improvements to existing units or by higher prices for newer units, but this problem should be limited to the post-'47 rent stabilized sector. While changes in rent levels in neither the pre-'47 stabilized nor controlled sectors are measured in terms of constant quality dwellings, it is unlikely that a significant portion of the post-1970 rent increase in these two inventories is due to improvements. In fact, available indicators of housing conditions in these sectors show no significant improvements during the 1970s (See Chapter 6).

TABLE 7-1. MEDIAN MONTHLY GROSS RENTS IN CURRENT AND CONSTANT (1967) DOLLARS, ALL RENTER-OCCUPIED UNITS, NEW YORK CITY, SELECTED YEARS

	Gross Rent				Percent Change			
	1970	1975	1978	1981	1970-'81	1970-'75	1975-'78	1978-'81
Current dollars	$109	$171	$210	$265	+143.1	+56.9	+22.8	+26.2
CPI*	116.9	163.4	192.2	253.9	+117.2	+39.8	+17.6	+32.1
Constant dollars	$ 93	$105	$109	$104	+ 11.8	+12.9	+ 3.8	- 4.6

*Consumer Price Index for All Urban Consumers for New York-Northeastern New Jersey (1967 = 100), March of each year, Bureau of Labor Statistics, U.S. Department of Labor.

NOTE: Rents in current dollars rounded to nearest dollar before calculating rents in constant dollars. Rents in constant dollars calculated by dividing rents in current dollars by the CPI for the appropriate year. Rents in constant dollars rounded to nearest dollar. Percent change figures calculated from rounded figures.

SOURCE: 1970, 1975 and 1978 data from Marcuse, p. 197; 1981 data from the U.S. Bureau of the Census, 1981 New York City Housing and Vacancy Survey.

The Changing Distribution of Rents

Analysis of New York City rents begins with an accounting of the number of occupied units renting at various levels and shows how the distribution has changed since 1978. The data are presented for both contract and gross rents to enable the reader to distinguish between the effects of increases in shelter rents and utilities on housing costs (Table 7-2).

TABLE 7-2. DISTRIBUTION OF RENTAL HOUSING BY CONTRACT AND GROSS RENTS, NEW YORK CITY, 1978 AND 1981

Contract Rent

	1978		1981		Percent Change
	Number	Percent	Number	Percent	1978-1981
Total reported*	1,841,793	100.0	1,872,781	100.0	+ 0.1
Less than $200	1,042,538	56.6	660,421	35.3	- 36.7
$200-299	541,167	29.4	694,769	37.1	+ 28.4
$300-399	149,625	8.1	279,386	14.9	+ 86.7
$400-499	55,365	3.0	112,337	6.0	+102.9
$500 or more	53,098	2.9	125,868	6.7	+137.0

Gross Rent

	1978		1981		Percent Change
	Number	Percent	Number	Percent	1978-1981
Total reported*	1,714,931	100.0	1,713,942	100.0	+ 1.7
Less than $200	768,309	44.8	437,219	25.5	- 43.1
$200-299	627,653	36.6	643,610	37.6	+ 2.5
$300-399	197,503	11.5	360,248	21.0	+ 82.4
$400-499	62,811	3.7	135,100	7.9	+115.1
$500 or more	58,655	3.4	137,765	8.0	+134.9

*No cash rent was included with Not Reported for 1978 and 1981.

NOTE: Percents may not add to 100 percent because of rounding.

SOURCES: 1978 data from Marcuse, p. 220; 1981 data from U.S. Bureau of the Census, 1981 New York City Housing and Vacancy Survey.

Between 1978 and 1981, there has been a sizeable reduction in the number of units renting for less than $200 a month. In 1978, more than three quarters of a million units had gross rents below $200, while now the number has dropped by 43 percent to 437,000.† The steep decline in the number of moderately priced rental units in the City is not surprising because utility costs alone have more than doubled since 1978, while the BLS index of operating costs has risen by 39 percent.

---

†Each time this symbol appears in the chapter, the probability is 95 percent that differences between the values referred to are not due to chance.

In both absolute and relative terms, the quantity of higher rent units has increased substantially since 1978. The number of apartments with gross rents of between $300 and $400 has risen by 82 percent, while the number renting for between $400 and $500 and for more than $500 a month has more than doubled in three years. In 1978, slightly more than one out of every 14 units had gross rents of $400 or more, while by 1981 the figure had climbed to more than one out of six.

Control Status

There are at least four important findings relative to changing rent levels and the control status of housing. First, consistent with the analysis in Chapter 2, median gross rents for controlled housing rose more rapidly than in either of the stabilized sectors. Since 1975, median controlled rents have increased by 60 percent, while for pre- and post-'47 stabilized housing the respective increases were 49 percent and 44 percent (Table 7-3 and Exhibit 7-1). One reason the stabilized sectors experienced different rates of rent increases, even though the Rent Guidelines Board orders apply equally to all stabilized units, is that each is characterized by different mixes of lease terms and tenant turnover rates. The greater the turnover rate, and the shorter the lease term, the greater the permissible increases have been under recent Board rent orders. While 22 percent of all renters moved into their pre-'47 stabilized units in either 1980 or 1981, the comparable rate in the post-'47 stock was just 13 percent.† Similarly, the average lease term is shorter in pre-'47 than in post-'47 apartments (2.1 versus 2.5 years), which leads to higher rent increases for the former during inflationary periods.*

Second, controlled rents have actually increased faster than the overall rate of inflation in recent years. This has been due to the combination of biennial increases in MBRs, annual rent increases of up to 7.5 percent and, more recently, to fuel pass-throughs. In real terms stabilized rents have declined since 1975: 5 percent for pre-'47 and 7 percent for post-'47 units. Controlled rents have increased 4 percent yet the median rent for pre-'47 stabilized apartments is $49 higher than that for controlled units. This suggests that the MBR system, while keeping rent increases in line with trends in operating costs, still has not accomplished its primary objective of closing the rent gap in the controlled sector.**

Third, rent levels vary significantly by control status (Table 7-3). Pre-'47 stabilized units rent for 23 percent more than do controlled apartments ($262 versus $213).† Similarly, post-'47 stabilized units cost 40 percent more than pre-'47 stabilized apartments, although in this case the higher rents signify higher quality housing.† This is not so for controlled

---

*When rent increases for the matched housing units in the pre- and post-'47 sectors are examined, average increases are much closer than when changes in medians throughout the inventory are compared. Between 1978 and 1981, for example, the sample of matched dwellings shows a 25 percent increase in median gross rents in the pre-'47 stabilized stock. Post-'47 rents in the longitudinal sample rose by 26 percent. See Chapter 9 for detailed analysis of additional longitudinal data.

**See Chapter 2 for further discussion of the MBR system.

TABLE 7-3. MEDIAN MONTHLY GROSS RENT IN CURRENT AND CONSTANT (1967) DOLLARS, BY CONTROL STATUS, ALL RENTER HOUSEHOLDS, NEW YORK CITY, 1975, 1978 AND 1981

	Current Dollars			Percent Change	
	1975	1978	1981	1975-1981	1978-1981
New York City	$171	$210	$265	+55.0	+26.2
Controlled	133	164	213	+60.2	+29.9
Decontrolled	191	222	271	+41.9	+22.1
Stabilized					
Pre-'47	176	209	262	+48.9	+25.4
Post-'47	255	296	368	+44.3	+24.3
CPI	163.4	192.2	253.9	+55.4	+32.1

	Constant Dollars			Percent Change	
	1975	1978	1981	1975-1981	1978-1981
New York City	$105	$109	$104	-1.0	-4.6
Controlled	81	85	84	+3.7	-1.2
Decontrolled	117	116	107	-8.5	-7.8
Stabilized					
Pre-'47	108	109	103	-4.6	-5.5
Post-'47	156	154	145	-7.1	-5.8

NOTE: Rents in current dollars rounded to nearest dollar before calculating rents in constant dollars. Rents in constant dollars calculated by dividing rents in current dollars by CPI for the appropriate year. Rents in constant dollars rounded to nearest dollar. Percent change calculated from rounded numbers.

SOURCES: 1975 and 1978 data from Marcuse, p. 256; 1981 data from U.S. Bureau of the Census, 1981 New York City Housing and Vacancy Survey.

versus pre-'47 stabilized units. More important than these rent differences, however, may be those between controlled and decontrolled housing.

Fourth, decontrolled rents tend to be higher than controlled rents ($271 versus $213 in 1981), although in recent years controlled rents have increased more rapidly.† This is true for the entire period 1975-1981 as well as for the most recent three years. The seeming paradox of a lower percentage rent increase in an unregulated sector might be used to support arguments in favor of abolishing rent regulation altogether. The more rapid rise for controlled and stabilized rents than for decontrolled ones could, however, reflect the phenomenon that MBR and Guidelines Board permissible rent increases become rent minima as well as rent maxima. If maximum permitted rent increases are likely to become the minimum charges landlords demand, then a system of administered price increases that reduces individual landlord uncertainty about market conditions and pricing, may have the unintended effect of raising housing costs to consumers.

The mere fact of a rent increase rate differential, however, cannot be depended on to support the proposition that rent ceilings become rent floors. This is so for at least two reasons: location and size. Decontrolled units are more likely than either controlled or stabilized apartments to be in Brooklyn, where total rents rose less rapidly than elsewhere in the City. Fifty-four percent of all decontrolled units are in Brooklyn, where median rents increased by 22 percent (versus 26 percent citywide) since 1978.

Because they are small, decontrolled buildings are much more likely than others to have their owners in residence. According to research literature, this implies a lesser tendency by owner-occupants to manage their buildings with an eye toward profit maximization in the traditional sense of the term.[4] Owner-investors are more likely than others to invest their own labor in maintenance on which they do not seek a return, to screen potential tenants, to assure compatibility with themselves, and to increase rents only upon a turnover in occupancy. Thus, the fact that owner-residents own 56 percent of all decontrolled and just 15 percent of all controlled apartments may be sufficient to explain a substantial portion of the difference in the recent rate of rent increases between these two sectors.

Borough

Housing costs in New York City vary substantially by borough, with median rents in Richmond and Manhattan being about 26 percent higher than those in the Bronx and Brooklyn (Table 7-4 and Exhibit 7-2).[†] More important than the absolute difference among the boroughs, however, is that the rent differential has widened considerably over the years, increasing the spatial segregation of New York City's rental market. In 1970, for example, median rents in Manhattan were just 10 percent higher than those in the Bronx. In 1975, the rent gap inched up to 11 percent, rose to 15 percent in 1978, and leapt to 26 percent in 1981.

The vigor of Manhattan's rental market is best reflected in the fact that, despite the dual system of rent control and stabilization, median rents there nearly tripled between 1970 and 1981, rising from $111 to $302. Because of the combination of strong demand, high turnover rates, vacancy lease increases above those permitted for lease renewals, and fuel pass-throughs, owners of rental housing in Manhattan were able to raise their rents substantially above the rate of inflation during the 1970s. During the 1970 to 1981 period, median rents in Manhattan increased by 25 percent more than the cost of living. In no other borough did real growth in rents exceed 11 percent. Even for the most recent three-year period during which the cost of living rose by 32 percent, Manhattan rents grew by 35 percent. In all other boroughs real rents declined between 1978 and 1981, by as much as 7 percent in the Bronx, and by 8 percent in Brooklyn and Queens.

TABLE 7-4. MEDIAN MONTHLY GROSS RENTS IN CURRENT AND CONSTANT (1967) DOLLARS, BY BOROUGH, ALL RENTER HOUSEHOLDS, NEW YORK CITY, SELECTED YEARS

					Percent Change			
	1970	1975	1978	1981	1970-81	1970-75	1975-78	1978-81
				Current Dollars				
New York City	$109	$171	$210	$265	+143.1	+56.9	+22.8	+26.2
Bronx	101	157	195	239	+136.6	+55.4	+24.2	+22.6
Brooklyn	102	162	199	243	+138.2	+58.8	+22.8	+22.1
Manhattan	111	175	224	302	+172.1	+57.7	+28.0	+34.8
Queens	135	194	230	283	+109.6	+43.7	+18.6	+23.0
Richmond	131	207	236	303	+131.3	+58.0	+14.0	+28.4
CPI	116.9	163.4	192.2	253.9	+117.2	+39.8	+17.6	+32.1
				Constant Dollars				
New York City	$93	$105	$109	$104	+11.8	+12.9	+3.8	-4.6
Bronx	86	96	101	94	+ 9.3	+11.6	+5.2	-6.9
Brooklyn	87	99	104	96	+10.3	+13.8	+5.1	-7.7
Manhattan	95	107	117	119	+25.3	+12.6	+9.3	+1.7
Queens	115	119	120	111	- 3.5	+ 3.5	+0.8	-7.5
Richmond	112	127	123	119	+ 6.3	+13.4	-3.1	-4.6

NOTES: 1. Rents in current dollars rounded to nearest dollar before calculating rents in constant dollars. Rents in constant dollars calculated by dividing rents in current dollars by CPI for the appropriate year. Rents in constant dollars rounded to nearest dollar. Percent change calculated from rounded numbers.

2. Consumer Price Index for all Urban Consumers for New York-Northeastern New Jersey. (1967=100), March of each year, Bureau of Labor Statistics, U.S. Dept. of Labor.

SOURCES: 1970, 1975 and 1978 data from Marcuse, pp. 206 and 221; 1981 data from U.S. Bureau of the Census, 1981 New York City Housing and Vacancy Survey.

EXHIBIT 7-1. MEDIAN MONTHLY GROSS RENT BY CONTROL STATUS, NEW YORK CITY, 1975, 1978 AND 1981

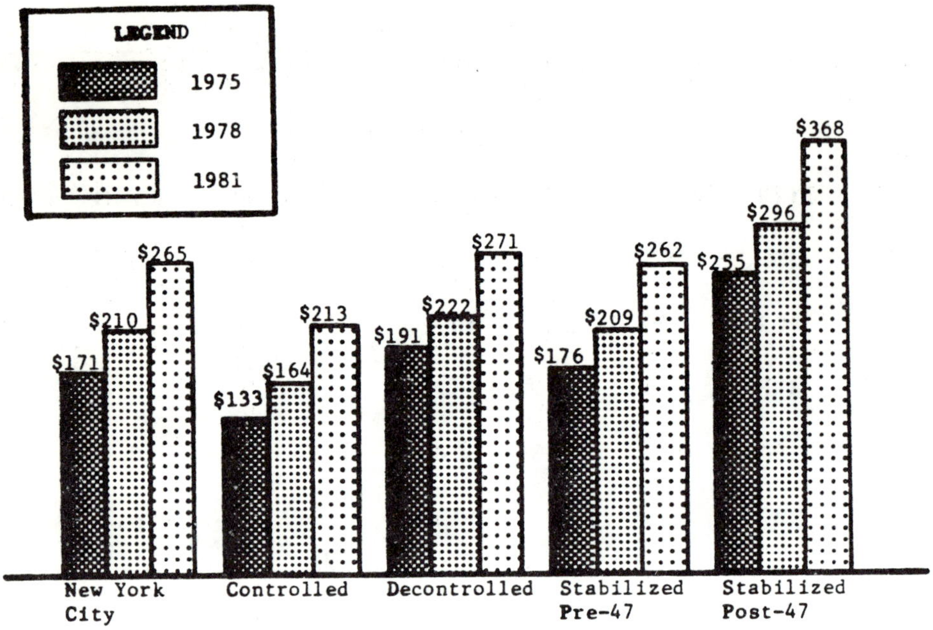

SOURCE: Table 7-3.

EXHIBIT 7-2. MEDIAN MONTHLY GROSS RENT BY BOROUGH, NEW YORK CITY, 1970 AND 1981

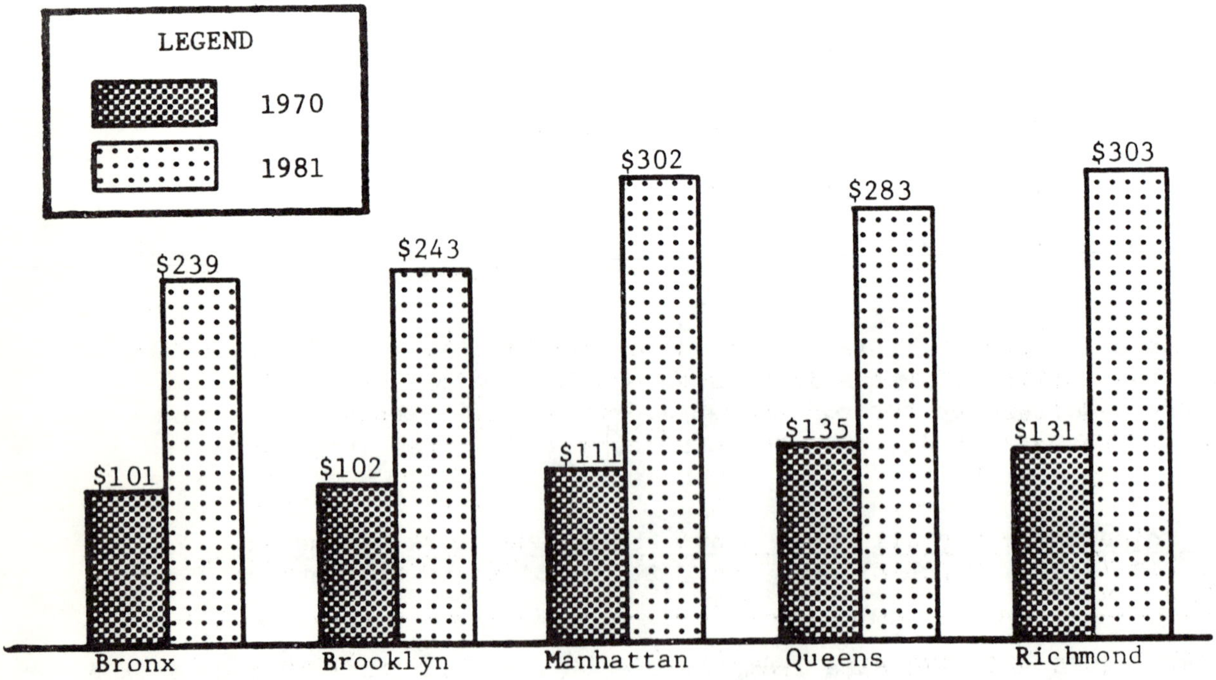

SOURCE: Table 7-4.

Number of Rooms

Holding quality constant, rents should vary with dwelling size, although not necessarily in a linear fashion. The addition of, say, a third bedroom is not likely to add the same increment to rent as would a second bedroom. Where rent levels are partially dependent on turnover rates and lease terms as they are in New York, the anticipated relationship between rent and dwelling size cannot be predicted with any degree of confidence. The distribution of median rents by the number of rooms in the dwelling confirms this point (Table 7-5). Rents do not vary much by apartment size in most control classes. For all occupied units, the difference between the median rent for one- and five-room units is just $44, or 18 percent ($244 versus $288). The difference is 21 percent for controlled units and 19 percent for pre-'47 stabilized units. In contrast, in the post-'47 stabilized stock, the difference in rents between one- and five-room apartments is 46 percent, $313 compared to $458. The larger difference between rents for small and larger apartments in this sector is partly due to the higher economic rents for new units that come onto the stabilized market. These rents reflect real differences in the respective development costs of older and newer apartments. As apartments of different sizes

TABLE 7-5. MEDIAN MONTHLY GROSS RENT, BY SELECTED CONTROL STATUS AND NUMBER OF ROOMS IN UNIT, FOR SELECTED CONTROL CATEGORIES, NEW YORK CITY, 1981

Rooms	All Renter Occupied Units	Controlled	Stabilized Pre-'47	Stabilized Post-'47
All renters	$265	$213	$262	$368
1 room	244	184	252	313
2 rooms	249	188	249	334
3 rooms	254	206	249	348
4 rooms	265	222	268	390
5 rooms	288	222	299	458
6 or more rooms	340	273	357	491
		Percent Change 1978-1981		
All renters	+27.1	+21.9	+23.5	+38.5
1 room	+31.1	+37.2	+31.1	+21.5
2 rooms	+26.4	+29.6	+25.1	+24.3
3 rooms	+25.0	+29.8	+24.7	+16.1
4 rooms	+26.9	+30.6	+23.0	+13.9
5 rooms	+20.1	+24.1	+19.0	+ 6.7
6 or more rooms	+26.2	+29.9	+25.4	+24.3

NOTE: Rents rounded to nearest dollar. Percent change figures calculated from rounded numbers.

SOURCES: 1978 data from Marcuse, p. 297; 1981 data from U.S. Bureau of the Census, 1981 New York City Housing and Vacancy Survey.

experience different mixes of lease terms and turnover rates, the relationships among their respective rents will change. If, for example, turnover rates are higher for smaller units than for bigger ones, the gap between their rents will narrow.

As suggested above, the lower than anticipated spread between rents for apartments of different size may be partially explained by the higher permissible rent increases under stabilization for vacancy than for renewal leases and by the higher turnover rates in smaller apartments. Also, one- and two-room apartments are disproportionately located in Manhattan where rents are generally higher for all housing. This has the effect of shifting the rent distribution for smaller units closer to that for larger ones.

Structure Type

Since 1978, median rents increased at a faster rate for apartments in Old Law tenements than for those in either New Law tenements or post-1929 multiple dwelling buildings (Table 7-6).

TABLE 7-6. MEDIAN MONTHLY GROSS RENT BY STRUCTURE CLASSIFICATION, ALL RENTER-OCCUPIED UNITS, NEW YORK CITY, 1975, 1978 AND 1981

	Median Gross Rent			Percent Change	
	1975	1978	1981	1975-1978	1978- 1981
New York City total	$171	$210	$265	+22.8	+26.2
Old Law tenement	136	174	232	+27.9	+33.3
New Law tenement	153	190	239	+24.2	+25.8
Multiple post-1929*	229	270	341	+17.9	+26.3
Public housing	101	132	144	+30.7	+ 9.0
1-2 Family houses	202	238	294	+17.8	+23.5

*Excludes public housing.

NOTE: Rents rounded to nearest dollar. Percent change figures calculated from rounded numbers.

SOURCES: 1975 and 1978 data from Marcuse, p. 209; 1981 data from U.S. Bureau of the Census, 1981 New York City Housing and Vacancy Survey.

The Old Law median rent, which was $232 in 1981, has increased by one-third since 1978, while rents for New Law tenements have risen by 26 percent to $239. Post-1929 apartments, which had a median rent of $291 in 1981, include the City's low-rent public housing stock. Excluding public housing, the median post-1929 apartment rent in 1981 increased by 26 percent to $341. Since 1978, median rents in public housing have risen by only 9 percent, from $132 to $144 a month.

Housing Quality

Holding dwelling size constant, housing costs should vary directly with quality. Because of the difficulties of measuring the condition of the occupied stock, analysis of the rent-quality relationship is, at best, incomplete. Nevertheless, the Housing and Vacancy Survey data do indicate that median gross rents, both on a dwelling unit and per room basis, are substantially greater for nondilapidated than for dilapidated housing. In 1981, the difference was $46 a month per dwelling unit, or 21 percent (Table 7-7).† On a per room basis, the difference between the median rent for dilapidated and nondilapidated units was 22 percent (Table 7-8).†

TABLE 7-7. MEDIAN MONTHLY GROSS RENT BY CONDITION, ALL RENTER-OCCUPIED UNITS, NEW YORK CITY, 1975, 1978 AND 1981

	Median Gross Rent			Percent Change	
	1975	1978	1981	1975-1978	1978-1981
New York City total	$171	$210	$265	+22.8	+26.2
Dilapidated units	126	182	222	+44.4	+22.0
Nondilapidated units	175	213	268	+21.7	+25.8

NOTE: Rents rounded to nearest dollar. Percent change calculated from rounded numbers.

SOURCE: 1975 and 1978 data from Marcuse, p. 210; 1981 data from U.S. Bureau of the Census, 1981 New York City Housing and Vacancy Survey.

TABLE 7-8. MEDIAN MONTHLY GROSS RENT PER ROOM, BY CONDITION, ALL RENTER-OCCUPIED UNITS, NEW YORK CITY, 1975, 1978 AND 1981

	Median Gross Rent Per Room			Percent Change	
	1975	1978	1981	1975-1978	1978-1981
New York City total	$49	$61	$76	+24.5	+26.2
Dilapidated units	36	49	63	+36.1	+28.6
Nondilapidated units	50	62	77	+24.0	+24.2

NOTE: Rents rounded to nearest dollar. Percent change calculated from rounded numbers.

SOURCES: 1975 and 1978 data from Marcuse, p. 211; 1981 data from U.S. Bureau of the Census, 1981 New York City Housing and Vacancy Survey.

Even at this level of analysis, there are two important aspects of the rent-quality relationship in New York City. On a dwelling unit basis, the rent for dilapidated housing increased by more than 20 percent since 1978, compared to the citywide rate of 26 percent. While this is an improvement over the previous three-year period when rents for this seriously inadequate stock rose by 44 percent, or twice the City average, the fact that demand for this housing is so strong is cause for concern. Another reflection of this problem is that the rents for dilapidated housing were 74 percent of the citywide median in 1975, but by 1981 they had risen to 84 percent of the City median. On a per room basis, the cost difference declined by a similar amount. The gross rent per room for dilapidated housing was 27 percent lower than the median for all housing in 1975, but only 17 percent lower in 1981.

In general, housing costs are inversely related to the number of maintenance deficiencies in the dwelling. Median contract rent for apartments with no deficiencies is $258 a month (Table 7-9), while for apartments with one or two deficiencies it is $236 and $230 respectively.* Rents tend to vary more between multiple-deficiency and deficiency-free apartments than between dilapidated and non-dilapidated units. In the latter case, dilapidated units

TABLE 7-9. MEDIAN MONTHLY CONTRACT RENT, BY NUMBER OF DEFICIENCIES IN MAINTENANCE AND EQUIPMENT, ALL RENTER-OCCUPIED HOUSING UNITS, NEW YORK CITY, 1981

		Number of Deficiencies					
	Total	None	One	Two	Three	Four	Five
1981 median contract rent	$235	$258	$236	$230	$212	$196	$190

NOTE: Data are not available by gross rent. Rents rounded to nearest dollar.

SOURCE: U.S. Bureau of the Census, 1981 New York City Housing and Vacancy Survey.

cost 18 percent less than nondilapidated ones, while apartments with five maintenance deficiencies cost 26 percent less than apartments with no maintenance problems. This greater difference reflects the premiums attached to high quality housing and the fact that deficiency-free apartments are disproportionately located in the decontrolled, post-'47, and state or city assisted sectors, three of the most expensive submarkets in New York (Table 7-10).

Household Characteristics

Chapter 8 will analyze the income distribution of renters in New York City. The long-term increase in relative housing expense burdens has leveled off since 1978, despite substantial increases in rents. Contrary to the 1975-'78 period, incomes and rents have risen at the same rates since 1978. In this section we concentrate on rents paid by various population groups during the period 1975 to 1981.

---

*The Housing and Vacancy Survey does not include data on maintenance deficiencies by gross rent.

TABLE 7-10. MEDIAN MONTHLY GROSS RENT, BY CONDITION AND CONTROL STATUS, ALL RENTER-OCCUPIED UNITS, NEW YORK CITY, 1981

	Median Gross Rent		
	Total	Not Dilapidated	Dilapidated
Total	$265	$268	$222
Controlled	213	216	162
Decontrolled	271	274	238
Stabilized pre-'47	262	265	234
Stabilized post-'47	368	368	293
State/City assisted	286	288	274

SOURCE: U.S. Bureau of the Census, 1981 New York City Housing and Vacancy Survey.

Race and Ethnic Origin of Householder. Median rents for the major racial and ethnic groups in New York increased by between 20 and 30 percent since 1978, which is somewhat more than between 1975 and 1978 (Table 7-11). Rents paid by White households increased by the highest percentage since 1975, to a level of $288 in 1981. Though still paying slightly less for their housing than Blacks, Puerto Rican households experienced the second highest six-year growth in median rents -- a 54 percent increase from $146 a month in 1975 to $225 in 1981. Median rents for Black households have increased by 48 percent since 1975, from $157 a month to $232.

TABLE 7-11. MEDIAN MONTHLY GROSS RENT BY RACE AND ETHNIC GROUP, ALL RENTER-OCCUPIED UNITS, NEW YORK CITY, 1975, 1978 AND 1981

	Median Gross Rent			% Change	% Change
	1975	1978	1981	1975-1978	1978-1981
All renters	$171	$210	$265	+22.8	+26.2
White	183	223	288	+21.9	+29.1
Black	157	192	232	+22.3	+20.8
Puerto Rican	146	180	225	+23.3	+25.0

NOTE: Rents rounded to nearest dollar. Percent change calculated from rounded numbers.

SOURCES: 1975 and 1978 data Marcuse, p. 216; 1981 data from U.S. Bureau of the Census, 1981 New York City Housing and Vacancy Survey.

Age and Sex. Between 1978 and 1981, median rents for both male and female householders 65 years and over increased by at least 28 percent (Table 7-12). Elderly men pay more for rent than do women --$236 versus $194. In general,

TABLE 7-12. MEDIAN MONTHLY GROSS RENT BY AGE AND SEX OF HOUSEHOLD HEAD, ALL RENTER-OCCUPIED UNITS, NEW YORK CITY, SELECTED YEARS

	1975	1978	1981	Percent Change 1975-1978	Percent Change 1978-1981
All renters	$171	$210	$265	+22.8	+26.2
Male Heads	178	219	282	+23.0	+28.8
Under 45	190	230	292	+21.1	+27.0
45-64	175	220	287	+25.7	+30.5
65 and over	142	184	236	+29.6	+28.3
Female Heads	159	194	245	+22.0	+26.3
Under 45	177	218	268	+23.2	+22.9
45-64	152	184	237	+21.1	+28.8
65 and over	123	151	194	+22.8	+28.5

NOTE: Rents rounded to nearest dollar. Percent change calculated from rounded numbers.

SOURCES: 1975 and 1978 data from Marcuse, pp. 216 and 218; 1981 data from U.S. Bureau of the Census, 1981 New York City Housing and Vacancy Survey.

this pattern holds for all age groups, no doubt because male incomes tend to be higher. The under-45-years age group of each sex tend to have the highest rents of all, $292 for males, $268 for females.

Household Size. Rents tend to increase with household size, although not proportionately, because income does not necessarily vary directly with household size, while nonhousing needs do (Table 7-13). At the median, single

TABLE 7-13. MEDIAN MONTHLY GROSS RENT BY HOUSEHOLD SIZE AND CONTROL STATUS, ALL RENTER-OCCUPIED UNITS, NEW YORK CITY, 1981

Persons	Total	Controlled	Decontrolled	Pre-'47 Stabilized	Post-'47 Stabilized
Total	$265	$213	$271	$262	$368
1	242	192	223	246	356
2	277	223	272	265	373
3	273	236	288	263	392
4	280	253	295	273	362
5	286	262	302	291	369
6 or more	284	246	332	315	361

SOURCE: U.S. Bureau of the Census, 1981 New York City Housing and Vacancy Survey.

person households in New York City spend 15 percent less for rent than do households of at least five persons ($242 versus $286). The differences in housing expenses among the remaining size classes are much smaller than this.

Two exceptions to the relation between rent and household size should, however, be noted. When disaggregated by control status, the rent-increasing effects of additional household members in the decontrolled sector is clear. There, median rents are almost one-third less for households of one versus households of six or more ($223 versus $332). This suggests that, since allowable rents in regulated sub-markets are heavily influenced by turnover rates and other factors unrelated to preferences for space and quality, the relation between rents and household size is less distinct than it might otherwise be.

The second exception concerns post-'47 stabilized housing, where smaller households are likely to be spending at least as much for rent as larger ones. Two-person households in this sector pay a median rent of $373, which is 3 percent more than that paid by households with at least six members. This phenomenon no doubt reflects the heavy influence of the Manhattan market, where a disproportionate share of the newer, smaller and more costly apartments in the City are located.

NOTES

1. The President's Commission on Housing, Interim Report, October 30, 1981, pp. 18, 19.

2. Ira S. Lowry, "Inflation Indexes for Rental Housing," cited in The President's Commission on Housing, Interim Report, October 30, 1981, p. 18.

3. Ibid., p. 19.

4. See, for example, George Sternlieb, The Tenement Landlord, New Brunswick, Center for Urban Policy Research, 1966, p. xiii and Chapter 7; and, Roger G. Krohn and Berkeley E. Fleming, "The Other Economy and the Urban Housing Problem: A Case Study of Older Residential Neighborhoods in Montreal." Cambridge, Joint Center for Urban Studies, Working Paper No. 11, 1972.

CHAPTER 8

THE INCOMES OF NEW YORK CITY RENTERS

From 1969 to 1980, the median income* for all renters in New York City increased by more than 50 percent, from $7,165 to $11,001 (Table 8-1, Exhibit 8-1). Between 1977 and 1980, incomes grew by 23 percent, triple the rate over the preceding three years when New Yorkers were still feeling the effects of the 1974-75 recession.** White renter incomes grew by 63 percent between 1969 and 1980, to $13,474. The gap between Black and White incomes has widened since 1969 because Black incomes rose at a lower rate. Black renters have a median income of $9,142, just 68 percent that of Whites. Puerto Rican renters have fallen further behind both Whites and Blacks. In 1969, the median income for Puerto Rican renters was $4,949, 60 percent of the White and 87 percent of the Black median. By 1977, Puerto Rican incomes had declined to 54 percent of White and 79 percent of Black renter incomes. By 1980, the Puerto Rican renter income had risen 11 percent to $6,460, an increase which was still less than half the rate enjoyed by both White and Black renters in the City. As a result, Puerto Rican renters now have an income less than half that of Whites and just 71 percent that of Blacks.

Incomes and the Cost of Living

Incomes have risen over 50 percent since 1969, but the cost of living in the City has more than doubled since then, so that all renters have lost purchasing power. Incomes for all renters fell by 28 percent in real terms between 1969 and 1980. For Whites and Blacks, the drop was 24 and 25 percent respectively, while for Puerto Ricans it was 39 percent over these 11 years. The uneven effects of inflation on racial and ethnic groups is particularly noticeable since 1977. Between 1977 and 1980, a period of intense inflation, the cost of living in New York City rose 28 percent. Whites almost kept pace with the cost of living, losing just 2 percent in real income, while Blacks lost around 4 percent in purchasing power. The real losers in the cost of living battle, however, were Puerto Rican households whose incomes rose at one-third the cost of living. As a result, their real incomes fell 14 percent between 1977 and 1980.

---

*See glossary for the definition of household income in 1981 and in past years. The reader should note that the 1981 Housing and Vacancy Survey, which was conducted from January to March 1981, collected income data for 1980. Similarly, the 1978 Housing and Vacancy Survey collected 1977 income data so that the relevant three-year comparison is 1977 to 1980. Finally, all incomes cited in this chapter are medians unless otherwise noted.

**Homeowner incomes rose by 31 percent, from $15,528 in 1977 to $20,333 in 1980, which widened the income gap between renters and owners. In 1977, renters had incomes which averaged 58 percent of those of homeowners, and just 54 percent in 1980.

TABLE 8-1. MEDIAN ANNUAL HOUSEHOLD INCOME OF RENTERS IN CURRENT AND CONSTANT (1967) DOLLARS, BY RACE AND ETHNIC ORIGIN, NEW YORK CITY, SELECTED YEARS

	1969	1974	1977	1980	Percent Change 1969-'80	1969-'74	1974-'77	1977-'80
				Current Dollars				
All renters	$7,165	$8,395	$8,979	$11,001	+ 53.5	+17.2	+ 7.0	+22.5
White	8,245	10,034	10,740	13,474	+ 63.4	+21.7	+ 7.0	+25.5
Black	5,681	7,263	7,427	9,142	+ 60.9	+27.8	+ 2.3	+23.1
Puerto Rican	4,949	5,468	5,848	6,460	+ 30.5	+10.5	+ 6.9	+10.5
CPI	110.8	154.8	185.5	237.2	+114.1	+39.7	+19.8	+27.9
				Constant Dollars				
All renters	$6,467	$5,423	$4,840	$4,638	-28.3	-16.1	-10.8	- 4.2
White	7,441	6,482	5,790	5,680	-23.7	-12.9	-10.7	- 1.9
Black	5,127	4,692	4,004	3,854	-24.8	- 8.5	-14.7	- 3.7
Puerto Rican	4,467	3,532	3,153	2,723	-39.0	-20.9	-10.7	-13.6

NOTE: CPI is average for year for all urban consumers, New York-Northeastern New Jersey, 1967 = 100, Bureau of Labor Statistics, Department of Labor.

SOURCES: 1969 data from Sternlieb, p. 101; 1974 and 1977 data from Marcuse, p. 38; 1980 data from U.S Bureau of the Census, 1981 New York City Housing and Vacancy Survey.

EXHIBIT 8-1. MEDIAN ANNUAL HOUSEHOLD INCOME OF RENTERS BY RACE AND ETHNIC ORIGIN, 1969 AND 1980

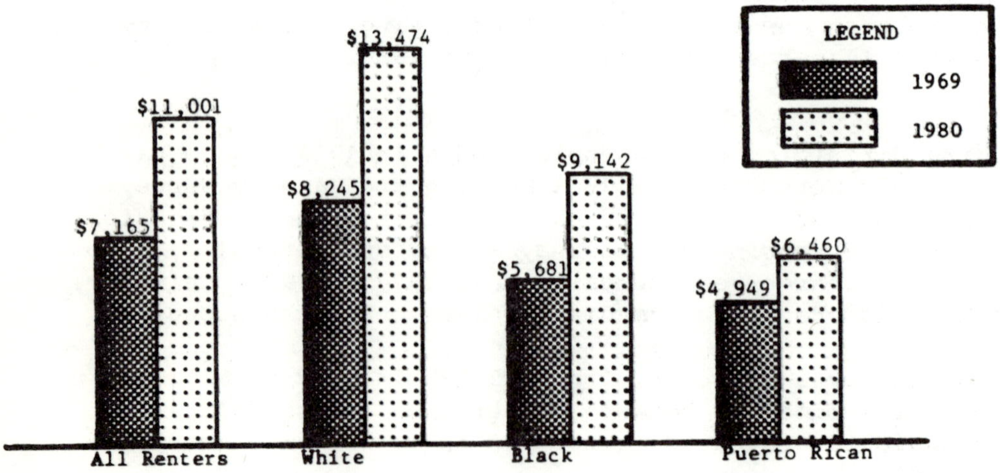

SOURCE: Table 8-1.

Age and Sex of Renters

Other things being equal, incomes for renters in New York City do not vary substantially by age except that incomes of households near the age of retirement fall dramatically (Table 8-2). The median income for the under-45 and 45-to-64 cohorts is $12,230 and $12,359 respectively. For householders who are at least 65 years old, the income in 1980 was $6,037, less than half that of younger cohorts.† More importantly, in constant dollars (i.e., 1967 dollars), older renters in New York City had incomes of $2,545 in 1980.*

Differences in income between men and women are harder to ascertain because of vagueness in the Census definition of "household head." The proliferation of nonconventional living arrangements,** and the sharing of household responsibilities among adults, have led the Census Bureau to stop using the term "household head." Instead, it refers to adult household members as "householders." The household is classified as male- or female-headed depending on the sex of the person who was named as the owner or tenant of record of the dwelling unit. Under the new Census classification, a household may be considered female-headed regardless of whether the woman identified as owner or tenant of record is married or is single and living with an adult male. For this reason the 1981 Housing and Vacancy Survey may not be consistent with earlier data on female-headed households. A growing number of single women and single mothers earn significantly less than men and rely on the rental stock for housing.*** It is therefore important to report household income data by age and sex.

---

†Unless otherwise noted, each time this symbol appears in the chapter the probability is 95 percent that differences between the values referred to are not due to chance.

*Current law exempts household heads who are at least 62 and have household incomes under $8,000 a year from rent increases if they live in rent regulated apartments. Landlords may deduct the full amount of these rent increase exemptions from their annual real estate taxes. In 1981, 17 percent of all household heads over the age of 62 benefited from the rent exemption. This included 25 percent of all older tenants in rent controlled apartments, 17 percent of elderly in pre-'47 stabilized apartments and 9 percent of those in post-'47 apartments.

**This term comprises households other than the traditional husband-wife or husband-wife-and-children sort, e.g., unrelated adults living together, single adults, single parents, etc.

***When interpreting the 1980 data, it is important to keep in mind that married households were previously classified as male-headed, whereas they are now classified as male- or female-headed, depending on how the Survey respondent characterized the household. Incomes of female-headed households may therefore appear higher than they really are, since there may be two earners in the household. The likelihood of this distortion is greater for the under-45 age cohort.

TABLE 8-2. MEDIAN ANNUAL HOUSEHOLD INCOME OF RENTERS IN CURRENT AND CONSTANT (1967) DOLLARS, BY AGE OF HOUSEHOLDER, NEW YORK CITY, 1980

Age of Household Head	Median Income: Current Dollars
All renters	$11,001
Under 45 years	12,230
45 to 64 years	12,359
65 or more	6,037
Age of Household Head	**Median Income: Constant (1967) Dollars**
All renters	$4,638
Under 45 years	5,156
45 to 64 years	5,210
65 or more	2,545

NOTE: CPI used to derive median income in constant dollars is average for year for all urban consumers, New York-Northeastern New Jersey, 1967 = 100, Bureau of Labor Statistics, Department of Labor.

SOURCE: U.S. Bureau of the Census, 1981 New York City Housing and Vacancy Survey.

Despite any possible upward bias, however, the income of male householders in 1980 was still twice that of females: $14,542 versus $7,280 (Table 8-3).† The gap between the two was even greater in 1969, but has narrowed because of the substantial progress made by women who are now over the age of 65. Because more women now receive social security on the basis of their own earnings, and because survivors' benefits have increased, the median income of older women has risen 126 percent since 1969, compared to 60 percent for similarly aged male renters. Female householders under 45 have also gained ground on their male peers between 1969 and 1980, especially since 1977. The incomes of younger women rose nearly 40 percent in three years, compared to 30 percent for similarly aged men. Although some of this increase could stem from the classification problem discussed above, the high rate is consistent with the growing number of professional single women who rent.

The same data must be analyzed in terms of constant dollars to illustrate the struggle for economic survival. When incomes are adjusted to account for inflation, young men and women have fared the best since 1969, although they, too, have lost ground. Elderly women, for the reasons mentioned above, were the only ones whose incomes rose more than the 11-year inflation rate. Nevertheless, despite a 5 percent growth in real incomes, their $2,094 median income (in constant dollars) is still extraordinarily low and scarcely higher than it was in 1969.

TABLE 8-3. MEDIAN ANNUAL HOUSEHOLD INCOME OF RENTERS IN CURRENT AND CONSTANT (1967) DOLLARS BY AGE AND SEX OF HOUSEHOLDER, NEW YORK CITY, SELECTED YEARS

	1969	1974	1977	1980	Percent Change 1969-80	1969-74	1974-77	1977-80
					Current Dollars			
All renters	$7,200	$8,395	$8,979	$11,001	+ 52.8	+16.6	+ 7.0	+22.5
Male heads	8,900	10,600	11,500	14,542	+ 63.4	+19.1	+ 8.5	+26.5
Under 45	9,000	11,600	12,400	16,099	+ 78.9	+28.9	+ 6.9	+29.8
45-64	11,000	11,800	12,500	16,974	+ 54.3	+ 7.3	+ 5.9	+35.8
65 or more	4,900	5,300	6,200	7,833	+ 59.9	+ 8.2	+17.0	+26.3
Female heads	4,100	5,100	5,700	7,280	+ 77.6	+24.4	+11.8	+27.7
Under 45	4,600	6,400	6,600	9,146	+ 98.8	+39.1	+ 3.1	+38.6
45-64	5,400	6,100	6,200	8,810	+ 63.1	+13.0	+ 1.6	+42.1
65 or more	2,200	3,200	<4,000	4,968	+125.8	+45.5	N.A.	N.A.
CPI	110.8	154.8	185.5	237.2	+114.1	+39.7	+19.8	+27.9
					Constant Dollars			
All renters	$6,498	$5,423	$4,840	$4,638	-28.6	-16.5	-10.8	- 4.2
Male heads	8,032	6,848	6,199	6,131	-23.7	-14.7	- 9.5	- 1.1
Under 45	8,123	7,494	6,685	6,787	-16.4	- 7.7	-10.8	+ 1.5
45-64	9,928	7,623	6,739	7,156	-27.9	-23.2	-11.6	+ 6.2
65 or more	4,422	3,424	3,342	3,302	-25.3	-22.6	- 2.4	- 1.2
Female heads	3,700	3,295	3,073	3,069	-17.1	-10.9	- 6.7	- 0.1
Under 45	4,152	4,134	3,558	3,856	- 7.1	-0.4	-13.9	+ 8.4
45-64	4,874	3,941	3,342	3,714	-23.8	-19.1	-15.2	+11.1
65 or more	1,986	2,067	<2,200	2,094	+ 5.4	4.1	N.A.	N.A.

NOTE: CPI is average for year for all urban consumers, New York-Northeastern New Jersey, 1967 = 100, Bureau of Labor Statistics, U.S. Department of Labor.

SOURCES: 1974, 1977 and 1979 data from Marcuse, pp. 54 & 57; 1980 data from the U.S. Bureau of the Census, 1981 New York City Housing and Vacancy Survey.

Borough

Because the racial, ethnic, age and household mix of the renter population varies significantly by borough, as does the rental housing stock, it follows that the distribution of incomes should also differ. The rate of income increase between 1969 and 1980 is 69 percent greater in Manhattan than in the City as a whole; Manhattan renters have the highest median income in New York (Table 8-4). Manhattan ranked only third in median income in 1969, behind Queens and Richmond, and was approximately $100 ahead of the Bronx and Brooklyn. As recently as 1977, renters in both Richmond and Queens had higher median incomes than those in Manhattan, but incomes in Manhattan have risen by 27 percent since 1977, in contrast to 8 and 17 percent increases in Richmond and Queens respectively. Today, the median income for renters in Manhattan is $13,024, 18 percent higher than for all renters citywide, nearly 50 percent greater than for renters in the Bronx, and almost 40 percent higher than for those in Brooklyn.

Since 1969, renters in all boroughs have suffered losses in real incomes, although less in Manhattan than elsewhere in the City. Save for Manhattan, where renters lost 11 percent of their purchasing power, renters in all other boroughs suffered real income declines of at least 33 percent. The greater relative strength of Manhattan's renters is best illustrated by the 1977-1980 inflationary period, when their real incomes remained virtually constant, rising point for point with the cost of living. At the same time, real incomes in the Bronx and Queens fell by 8 percent, and in Richmond by 16 percent. The size of the latter decline may be partially explained by the increase in Richmond's low-rent housing stock since 1977, and the fact that its renter population is small enough to be substantially affected by the addition of relatively few lower-income households.

Household Size. Two-person households in New York enjoy the highest income of all renters (Table 8-5). With a 1980 median of $12,602, two-person households have incomes twice as high as single people, slightly greater than three- and four-person households and 15 percent higher than households of five or more.*

This relationship holds for renters in the Bronx, Brooklyn and Manhattan, but not in Queens or Richmond, where three-person households have the highest median income and the decline in incomes for larger households is more gradual. The higher income for larger families in these two boroughs may be partly explained by the higher incidence of one- and two-family rental units which provide a living environment attractive to more affluent households with children.

---

*While the Housing and Vacancy Survey data do not explain why two-person households are financially better off than those with more members, these households are more likely to be childless working adults. Eighty-six percent of all two-person households have no members under 18, compared to 34 percent of all three-person, 17 percent of all four-person, 11 percent of all five-person, and 6 percent of all six-or-more-person households.

TABLE 8-4. MEDIAN ANNUAL HOUSEHOLD INCOME OF RENTERS IN CURRENT AND CONSTANT (1967) DOLLARS, BY BOROUGH, NEW YORK CITY, SELECTED YEARS

					Percent Change			
	1969	1974	1977	1980	1969-80	1969-74	1974-77	1977-80
				Current Dollars				
All renters	$7,165	$8,395	$8,979	$11,001	+53.5	+17.2	+ 7.0	+22.5
Bronx	6,709	7,286	7,488	8,775	+30.8	+ 8.6	+ 2.8	+17.2
Brooklyn	6,728	7,559	7,713	9,400	+39.7	+12.4	+ 2.0	+21.9
Manhattan	6,836	8,400	10,225	13,024	+90.5	+22.9	+21.7	+27.4
Queens	8,958	10,929	10,710	12,572	+40.3	+22.0	- 2.0	+17.4
Richmond	8,537	11,012	11,356	12,230	+43.3	+29.0	+ 3.1	+ 7.7
CPI	110.8	154.8	185.5	237.2	+114.1	+39.7	+19.8	+27.9
				Constant Dollars				
All renters	$6,467	$5,423	$4,840	$4,638	-28.3	-16.1	-10.8	- 4.2
Bronx	6,055	4,707	4,037	3,699	-38.9	-22.3	-14.2	- 8.4
Brooklyn	6,072	4,883	4,158	3,963	-34.7	-19.6	-14.8	- 4.7
Manhattan	6,170	5,426	5,512	5,491	-11.0	-12.1	- 1.6	- 0.4
Queens	8,085	7,060	5,774	5,300	-34.4	-12.7	-18.2	- 8.2
Richmond	7,705	7,114	6,122	5,156	-33.1	- 7.7	-13.9	-15.8

NOTE: CPI is average for year for all urban consumers, New York-Northeastern New Jersey, 1967 = 100, Bureau of Labor Statistics, U.S. Department of Labor.

SOURCES: 1969 data from Sternlieb, p. 97; 1974, 1977 income data from Marcuse, pp. 54, 57; 1980 data from the U.S. Bureau of the Census, 1981 New York City Housing and Vacancy Survey.

TABLE 8-5. MEDIAN ANNUAL RENTER HOUSEHOLD INCOME, BY BOROUGH AND SIZE OF HOUSEHOLD, NEW YORK CITY, 1980

	All Households	Number of Persons in Household 1	2	3	4	5 or more
All Boroughs	$11,001	$8,389	$12,602	$12,075	$11,968	$10,972
Bronx	8,775	5,785	10,743	9,914	9,648	9,859
Brooklyn	9,400	6,133	11,306	9,912	11,980	9,943
Manhattan	13,024	12,196	16,777	13,503	10,623	11,282
Queens	12,572	8,665	14,294	17,100	16,552	14,599
Richmond	12,230	9,139	15,602	18,514	15,499	16,118

SOURCE: U.S. Bureau of the Census, 1981 New York City Housing and Vacancy Survey.

Concentrations of Rich and Poor Households by Borough. Changes in the extent of poverty and in the concentration of rich and poor by borough also indicate how renters have redistributed themselves by income within the City. Overall, one-quarter of New York renters had an income in 1980 that was below the official federal poverty level (Table 8-6; Exhibit 8-2). This represents a nearly 13 percent increase in the citywide renter poverty rate since 1977.† The largest three-year increase in the incidence of poverty was in the Bronx, where 36 percent of all renters were poor in 1980, representing a 22 percent increase since 1977. The growth in the rate of the near-poor* in the Bronx has increased more slowly than the poverty rate. Today almost half of all Bronx renters have incomes below 125 percent of the poverty level. The 16 percent increase in the number of near-poor since 1977 is slower than the growth rate for the very-poor,**indicating that the number of very-poor in the Bronx is increasing more rapidly than the near-poor. This is also happening in all of the other boroughs except Richmond, where the number of near-poor grew at twice the rate of the very-poor. Queens is virtually tied with Richmond in terms of the percentages of poor and near-poor, but their rates of increase vary. Although the increase in Brooklyn's poverty rate is the lowest in the City, 31 percent of its households are below poverty level and 41 percent are below 125 percent of the poverty level. Manhattan's dual personality is reflected in its poverty statistics. Twenty-one percent of all renters in Manhattan have incomes below the poverty level, while 28 percent are below 125 percent of poverty.

---

*The near-poor are defined as those with incomes between 100 and 125 percent of the poverty level.

**The very-poor are those with incomes below 100 percent of poverty level.

TABLE 8-6. DISTRIBUTION OF RENTER HOUSEHOLDS WITH INCOMES BELOW FEDERAL POVERTY OR NEAR-POVERTY LEVEL, BY BOROUGH, NEW YORK CITY, 1974, 1977 AND 1980

	Percent of All Renters Below Federal Poverty Level				Percent of All Renters Below 125% of Federal Poverty Level			
	1974	1977	1980	Percent Change 1977-'80	1974	1977	1980	Percent Change 1977-'80
All renters	16.5	22.5	25.3	+12.4	26.3	32.1	34.3	+ 6.9
Bronx	22.1	29.1	35.5	+22.0	33.7	39.6	46.0	+16.2
Brooklyn	19.6	27.7	30.7	+10.8	31.2	38.5	40.6	+ 5.5
Manhattan	16.0	18.9	21.1	+11.6	24.6	27.1	28.0	+ 3.3
Queens	8.4	13.4	15.3	+14.2	15.4	22.2	24.9	+12.2
Richmond	9.6	13.5	14.8	+ 9.6	18.5	19.5	23.1	+18.5

SOURCES: 1974, 1977 data from Marcuse, p. 32; 1980 data from U.S. Bureau of the Census, 1981 New York City Housing and Vacancy Survey.

It was necessary to redefine poverty in order to see where high- and low-income renters live in New York and if their distribution has changed in recent years. For purposes of this analysis, low-income households are defined as those with incomes in the bottom 20 percent of the citywide renter income distribution, or below $4,960 in 1980. Similarly, high-income

EXHIBIT 8-2. DISTRIBUTION OF RENTER HOUSEHOLDS WITH INCOMES BELOW POVERTY OR NEAR-POVERTY LEVEL, BY BOROUGH, NEW YORK CITY, 1980

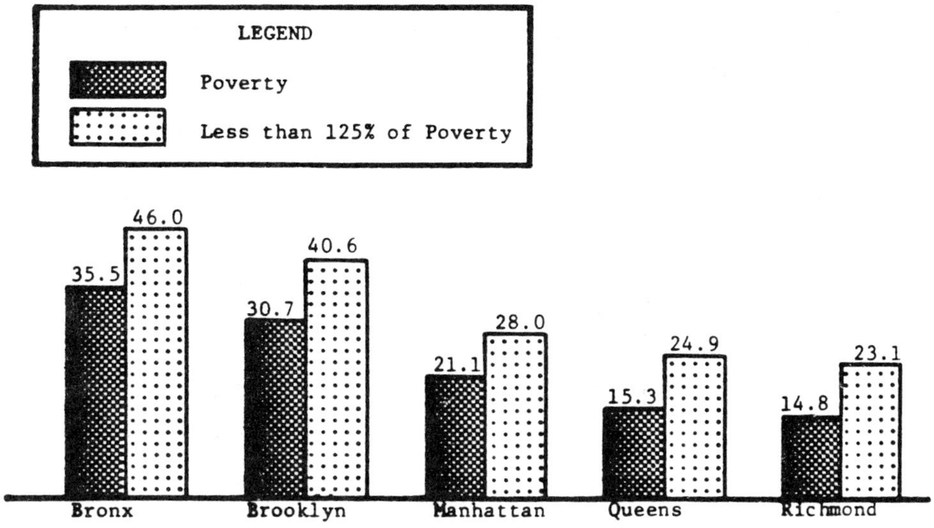

SOURCE: Table 8-6.

EXHIBIT 8-3. GAIN OR LOSS OF RENTER HOUSEHOLDS IN BOTTOM AND TOP INCOME QUINTILES, BY BOROUGH, NEW YORK CITY, 1977 AND 1980

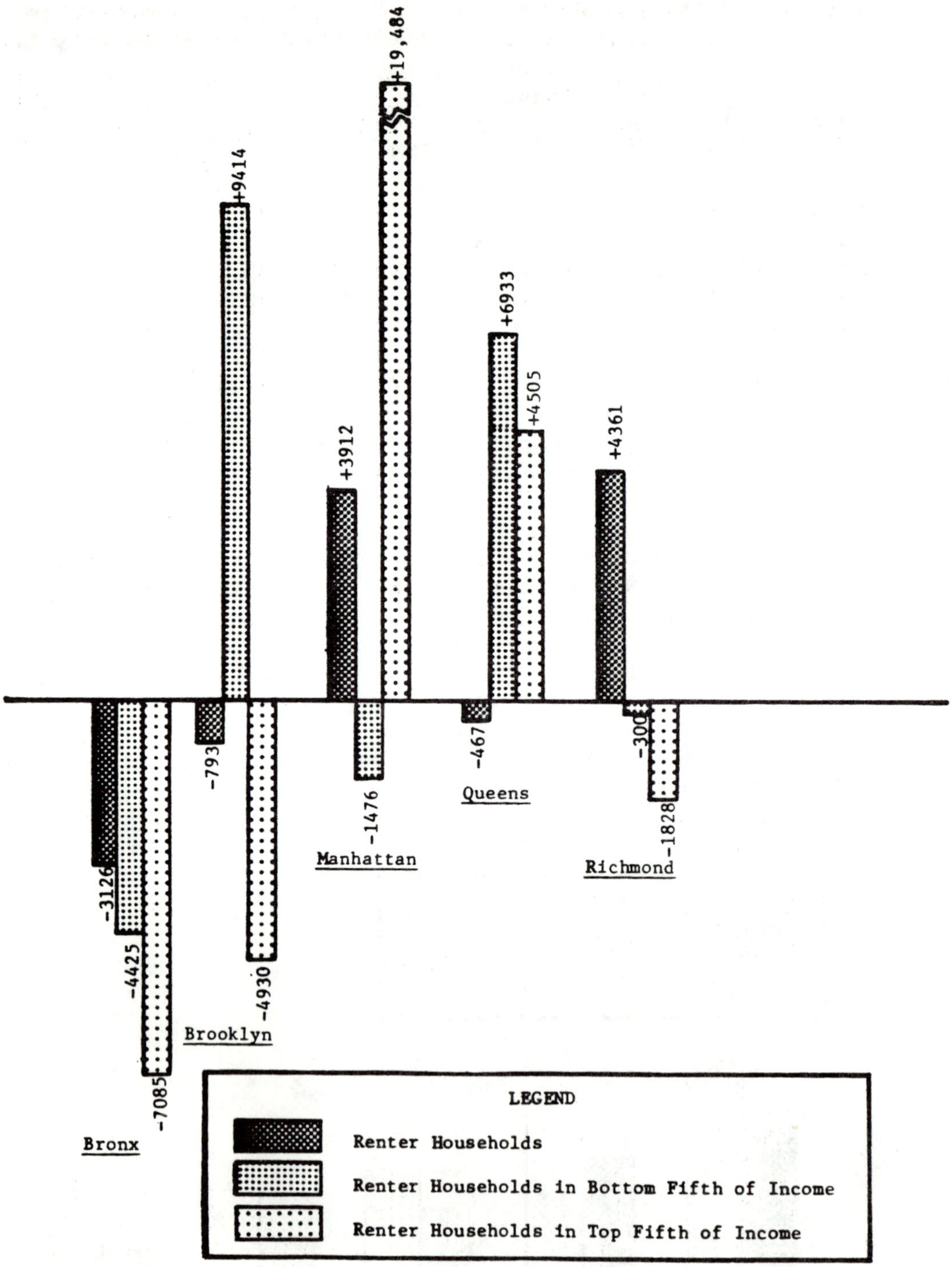

SOURCE: Table 8-8.

TABLE 8-7. RELATIVE CONCENTRATION OF UPPER AND LOWER INCOME RENTERS IN NEW YORK CITY, BY BOROUGH, 1977 AND 1980

	% of All Renters by Borough		% of All Renters in City's Bottom Income Quintile		% of All Renters in City's Top Income Quintile		Ratio of % in Bottom Quintile to Borough's Share of All Renters		Ratio of % in Top Quintile to Borough's Share of All Renters	
	1977	1980	1977	1980	1977	1980	1977	1980	1977	1980
Total	100.0	100.0	100.0	100.0	100.0	100.0	N.A.	N.A.	N.A.	N.A.
Bronx	17.0	16.9	24.5	22.1	13.7	10.8	1.44	1.31	0.81	0.64
Brooklyn	30.1	30.1	34.2	36.2	22.7	20.2	1.14	1.20	0.75	0.67
Manhattan	30.1	30.2	26.5	25.1	37.2	42.6	0.88	0.83	1.24	1.41
Queens	20.8	20.8	13.4	15.3	23.7	24.5	0.64	0.74	1.14	1.18
Richmond	1.9	2.1	1.4	1.3	2.7	1.9	0.74	0.62	1.42	0.90
Income	N.A.	N.A.	$4,109	$4,960	$17,746	$22,744	N.A.	N.A.	N.A.	N.A.

SOURCES: 1977 data from Marcuse, p. 54; 1980 data from U.S. Bureau of the Census 1981 New York City Housing and Vacancy Survey.

TABLE 8-8. GAIN OR LOSS OF RENTER HOUSEHOLDS IN BOTTOM AND TOP INCOME QUINTILE, BY BOROUGH, NEW YORK CITY, 1977 AND 1980

	Gain or Loss in Renter Households 1977-1980	Gain or Loss in Households in Bottom Fifth of Income	Gain or Loss in Households in Top Fifth of Income
Bronx	-3,126	-4,425	- 7,085
Brooklyn	- 793	+9,414	- 4,930
Manhattan	+3,912	-1,476	+19,484
Queens	- 467	+6,933	+ 4,505
Richmond	+4,361	- 300	- 1,828

NOTE: In 1977 bottom fifth of income was below $4,109; in 1980 it was $4,960. In 1977 top one-fifth of income was $17,746 or above; in 1980 it was $22,744.

SOURCES: 1977 data from Marcuse, p. 54; 1981 data from U.S. Bureau of the Census, 1981 New York City Housing and Vacancy Survey.

households are defined as those with incomes in the top 20 percent of the total renter population, which in 1980 amounted to an income over $22,744. Using these two income limits to define high and low income, the Bronx housed just 11 percent of all high-income and 22 percent of all low-incomw renters in 1980 (Table 8-7). In contrast, Brooklyn had one-fifth of all the high-income and more than one-third of all the low-income renters. In Manhattan, the reverse was true: 43 percent of all high-income renters lived there in 1980, compared to 25 percent of all low-income households.

Proportion of Rich and Poor Renters by Borough. By dividing a borough's share of high- and low-income renters by its share of the City's rental stock one can control for the effects of borough size. If each borough's proportion of high- and low-income renters equalled its proportion of the rental stock, the ratio of the borough's percent of the City's high- or low-income households to each borough's proportion of the total rental housing stock would equal one. A ratio greater than one means that, relative to the size of its rental housing stock, a particular borough has a higher than expected share of high- or low-income renters. The Bronx's ratio of 1.31 of the lowest-income households to its stock means that it houses 31 percent more of the City's low-income renters than expected. For the high-income, the Bronx's ratio of 0.64 shows that its share of the City's high-income is 36 percent below its proportionate share. Moreover, the fact that the ratio for low-income households has declined much more gradually since 1977 than the ratio for high-income ones means that the Bronx's recent household losses were disproportionately from the upper 20 percent of the city's renter income distribution (Table 8-8; Exhibit 8-3).

Brooklyn is the only borough in which the concentration of low-income is disproportionately high and growing at the same time that its below-average share of high-income renters continues to decline. Between 1977 and 1980, Brooklyn gained almost 9,000 households with incomes in the bottom 20 percent, while it lost nearly 5,000 with incomes in the top 20 percent of the City's renters.

The recent experiences of the remaining boroughs have been different. Queens' share of the City's low-income renters has risen somewhat since 1977 but still remains substantially below its proportionate share. In contrast, its disproportionately high share of the City's high-income renters has declined slightly since 1977. Richmond's share of the City's renter population grew faster than its share of the City's low-income and high-income, with the result that both ratios have declined since 1977. Overall, Richmond's renters have become more middle-income since 1977.

In sharp contrast to the rest of the City, Manhattan's relative share of the City's low-income renters has declined since 1977, while its concentration of high-income renters has grown substantially. In 1980, Manhattan's share of the City's high-income renters was 41 percent greater than its share of all occupied rental units, a 17 percent increase since 1977. From a level 12 percent below its fair share of low-income renters in 1977, Manhattan's proportion fell to 17 percent below its expected share in 1980. Between 1977 and 1980, in other words, Manhattan lost 1,476 households with incomes in the bottom 20 percent of the New York distribution and gained nearly 20,000 households with incomes in the top 20 percent in the City.

Income and Structure Type

The relationship between household income and structure type is not straightforward because certain structure types are concentrated in sections of the City that are characterized by particular income levels. For example, New Law tenements are concentrated in the Bronx where the incidence of poverty is very high (Table 8-9). The median income of occupants of New Law tenements is lower than that of renters in all other structure types, including Old Laws ($8,923 versus $9,475). The median income for occupants of post-'29 buildings, excluding public housing, is $16,400, the highest by far for any structure type including households in one- and two-family rental houses.

TABLE 8-9. MEDIAN INCOME OF RENTER HOUSEHOLDS BY STRUCTURE TYPE, NEW YORK CITY, 1980

	Median Household Income
Old Law tenement	$9,475
New Law tenement	$8,923
Post-1929 multiple*	$16,401
1- or 2-family converted to apartment	$11,881
1- or 2-family house	$12,979

*Excludes public housing. With public housing included, median 1980 household income was $12,326.

SOURCE: U.S. Bureau of the Census, 1981 New York City Housing and Vacancy Survey.

Although it is true that New York City's more than 784,000 tenements house a disproportionately large share of the City's lower-income population, this old stock is an important resource for the nonpoor as well. Almost one-third of the occupants of both Old and New Law tenements have incomes of at least $12,500, while 10 percent have incomes of $25,000 or more (Table 8-10). Viewed another way, while 55 percent of all households with incomes below $6,500 live in Old or New Law tenements, fully 30 percent of those with incomes of at least $25,000 do also (Table 8-11). Most of these wealthier families are in New Law tenements, probably concentrated in upper Manhattan, i.e., below 96th Street.

TABLE 8-10. INCOME BY STRUCTURE CLASSIFICATION, ALL RENTER-OCCUPIED UNITS, NEW YORK CITY, 1981

	Total	Less Than $6,500	$6,500-$12,499	$12,500-$24,999	$25,000 or More
		Percent Distribution			
Multi-unit buildings	100.0	32.1	26.6	25.3	16.0
Old Law tenement	100.0	37.2	30.2	22.2	10.4
New Law tenement	100.0	38.4	28.5	22.9	10.2
Post-'29 multiple	100.0	27.0	23.8	26.9	22.3
1- or 2-family house converted to apartment	100.0	25.8	27.8	32.1	14.3
1- or 2-family house	100.0	23.4	25.5	32.3	18.8

SOURCE: U.S. Bureau of the Census, 1981 New York City Housing and Vacancy Survey.

TABLE 8-11. STRUCTURE TYPE BY INCOME, ALL RENTER-OCCUPIED UNITS, NEW YORK CITY, 1981

Structure Type	Income: Less Than $6,500	Income: $6,500-$12,499	Income: $12,500-$24,999	Income: $25,000 or More
	Percent Distribution			
Multi-unit buildings	100.0	100.0	100.0	100.0
Old Law tenement	13.5	13.3	10.3	7.6
New Law tenement	42.7	38.7	32.7	23.0
Post-'29 multiple	36.9	39.6	47.3	61.9
1- or 2-family house converted to apartment	5.2	6.9	8.4	5.9
Other multiple	1.7	1.5	1.2	1.6

SOURCE: U.S. Bureau of the Census, 1981 New York City Housing and Vacancy Survey.

Control Status

Because of their more advanced age, households living in rent controlled apartments are likely to have lower incomes than those in noncontrolled dwellings (Table 8-12). The median income of households in rent controlled

TABLE 8-12. MEDIAN INCOME OF RENTER HOUSEHOLDS BY CONTROL STATUS, NEW YORK CITY, 1977 AND 1980

Control Status	Median Income 1977	Median Income 1980	Percent Change 1977-1980
All renter-occupied	$8,979	$11,001	+22.5
Controlled	7,338	8,918	+21.5
Decontrolled	8,549	11,315	+32.4
Pre-'47 stabilized	8,218	10,355	+26.0
Post-'47 stabilized	15,536	18,788	+20.9

SOURCES: 1977 data from Marcuse, p. 254; 1980 data from U.S. Bureau of the Census, 1981 New York City Housing and Vacancy Survey.

units was $8,918 in 1980, nearly $1,500 lower than the median for tenants in pre-'47 stabilized apartments and more than $2,000 below that for tenants in decontrolled units.† Incomes of tenants in controlled units increased at just about the citywide rate between 1977 and 1980, although their incomes lagged behind those of households in decontrolled apartments, whose median income increased by nearly one-third.

The lower the income of the household in a controlled apartment, the longer its occupancy in that unit (Table 8-13). Nearly 40 percent of all tenants with incomes under $6,500 living in controlled units have not moved since 1953 or earlier, a tenancy of at least 28 years. For households with incomes between $6,500 and $12,499, the comparable figure is 33 percent. The incidence of very long tenancy falls as income increases. Even for high-income households, however, far more tenants in controlled apartments have stayed put for a long time. One in five tenants in controlled housing with incomes of at least $25,000 have lived in their apartments since 1953, compared to just one out of every 10 renter households citywide.

Because the incomes of tenants in post-'47 stabilized apartments and of homeowners are very similar, these tenants might seem to have more in common with homeowners than with other renters. This is not the case, however, with regard to household composition. The proportion of single-person households in post-'47 stabilized units is more than twice that of homeowners, whereas the proportion of married couples in the post-'47 stabilized stock is 57 percent as high as the proportion of homeowning couples (Table 8-14). Twice as many married couples who own homes are 65 years or more

---

†The probability is .95 that rent controlled households have a median income lower than the median income of decontrolled households. The probability is .68 that rent controlled households have a lower median income than pre-'47 stabilized households.

TABLE 8-13. INCOME OF HOUSEHOLDS IN RENT CONTROLLED APARTMENTS BY YEAR MOVED IN, NEW YORK CITY, 1980

	1980 Household Income			
	Less Than $6,500	$6,500- $12,499	$12,500- $24,999	$25,000 or More
Year Moved In	Percent Distribution			
Total	100.0	100.0	100.0	100.0
1971*	7.9	13.2	11.9	14.5
1960-1971	42.8	44.0	57.6	48.3
1954-1959	10.7	10.2	12.3	16.6
1943-1953	17.3	15.1	11.5	12.9
1942 or earlier	21.3	17.5	6.7	7.7

*Rent controlled apartments vacated after June 30, 1971 entered the rent stabilized stock. Consequently, a response in this category either represents a household that moved into a rent controlled unit between January 1 and June 30, 1971 or nonsampling error.

SOURCE: U.S. Bureau of the Census, 1981 New York City Housing and Vacancy Survey.

TABLE 8-14. HOUSEHOLD COMPOSITION OF HOMEOWNERS AND POST-'47 STABILIZED RENTER HOUSEHOLDS, NEW YORK CITY, 1981

Household Characteristics	Homeowner	Post-'47 Stabilized
	Percent Distribution	
Total	100.0	100.0
2-or-more person households	79.3	53.8
Married, no nonrelatives	64.2	36.4
Under 45 years	21.1	17.3
45-64 years	30.3	12.9
65 years or older	12.9	6.2
Other male householder	4.7	4.0
Under 65 years	3.8	3.5
65 years or older	0.9	0.5
Female householder	10.4	13.3
Under 65 years	7.6	12.2
65 years or older	2.8	1.1
1-person households	20.7	46.2
Under 65 years	10.9	35.0
65 years or older	9.8	11.3

SOURCE: U.S. Bureau of the Census, 1981 New York City Housing and Vacancy Survey.

(13 percent versus 6 percent of couples in the post-'47 stock). Nearly one-third more women rent post-'47 stabilized apartments than own their homes. Finally, 8 percent of the tenants in this sector are elderly, compared to 27 percent of homeowners.

Condition

The incidence of both dilapidated and inadequate housing declines as income rises (Tables 8-15, 8-16). Seven percent of all renters with incomes below $6,500 live in dilapidated housing, compared to 3 percent with incomes between $12,500 and $24,999, and just 1 percent of those earning over $25,000. Similarly, 31 percent of the poorest tenants and just 11 percent of the richest live in apartments with multiple maintenance deficiencies. This relationship between housing condition and income is not quite as clear when the stock is disaggregated by control status. The dilapidation rate seems to vary less by tenant income in the controlled sector than in other market sectors. While definition of the income groups could affect this relationship, the dilapidation rate is fixed at between 6 and 7 percent for tenants in controlled apartments who earn between $6,500 and $25,000. In the pre-'47 stabilized sector, 11 percent of the apartments occupied by the poorest households are dilapidated, compared to just 4 percent of those inhabited by households with incomes between $12,500 and $24,999.

TABLE 8-15. DILAPIDATION RATES FOR RENTER-OCCUPIED UNITS BY CONTROL STATUS AND INCOME, NEW YORK CITY, 1981

1980 Income	All Renter Occupied	Controlled	Decontrolled	Stabilized Pre-'47	Stabilized Post-'47
Less than $6,500	7.1%	6.1%	9.2%	11.1%	0.7%
$6,500-12,499	5.4	6.7	7.2	6.2	0.4
$12,500-24,999	3.0	6.7	3.2	3.9	--
$25,000 or more	1.3	0.8	2.0	2.1	--

SOURCE: U.S. Bureau of the Census, 1981 New York City Housing and Vacancy Survey.

Dilapidation rates for decontrolled housing parallel those for pre-'47 stabilized apartments, ranging from a high of 9.2 percent of all units occupied by households with incomes below $6,500 to a low of 2 percent of the stock occupied by the highest-income renters. Less than 1 percent of the post-'47 stabilized stock is dilapidated, and all of that is occupied by households with incomes below $12,500.

Especially for lower-income tenants, rent controlled apartments appear to be in better condition than pre-'47 stabilized apartments. Less than 31 percent of the tenants in controlled units who earn less than $6,500 report

TABLE 8-16. MULTIPLE MAINTENANCE DEFICIENCY RATES FOR RENTER OCCUPIED UNITS, BY CONTROL STATUS AND INCOME, NEW YORK CITY, 1981

1980 Income	All Renter Occupied	Controlled	Decontrolled	Stabilized Pre-'47	Stabilized Post-'47
Less than $6,500	30.8%	27.6%	25.9%	46.6%	9.2%
$6,500-12,499	25.1	28.5	20.0	36.1	11.3
$12,500-24,999	18.6	29.4	11.3	29.0	10.8
$25,000 and more	10.5	23.6	5.9	14.9	7.4

SOURCE: U.S. Bureau of the Census, 1981 New York City Housing and Vacancy Survey.

at least three maintenance deficiencies, compared to nearly half of equally poor tenants in pre-'47 stabilized housing. As with the incidence of dilapidation, multiple deficiences in the controlled sector occur in around 28 percent of the stock across a broad range of household incomes. Between 7 and 11 percent of all post-'47 stabilized apartments have multiple deficiencies regardless of tenant income. In the pre-'47 stabilized inventory, the incidence of multiple maintenance problems does decline dramatically with an increase in tenant income. The percentage of households in the pre-'47 stabilized stock reporting three or more maintenance problems falls from 47 percent among those with incomes below $6,500 to 29 percent for those with incomes between $12,500 and $24,999, down to just 15 percent of households with incomes above $25,000.

Rent-Income Ratios

Because of the changing characteristics of the renter population and housing inventory, it is very difficult to assess the policy significance of recent changes in housing expense burdens. Increases in rent-income ratios can reflect the loss of higher-income families to the homeownership market, a disproportionately high rate of growth in traditionally poor socioeconomic groups, across-the-board stagnation in incomes, substantial rent inflation, or combinations of the above. Also, as the President's Commission on Housing implies, some of today's higher nominal rents may be attributable to increases in the quality and amount of space that families buy.[1]

Whatever the reasons, the median gross rent-income ratio for households in New York City has increased by nearly 50 percent since 1950, from 19 to 28 percent (Table 8-17). About 12 percent of this long-term increase occurred between 1950 and 1970, with the remainder occurring from 1970 to 1978. Since 1978, the median rent-income ratio in New York City has remained constant at 28 percent.

According to the President's Commission, the old rule of thumb that households spending more than one-quarter of their incomes for rent are spending too much for housing has lost much of its significance now that such expense burdens have become the rule rather than the exception (Table 8-18; Exhibit 8-4). Even with rent regulation, 57 percent of all renters in New York spend at least one-quarter of their incomes for housing. This

TABLE 8-17. MEDIAN GROSS RENT-INCOME RATIO, ALL RENTER HOUSEHOLDS, NEW YORK CITY, SELECTED YEARS

	1950	1960	1965	1968	1970	1975	1978	1981
Median Gross Rent-Income Ratio	18.9%	18.7%	20.4%	21.0%	20.0%	24.7%	28.3%	28.0%

SOURCES: 1950-1978 data from Marcuse, p. 197; 1981 data from the U.S. Bureau of the Census, 1981 New York City Housing and Vacancy Survey.

suggests that, in the foreseeable future, the more serious challenge to creating and maintaining a healthy rental market might be incomes, not the unresponsiveness of rent regulations to the costs of doing business. Nearly half of all tenants in the City now spend at least 30 percent of their incomes for rent and utilities. This group has grown considerably over the past decade. The highest growth-rate in the City was among those households for whom rent consumes at least 40 percent of income. In 1981, three out of every 10 renters in New York City fell into this category, an 83 percent increase since 1968.

TABLE 8-18. PERCENT OF HOUSEHOLDS WITH RENT-INCOME RATIOS OVER SPECIFIED LEVELS, NEW YORK CITY, SELECTED YEARS

	Percent of Households with Rent-Income Ratio over Specified Level							
Gross rent-income ratio	1950	1960	1965	1968	1970	1975	1978	1981
25% or more	N.A.	N.A.	34.9	37.2	35.5	49.1	57.1	56.6
30% or more	25.0	24.0	25.3	27.4	N.A.	38.1	46.3	45.6
35% or more	N.A.	19.0	18.7	21.2	23.2	30.8	38.0	37.1
40% or more	N.A.	N.A.	14.5	16.7	N.A.	25.2	31.6	30.5

SOURCES: Gross rent-income ratios 25% or more, 30% or more, and 35% or more, 1950-1978, Marcuse, p. 198; gross rent-income ratios 40% or more, 1965 and 1968 from Niebanck pp. 149-50, 1981 data from the U.S. Bureau of the Census, 1981 New York City, Housing and Vacancy Survey.

EXHIBIT 8-4. PERCENT OF HOUSEHOLDS WITH RENT-INCOME RATIOS OVER FORTY PERCENT, NEW YORK CITY, 1965, 1975 AND 1981.

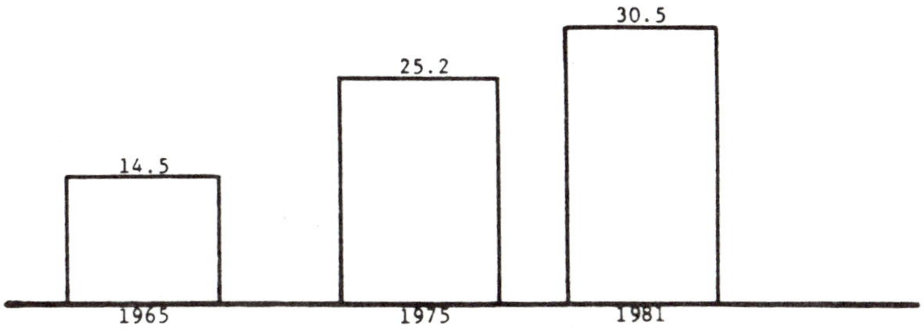

SOURCE: Table 8-18.

TABLE 8-19. MEDIAN GROSS RENT-INCOME RATIO, BY AGE AND SEX OF HOUSEHOLD HEAD, NEW YORK CITY, 1978 AND 1981

	1978	1981
Male		
Under 45	22.7%	22.8%
45-61	20.7	20.8
62-64	21.0	23.9
65 and over	31.7	31.4
Median	23.5	23.5
Female		
Under 45	37.8	34.7
45-61	32.8	29.4
62-64	35.0	33.5
65 and over	42.4	39.1
Median	38.2	35.1

SOURCES: 1978 data from Marcuse, p. 218; 1981 data from U.S. Bureau of the Census, 1981 New York City Housing and Vacancy Survey.

Age and Sex. Male renter householders have experienced a greater degree of stability in the housing-income relationship than have female householders. Female householders have much higher relative housing expense burdens than males because their incomes are much lower (Table 8-19). While there is virtually no floor below which incomes can fall, the level of

TABLE 8-20. GROSS RENT-INCOME RATIOS OF HOUSEHOLD HEADS AGED 65 YEARS AND OLDER, NEW YORK CITY, 1978 AND 1981

	All Renter Households		Aged 65 and over	
Gross Rent-Income Ratio	1978	1981	1978	1981
	Percent Distribution			
Total	100.0	100.0	100.0	100.0
Less than 15%	13.7	14.0	6.9	6.3
15% to 24%	29.2	29.3	18.5	21.1
25% to 39%	25.4	26.2	30.4	31.1
40% or more	31.7	30.5	44.3	41.4

NOTE: Data is based on the number of household heads reporting on age, sex, rent and income.

SOURCES: 1978 data from Marcuse, p. 217; 1981 data from U.S. Bureau of the Census, 1981 New York City Housing and Vacancy Survey.

operating costs sets the practical floor below rents. The median rent-income ratio of female householders has fallen slightly since 1978, but it is still 35 percent compared to 24 percent for males. To the extent that female householders become an increasingly larger segment of total rental housing demand, the long-term picture for the older rental stock is not especially bright. This is also the case for older people: among both male and female householders, rent-income ratios are higher for those aged 65 or more. Elderly male householders have a median rent-income ratio of 31 percent, while for females it is 39 percent. The share of older renters suffering high rent burdens has dropped about 7 percent since 1978 because of the rise in the incomes of elderly female householders, but is still high (Table 8-20). Today, 40 percent of elderly households spend more than 40 percent of their income for housing, whereas only 30 percent of all renters do.

Race and Ethnic Origin. The stability in the citywide housing-income relationship between 1978 and 1981 is shown in the data for racial and ethnic groups (Table 8-21). Following an 11 percent increase between 1975 and 1978, the median rent-income ratio for Whites remained steady at 26 percent over the succeeding three years. The median for Black renters declined slightly to 29 percent, after a 21 percent increase in the rent-income ratio between 1975 and 1978. Puerto Rican households continue to have the highest housing expense burdens in the City, with a median of 36 percent. Between 1975 and 1978, their median rent-income ratio increased by 17 percent.

TABLE 8-21. RACE AND ETHNIC GROUP BY GROSS RENT-INCOME RATIO, NEW YORK CITY, 1975, 1978, 1981

	Median Rent-Income Ratio		
	1975	1978	1981
All households	24.7%	28.3%	28.0%
White	23.7	26.4	26.3
Black	25.3	30.5	28.8
Puerto Rican	31.1	36.3	35.7
Other	22.9	25.2	28.0

NOTE: Table based on those reporting race and ethnic group, income and rent.

SOURCES: 1975 and 1978 data from Marcuse, p. 219; 1981 data from U.S. Bureau of the Census, 1981 New York City Housing and Vacancy Survey.

With respect to race and ethnic groups, household incomes are inversely related to rent-income ratios. The median income is nearly $30,000 among households who pay less than 15 percent of their incomes for rent (Table 8-22). For Whites, it is $33,000, while for Black and Puerto Rican renters,

TABLE 8-22. MEDIAN INCOME OF RENTERS, BY GROSS RENT-INCOME RATIO AND RACE AND ETHNIC ORIGIN, NEW YORK CITY, 1980

	Median Household Incomes			
Gross Rent-Income Ratio	All Renters	White	Black	Puerto Rican
All renters	$11,001	$13,474	$9,142	$6,460
Less than 15%	29,753	32,916	23,697	20,766
15-19%	19,403	22,379	15,875	14,523
20-24%	14,896	17,190	11,457	11,722
25-29%	11,739	12,939	10,580	9,710
30-39%	9,488	10,159	8,927	8,048
40% or more	4,946	5,401	4,469	4,394

SOURCE: U.S. Bureau of the Census, 1981 New York City Housing and Vacancy Survey.

median incomes are $24,000 and $21,000 respectively. As rent-income ratios increase, incomes fall, while the gaps among the groups narrow in both absolute and relative terms. Thus, among households with the lowest rent-income ratios, for example, Puerto Rican incomes are 37 percent lower and Black incomes are 28 percent lower than Whites'. Among households with rent burdens equal to at least 40 percent of income, Puerto Rican and Black incomes are 19 and 17 percent lower than the median income for Whites.

Regardless of race or ethnic origin, New York households with incomes below $6,000 are very likely to spend at least half of their resources for housing (Table 8-23). Median rent-income ratios remain high until household income reaches $10,000. Increasingly large numbers of households with incomes above $10,000 pay less than one-quarter of their incomes for rent. Around two-thirds of all renters with incomes between $12,500 and $20,000 have rent-income ratios of less than 25 percent. This proportion grows to 83 percent for households with incomes between $20,000 and $25,000, and rises to more than 90 percent for those with incomes above $25,000 (Table 8-24).

Rent-Income Ratios by Rent. The distribution of rent-income ratios by rent is narrower than that by income (Table 8-25). The median rent-income ratio for households paying less than $100 on rent is 23 percent, compared to the median of 26 percent for households paying rent of at least $500 a month. The tightness in the distribution is due largely to the substantial numbers of lower- and moderate-income households represented in the upper reaches of the rent distribution. Thus, despite the fact that median income increases with rent, nearly 100,000 households with incomes of less than $10,000 a year pay at least $300 a month for housing. The financial squeeze on the lower-income families in the City is also reflected in the fact that the 198,235 renter households with incomes of less than $4,000 a year compete with each other for the 66,159 apartments which rent for less than $100 a month. This partially explains the difference in the rent-income ratio between occupants of apartments renting for less than $100 a month and those renting for between $100 and $250 a month.

TABLE 8-23. MEDIAN GROSS RENT-INCOME RATIOS BY RACE/ETHNIC ORIGIN AND INCOME, ALL RENTER HOUSEHOLDS, NEW YORK CITY, 1981

	All Renters	<$4,000	$4,000-5,999	$6,000-6,499	$6,500-7,999	$8,000-9,999	$10,000-12,499	$12,500-14,999	$15,000-19,999	$20,000-24,999	$25,000-34,999	$35,000 or more
All Renters	28.0%	50.0+%	50.0+%	44.2%	39.0%	33.3%	28.5%	24.4%	21.0%	18.3%	15.0%	13.6%
White	26.3	50.0+	50.0+	45.3	39.4	36.2	30.4	25.2	21.8	19.0	15.9	13.8
Black	28.8	50.0+	50.0+	38.3	35.3	30.2	26.6	24.3	19.4	17.2	13.6	10.0-
Puerto Rican	35.7	50.0+	50.0+	44.7	39.5	32.0	24.9	21.9	18.2	16.9	13.2	10.0-
Other	28.0	50.0+	50.0+	49.1	43.9	32.0	29.6	23.2	21.2	18.5	14.1	13.9

SOURCE: U.S. Bureau of the Census, 1981 New York City Housing and Vacancy Survey.

TABLE 8-24. GROSS RENT-INCOME RATIOS BY INCOME OF HOUSEHOLD, ALL RENTER HOUSEHOLDS, NEW YORK CITY, 1978 AND 1981

	Percent with 25% or Higher Gross Rent-Income Ratio	
	1978	1981
Total Households	57.1	56.6
Less than $4,000	94.3	91.6
$4,000-5,999	94.4	92.5
$6,000-6,4999	90.0	90.8
$6,500-9,999	69.2	80.8
$10,000-12,499	43.3	65.7
$12,500-19,999	17.1	32.7
$20,000-24,999	12.7	16.6
$25,000-34,999	5.3	9.5
$35,000 or more	4.0	9.4

NOTE: Household incomes are from years 1977 and 1980.

SOURCES: 1978 data from Marcuse, p. 201; 1981 data from U.S. Bureau of the Census, 1981 New York City Housing and Vacancy Survey.

TABLE 8-25. MEDIAN RENT-INCOME RATIO BY GROSS RENT, ALL RENTER HOUSEHOLDS, NEW YORK CITY, 1978 AND 1981

	Median Gross Rent-Income Ratio		
Gross Rent	1978	1981	Median Income
Total Households	28.3%	28.0%	$11,001
Less than $100	25.1	22.7	<4,000
$100-$149	30.6	29.8	5,516
$150-$199	29.6	31.2	6,807
$200-$249	29.0	29.9	9,481
$250-$299	28.1	29.2	11,614
$300-$399	26.1	27.5	15,615
$400-$499	25.9	24.8	22,675
$500-$749	26.1	24.2	32,733
$750 or more	N.A.	30.5	35,000+
Median rent	$210	$265	N.A.

SOURCES: 1978 data from Marcuse, pp. 202 and 224; 1981 data from the U.S. Bureau of the Census, 1981 New York City Housing and Vacancy Survey.

Condition. Another reflection of the tight rental market for lower-income families is the high rent burden for households living in the City's oldest and lowest-quality housing. Although the proportion is somewhat lower than three years ago, 38 percent of the occupants of Old Law tenements pay at least 40 percent of their income for rent. This figure is 24 percent higher than the citywide rate (Table 8-26). Similarly, 45 percent of the occupants of dilapidated housing also have rent-income ratios of at least 40 percent. Financial sacrifice by poor New Yorkers does not guarantee occupancy of adequate housing, nor does the acceptance of inadequate housing necessarily imply a low housing expense burden.

TABLE 8-26. GROSS RENT-INCOME RATIO BY SELECTED CHARACTERISTICS, ALL RENTER HOUSEHOLDS, NEW YORK CITY, 1978 AND 1981

	1978			1981		
	Total	Dilapidated	Old Law	Total	Dilapidated	Old Law
Rent-income ratio						
Less than 15%	13.7%	9.4%	15.0%	13.9%	11.3%	13.8%
Less than 25%	42.9	28.7	36.4	43.4	31.5	40.2
40% or more	31.7	49.9	41.3	30.5	45.4	37.7
Median rent-income ratio	28.3	40.0	33.2	28.0	36.9	30.0

SOURCES: 1978 data from Marcuse, p. 211; 1981 data from the U.S. Bureau of the Census, 1981 New York City Housing and Vacancy Survey.

Control Status. With the relatively substantial rent increases for controlled units since 1970, the 29 percent median rent-income ratio for controlled housing is about the same as for the City as a whole, and has not changed since 1978 (Table 8-27). Due to a higher-than-average increase in tenant incomes and a lower-than-average increase in rents over the period, the median rent-income ratio for households in decontrolled apartments has declined from 33 percent in 1978 to 29 percent in 1981. The higher expense burden for tenants in pre-'47 stabilized units than for those in controlled housing is due principally to the higher rent to which landlords are entitled when controlled units are vacated and move into the stabilized sector. The net effect of these adjustments is a rent difference of $49 at the median between the two sectors of housing. This means that, at the median, a tenant who moves into a newly vacated controlled apartment will pay 23 percent more in rent than the tenant who moved out.* Despite the even greater difference between the median rent for post-'47 stabilized apartments and other rental housing in the City, the median rent-income ratio for households in the City's newer inventory is lower than it is in other sectors. This comes from household incomes being disproportionately higher in the post-'47 stock. While post-'47 stabilized rents are 40 percent higher than pre-'47 rents, households in post-'47 housing have incomes 81 percent higher than those in pre-'47 apartments.

---

*This issue is discussed more fully in Chapter 9.

TABLE 8-27. GROSS RENT-INCOME RATIO BY CONTROL STATUS, ALL RENTER HOUSEHOLDS, NEW YORK CITY, 1981

	Gross Rent-Income Ratio		
	1968	1978	1981
All renters	21.0%	28.3%	28.0%
Controlled	21.0	28.6	28.6
Decontrolled	22.4	32.9	28.8
Pre-'47 stabilized	N.A.	32.3	31.7
Post-'47 stabilized	N.A.	24.6	25.4

SOURCE: 1968 data from Niebanck, p. 150; 1978 data from Marcuse, p. 268; 1981 data from U.S. Bureau of the Census, 1981 New York City Housing and Vacancy Survey.

Rent Regulation and Housing Need

Some observers have criticized the City's system of rent control since it was first studied, claiming that the benefits of rent control are distributed randomly and without due regard to housing need. This unequal distribution results from the combination of vacancy rent increases, vacancy decontrol and variations in moving behavior among different household groups. Consequently, large numbers of lower-income families live in noncontrolled apartments and large numbers of middle- and upper-income families occupy controlled units. Since the controlled stock is now only 15 percent of the occupied rental inventory, the issue of who is benefiting under rent control is not as urgent a question as it once was. Nevertheless, the control categories housing the City's most needy were examined to determine who is benefiting from rent regulation. The indices used to assess need were the Bureau of Labor Statistics (BLS) lower family budget and the federal poverty level. The analysis was completed in two steps. First, the percentage of households in each control class with incomes below each of these indices was computed. Then each of these percentages was divided into the percentage each control category is of the City's total occupied rental stock. A ratio of one means that a particular market sector is housing its proportionate share of the City's households with urgent needs. A ratio of less than one means that needy households are underrepresented, and a ratio of more than one means that they are over represented in a particular market sector.

The fraction of households with incomes below the BLS lower budget level for the New York metropolitan area varies from a low of 12 percent in rent controlled units to 36 percent in pre-'47 stabilized apartments (Table 8-28). A higher proportion of households in decontrolled than in controlled apartments have incomes below the BLS budget. Sixteen percent of the households in decontrolled apartments are below the BLS minimum. Since decontrolled units account for 15 percent of all occupied apartments, this market sector contains a proportionate share of the City's needy population. In contrast, 36 percent of the occupants of pre-'47 stabilized apartments fall below the BLS threshold, which is 15 percent higher than the share of stock accounted for by such housing. Using the BLS lower budget as the measure of need, poor people are underrepresented by some 20 percent in the rent controlled sector. Underrepresentation of needy households in controlled apartments increases to 23 percent if the more restrictive measure of need -- i.e., the official federal poverty level -- is used.

TABLE 8-28. RELATIVE REPRESENTATION OF INCOME DEPRIVED RENTER HOUSEHOLDS, BY CONTROL STATUS, NEW YORK CITY, 1981

	I	II	III	Relative Representation of Income-Deprived Households	
	All Renter Households	Households Below BLS budget Level*	Households Below Poverty Level	Ratio of Column II to Column I	Ratio of Column III to Column I
	Percent Distribution				
Total	100.0	100.0	100.0	--	--
Controlled	14.8	11.8	11.4	0.797	0.770
Decontrolled	14.6	15.5	14.7	1.062	1.007
Pre-'47 Stabilized	31.8	36.4	37.6	1.145	1.182
Post-'47 Stabilized	16.2	6.4	5.3	0.395	0.327
State/City Assisted	2.1	1.3	1.5	0.619	0.714

*The number of households below the BLS minimum budget level were computed separately for one- and two-person households under age 65 and over age 65 and for three-, four-, five- and six or more person households, with the head assumed to be under age 65. These individual estimates were then aggregated for the City and by control status.

NOTE: Both the BLS and poverty figures are the percent of all households below the respective cutoffs who live in each of the control categories. Percents in columns I, II and III do not equal 100.0 because the distribution includes Public Housing and Other Rental Housing which are not displayed in the table.

SOURCES: Budget data for New York-Northeastern New Jersey are from Autumn 1980 Urban Family Budgets and Comparative Indices for Selected Urban Areas; Release USDL 81-195, April 22, 1981, Bureau of Labor Statistics, U.S. Department of Labor; Housing unit counts from U.S. Bureau of the Census, 1981 New York City Housing and Vacancy Survey.

Redefining Housing Need

Until now, housing need has been measured in terms of the fraction of income households allocate to rent. While the old rule of one week's wages for one month's shelter has been replaced in recent federal low-income housing legislation by a higher rent contribution requirement of 30 percent of income, neither the new nor the old standards can be said to seriously address the issue of affordability. Michael Stone, among others, argues that some families are simply too poor to be able to afford to pay anything for housing -- not 20 percent, not 15 percent, nor even 10 percent of their meager incomes.[2] This is so if affordability is defined as the difference between total income and the costs of all nonhousing necessities. If the costs of minimum purchases of food, clothing, health care and other such necessities equal or exceed a household's total income, then that household cannot afford any housing expense, not even 10 percent of its income.

Stone demonstrates that when affordable housing expenses are considered as a residual in the poor person's budget, very large numbers of families cannot spend anything for shelter unless they sacrifice nonhousing necessities. Building on his analytical framework, BLS budget data for the lower living standard for the New York metropolitan area were adjusted to remove the housing component.* The BLS minimum nonhousing budget needs in New York City range from a low of $3,735** for one-person households to $15,492 a year for families of six of more (Table 8-29).

Nearly one-half million renters, or 30 percent of the City total are, by Stone's standard, too poor to afford rent of any amount. Of course, this does not consider the additional hundreds of thousands of renters whose incomes are higher than the adjusted BLS nonhousing budget but not high enough to pay the full cost of adequate housing.

The policy significance of this different perspective on housing needs is not simply that it produces a much larger gap between the cost of adequate housing and the ability of the poor to pay shelter costs than do more conventional measures. Using 80 percent of the median city gross rent of $265 as the subsidy standard, for example, produces an income gap for these house-poor of more than 96 million dollars a year in New York City alone. More importantly, compared to a housing assistance program in which aid is allocated according to excessive rent-income ratios, the BLS residual approach would redistribute housing subsidies away from individuals toward families and, further, from smaller to larger families.

To illustrate this point, Table 8-29 shows the percentage of each household size category that is considered house-poor using both the adjusted BLS budget definition and a rent-income ratio greater than 40 percent. Nearly 525,000, or 31 percent of the total renter population, pay more than

---

*The private automobile allowance in the budget was eliminated under the assumption that public transportation in New York City is adequate to meet the transportation needs of lower-income families.

**Aggregated for renters above 65 and below 65 years of age.

TABLE 8-29. RENTER HOUSEHOLDS CLASSIFIED AS HOUSE-POOR, USING AN ADJUSTED BLS LOWER BUDGET REQUIREMENT AND CONVENTIONAL RENT-INCOME RATIOS, NEW YORK CITY, 1981*

Household Size	BLS Adjusted Lower Budget Requirement	Percent of Households Below BLS Adjusted Lower Budget Requirement	Percent of Households with Rent-Income Ratios Greater Than 40 Percent
Total housepoor households	435,853	29.6	30.7
1 person	$3,735**	20.9	34.5
2 persons	$6,436**	20.9	24.7
3 persons	$9,090	37.0	31.3
4 persons	$11,113	45.6	30.3
5 persons	$13,247	56.6	33.6
6 or more persons	$15,492	70.0	33.6

*The BLS adjusted nonhousing lower budget requirement was derived by subtracting the costs of housing and household furnishings. The BLS computes the transportation budget requirement for lower-income families assuming a 50 percent automobile ownership rate, in the case of New York City. We recomputed this component assuming 100 percent use of public transportation. For a family of four, the net effect of the two adjustments is to reduce the BLS lower budget nonhousing requirement from $14,393 to $11,113.

**To derive these figures the BLS budget requirement was weighted to account for one- and two-person households above and below 65 years of age.

SOURCES: U.S. Department of Labor, Bureau of Labor Statistics, Publication 81-195, Autumn 1980 Urban Family Budgets and Comparative Indexes for Selected Urban Areas, and U.S. Bureau of the Census, 1981 New York City Housing and Vacancy Survey.

40 percent of their incomes on rent. The proportion of households with excessive rent-income ratios does not vary directly with household size, ranging between 25 and 35 percent of each size class. Presumably, therefore, a roughly equal proportion of each size class would be eligible for housing assistance when need is determined by excessive rent-income ratio.

On the other hand, the proportion of renters with incomes below the adjusted BLS budget standard does vary directly with household size. One-fifth of one- and two-person renter households fall completely below the standard. For four-person households, the failure rate is 46 percent and rises to 70 percent for families with six or more members.

NOTES

1. The President's Commission on Housing, Interim Report, October 30, 1981, pp. 18, 19.

2. Michael Stone, "Housing, Mortgage Lending and the Contradictions of Capitalism," in Marxism and the Metropolis, edited by W. K. Tabb and L. Sawers (New York: Oxford University Press, 1978).

CHAPTER 9

RENTAL HOUSING MARKET DYNAMICS

Introduction

Thus far, the analysis of changes in housing conditions, rents and occupancy patterns has been carried out using cross-sectional data from different years. This analysis has been useful in assessing the general nature and magnitude of changes in housing quality, rents, vacancies and racial distributions. Cross-sectional studies do not, however, control for variations in the size and composition of the stock, nor do they indicate much about the processes or location of change. To deal with these inadequacies, the Housing and Vacancy Survey used the same basic sample in 1975, 1978 and 1981, allowing one to investigate changes in individual units. The analysis of losses from the housing inventory between 1978 and 1981, and the assessment of "returning losses" demonstrate the strength of the longitudinal sample. Studying matched dwelling units also permits a more definitive appraisal of the changes in occupancy and household characteristics that accompany the transition of rent controlled apartments into the stabilized inventory.

This chapter focuses on the rental housing market dynamics in New York City in the years 1978-1981. The data studied in the latter part of the chapter come from the longitudinal portion of the Housing and Vacancy Survey of the 13,348 households who responded to both the 1978 and 1981 surveys. An overview of changes in New York's housing inventory in the years since 1978 opens this chapter. Subsequent sections discuss two key components of change: new construction and inventory losses. The concluding section of the chapter draws on the longitudinal data to analyze changes in occupancy patterns in New York between 1978 and 1981.

Components of Inventory Change

Additions. As reported in Chapter 4, the housing inventory in New York City is reported to have increased from 2,783,000 to 2,792,000 units since 1978. The 1978 total presented here is drawn from Marcuse's 1978 report, but evidence suggests that the actual inventory may have included 16,000 more units than were reported. This discrepancy arises because the New York City Building Department list of Certificates of Occupancy, from which the Housing and Vacancy Survey sample of new construction was drawn, excludes approximately 16,000 apartments sponsored by the New York State Urban Development Corporation. These 16,000 dwelling units were financed by a State agency and therefore did not require Certificates of Occupancy. Approved for occupancy between the 1970 Census and the 1978 Housing and Vacancy Survey, they appear in both the 1980 Census and the 1981 Housing and Vacancy Survey. The analysis of inventory change in the last three years adds these 16,000 UDC units to the 1978 inventory because they were inadvertently omitted from previous surveys and were then included in the 1981 stock (Table 9-1).

TABLE 9-1. CHANGES IN TOTAL HOUSING INVENTORY, NEW YORK CITY, 1978-1981

Revised 1978 actual inventory	2,799,000
1978 Actual inventory	2,783,000
Previously uncounted UDC construction*	16,000
Additions to the stock, 1978-1981:	
New construction	28,000
Lofts and other conversions from non-residential to residential use	3,000
Net conversions within residential sector	9,000
Returning losses	33,000
Gross losses from the stock, 1978-1981	81,000
1981 Estimated inventory	2,791,000
1981 Actual inventory	2,792,000

*See text for discussion of UDC-sponsored construction for the period 1970-1978.

SOURCE: U.S. Bureau of the Census, 1981 New York City Housing and Vacancy Survey.

In addition to the never-counted UDC units, the 1978 inventory is adjusted to reflect the reported addition of 28,000 new dwellings built since 1978.* The conversion of previously nonresidential space to housing contributes further to the expansion of the rental inventory. The bulk of the reported 3,000 housing units added to the supply from such conversions since 1978 is probably residential lofts. Residential conversions other than lofts have added another 9,000 apartments to the City's housing supply since 1978. In 1981, Census enumerators identified conversions, or "extra housing units," when they returned to buildings they had surveyed three years earlier and discovered additional dwellings at those sites. In some cases, a sampled dwelling was found to no longer be a separate apartment, while in others single and multi-unit buildings had been converted into additional living units. Overall, 9,000 additional housing units are reported in New York as a result of this type of conversion activity between 1978 and 1981.

<u>Losses</u>. A substantial number of housing units have dropped out of the inventory since 1978 (see later sections of this chapter). The Census

---

*A detailed analysis of new supply and privately and publicly supported construction is presented later in this chapter.

reports that 81,000 housing units have been lost from the inventory since 1978. The Census defines losses to include demolitions, units condemned by a public authority, units boarded-up, burned-out or vacant and open to the elements, conversions to nonresidential uses, or mergers with other apartments. Although gross losses to the stock since 1978 are twice as numerous as additions, the loss rate has slowed significantly from what it was through most of the 1970s. Moreover, at the same time that 81,000 housing units were dropping out of the inventory, 33,000 apartments, which were losses in 1978 were back in the 1981 inventory. This phenomenon of returning losses, about which not much is known, demonstrates that many units previously withdrawn from the inventory can be brought back into the supply. More will be said about returning losses later, but it is important to note here that they, together with nonresidential and residential conversions, account for 62 percent of the gross additions to the City's housing supply since 1978, and are also 61 percent higher than the number of newly constructed units.

New Construction

Policy Debates. The pattern of housing starts over time must be studied because new additions are not only a significant part of the City's housing picture, but variations in the volume and composition of starts have become a key element in rent regulation policy discussions. With respect to these discussions, Louis Winnick of the Ford Foundation, author of many works on rental housing markets, has put the issue quite bluntly: "The politicization of rental housing has dealt a mortal blow to this segment of the debt market ... the debt investor cannot rationally assess the ratio of risk to reward ... [because] rental housing is the one real estate market that has to contend with not only the usual economic uncertainties but with the far less calculable political uncertainties."[1]

Frank Kristof, former Chief Economist for the New York State Urban Development Corporation and former President of the Rent Stabilization Association, also holds that the reimposition of regulations in New York City via rent stabilization was principally to blame for the fact that "since 1969 ... new additions to the privately financed rental housing supply have dropped to one-quarter of the pre-1969 rate."[2] In this section, the Winnick-Kristof view will be examined by reference to data on statewide housing starts. Despite the elegance and simplicity of the theoretical arguments on the supply-effects of rent regulation, the empirical explorations by rent regulation critics are not unassailable, partly because of inherent limitations in the data, and partly because the regulatory system actually in place is by no means as pure as the underlying economic theory might imply. The conclusion one draws from the analysis is that even if private rental housing construction has suffered since the introduction of rent stabilization, it is not at all clear that total housing construction has been affected to the same degree, if at all. Moreover, a close look at the composition of the local housing supply and the high degree of public intervention in the local housing market suggests that it is difficult to single out one form of intervention like rent stabilization and demonstrate irrefutably that it has been the most important determinant of the changing levels of private housing investment in New York over the last 10 years.

Notes on the Data Sources. Before beginning the analysis, the nature of the data and its limitations should be noted. There are three possible data sources on new supply. The first is Building Department records on Certificates of Occupancy (C's of O) issued for buildings approved for occupancy during the period under consideration. The Census Bureau uses C's of O to define housing additions. According to C of O data, 28,000 new housing units were built in New York between 1978 and 1981. A second source of information on new supply is the 1981 Housing and Vacancy Survey during which enumerators asked respondents to estimate the year in which their apartment or building was built. The age of vacant units was estimated through interviews with superintendents or managing agents. Less reliable than C of O data, respondents are still useful as a source to confirm other independent estimates of new supply. Survey respondents placed the level of new housing construction in New York City between 1978 and 1981 at 26,831 units. The third source, and the one which will be used here, is official building permit records for New York City and State. Estimates of new supply derived from these data will differ from those obta-ined from C's of O because some buildings for which permits have been issued never get built.

Permits reflect the commitment to build, while C's of O indicate that the building has been completed. Also, because permits start the building cycle, the gap between estimates of additions based on the number of permits issued and data based on C's of O will depend on what point in the building cycle is being examined. For the period January 1978 through April 1981, building permits were authorized for 37,619 housing units in New York City. This number is 9,600 units more, (or one-third greater) than the number of Certificates of Occupancy issued for that same period.

Because permits are issued at the beginning of the cycle, investor responses to change in the construction climate will show up first in changes in the number and kind of building permits issued. For this reason and because permit data are readily available for New York City and the State as a whole back to 1960 -- a decade before rent stabilization -- they are a good source for an analysis of new supply. The permit data cannot be used to test the hypothesis that stabilization has caused the collapse of the City's private rental market since 1969 for two reasons: they include single- as well as multi-family dwellings and owner as well as renter housing. From the standpoint of the housing welfare of New Yorkers, though, total new additions to the inventory are more relevant than just new private multi-family rental starts.

Like the first possible source of data, permits are issued for subsidized and unsubsidized housing; the former includes projects built under the Mitchell-Lama program and federal low rent public housing as well as other lower- and moderate-income housing assistance programs. Finally, since the data on building permits do not account for all rehabilitation, and rehabilitation has grown considerably as a proportion of residential development over the past five years, the available data present an incomplete picture of the true extent of recent construction in New York City.

This background information allows us to examine the pattern of new housing authorized in New York City and State since 1960 (Table 9-2). The

TABLE 9-2. NUMBER OF NEW HOUSING UNITS IN NEW YORK STATE AND NEW YORK CITY, BASED ON BUILDING PERMITS ISSUED 1960-1981

Years	New York State	New York City	NYC as Percent of New York State
1960-1969	905,805	368,700	40.7%
1960-1964	510,957	258,576	50.6
1960	92,679	46,792	50.5
1961	117,629	70,606	60.0
1962	121,758	70,686	58.1
1963	103,458	49,898	48.2
1964	75,433	20,594	27.3
1965-1969	394,848	110,124	27.9
1965	91,170	25,715	28.2
1966	75,420	23,142	30.7
1967	77,003	22,174	28.8
1968	80,960	22,062	27.3
1969	70,295	17,031	24.2
1970-1979	605,650	171,343	28.3
1970-1974	414,453	128,840	31.1
1970	68,831	22,365	32.5
1971	103,233	32,254	31.2
1972	111,282	36,061	32.4
1973	79,470	22,417	28.2
1974	51,637	15,743	30.5
1975-1979	191,197	42,503	22.2
1975	32,623	3,810	11.7
1976	33,370	5,434	16.3
1977	41,611	7,639	18.4
1978	43,751	11,096	25.4
1979	39,842	14,524	36.5
1978-1981*	120,082	37,619	31.3
1980-1981*	36,489	11,999	32.9

*1981 data are for January through April only.

SOURCE: New York State Division of Housing and Community Renewal, April 1981, Table 1, p. 1.

high levels of new construction between 1961 and 1963, immediately preceding implementation of the City's new zoning code, have not been achieved again. New authorizations totaled more than 70,000 units a year in 1961 and 1962, and averaged almost 52,000 a year for the five-year period 1960-1964. During this time, over half of the State's total new housing construction was in New York City. This level has not been sustained in any five-year period since the early sixties. Despite the two high years (1961 and 1962), when the City's share of total State production was 60 and 58 percent respectively, new City authorizations averaged 41 percent of the State total for the decade. This is due to the fact that in the five years immediately preceding implementation of rent stabilization, new units authorized in New York City averaged 22,000 a year, while its share of the State total declined to 28 percent. In the second half of the decade, new units in the City ranged from a high of 25,700 in 1965 to a low of 17,000 in 1969, and the ratio of City to State authorizations varied in similar fashion.

From the standpoint of the City's housing picture, the decade of the seventies can be divided into two parts: pre- and post-recession, with the recession and the enactment of ETPA, which terminated vacancy decontrol, occurring at the same time. From 1970 to 1974, new housing units authorized in New York City totaled nearly 129,000, or close to 26,000 per year, resulting in an annual rate substantially over the pre-rent stabilization rate during 1965-1969. During the period between 1970 and 1974, City permits made up 31 percent of State authorizations, a share matched only once in the five years immediately preceding rent stabilization. In 1975, however, the bottom fell out of the market and the recession and ETPA began to affect the number of permits issued. Annual additions authorized in New York limped along in 1975 and 1976 at historically low levels of 3,800 and 5,400 units respectively. The City's housing picture was all the more gloomy when compared to that of the State. Through 1977, the City's share of total State permit authorizations ranged between 12 and 18 percent, the lowest levels in at least 15 years.

While the available data do not permit us to distinguish between the effects of ETPA and those of the recession, it is noteworthy that in the next two years the housing market recovered somewhat, with authorizations in the City climbing to 11,000 units in 1978 and to 14,500 units in 1979. In each of these years, the City's recovery exceeded the State's, with the result that the ratio of City to State activity again climbed to respectable levels. For the 16-month period between January 1, 1980 and April 30, 1981, 12,000 units were authorized in New York City, or 9,000 units annually. This depressed level of construction was still one-third of all statewide authorizations for that period. This is impressive, given the national housing slump. Because the regulatory system has not changed since 1974, and the City's housing recovery (1978 and 1979) and slump (1980 and 1981) coincide with the general building cycle, it would seem that at least some of the fluctuation in City housing starts since 1970 can be attributed to economic conditions in the City and not solely to the enactment of rent stabilization and ETPA.

<u>The Level of Housing Subsidies in New York City</u>. Undoubtedly, the City's recent construction levels have been buoyed by the more than 5,000 new and 9,000 substantial rehabilitation Section 8 units that have been built in New York since 1978. Indeed, the City has long been an effective user of all forms of federal housing assistance and also has a tradition, as does New York State, of providing direct assistance to for-profit and not-for-profit housing developers. This tradition, while for the most part postdating the initial imposition of wartime rent controls, goes back many years and was not begun to counter the adverse investment effects of controls. Public intervention in the City's housing market has not been countercyclical to the level of private housing starts. Indeed, Mitchell-Lama and other sources of State or City housing assistance have tended over the years to move with rather than against the building cycle.

The largest volume of publicly assisted housing in New York was built when inflation was low, operating cost ratios stable, and arguments about the disincentives caused by rent control far milder than they became when inflation soared in the mid-seventies. Public housing and Mitchell-Lama units accounted for one-quarter of all new rental units built in New York City between 1960 and 1969.*

Not only do the City's more than 41,000 state- or city-sponsored Mitchell-Lama housing units constitute one of the nation's largest nonfederal middle-income housing programs, but New York also has the nation's largest federally supported low-rent public housing program (currently more than 171,000 units)(Table 9-3). Add to these inventories more than 30,000 other apartments newly built or rehabilitated with federal subsidies over the years, and the proportion of the City's occupied rental stock benefiting from direct subsidies in 1981 is around 13 percent.

Demand. Beyond these direct supply-side subsidies, of course, are the housing assistance payments that lower-income families use to help pay the rent in existing private housing. The two principal sources of housing allowances are the welfare and Section 8 rental assistance programs. There are over 163,000 households receiving public assistance who live in otherwise unsubsidized apartments. Another 34,000 households who occupy privately owned rental housing receive Section 8 existing housing payments. Collectively, these two demand-side programs assist more than 200,000 households who occupy either rent controlled, decontrolled or stabilized apartments. Supply and demand programs together provide more than 400,000 households, i.e., one out of every five renters in New York City, with some form of direct housing subsidy.**

One must recognize the effects of the substantial government involvement in New York's housing market. It affects the analysis that housing economists such as Winnick and Kristof do on the results of regulation, and by its sheer magnitude, it also influences housing expenditure patterns and changes in relative rent burdens. As an example, recent Congressional action to raise tenant contributions for rents in public and other assisted housing to 30 percent of income will have a noticeable effect on the aggregate housing expense burden of renter households in New York City.

Long-Term Losses

Because the Housing and Vacancy Survey is not designed to establish components of inventory change, for which very specialized techniques are required, analysis of housing loss data from the survey must be done with

*A total of 58,812 Mitchell-Lama and public housing units were built between 1960 and 1969, i.e., 24.1 percent of the 244,006 renter-occupied units built in New York City during the sixties.

**Excluding recipients of Supplemental Security Income, which replaced Old Age Assistance, and Aid to the Blind and Disabled, both of which were once part of public assistance. As of December 31, 1981, 209,197 elderly individuals in New York City were receiving SSI payments. How many of these people live in separate households and how many live in rental, as opposed to owner, housing cannot be determined from the data provided by the New York City Department of Social Services.

TABLE 9-3. SELECTED DATA ON SUBSIDIZED RENTAL HOUSING AND HOUSEHOLDS RECEIVING HOUSING ASSISTANCE IN NEW YORK CITY, 1981

Form of Assistance	Number of Housing Units	Percent of Occupied Rental Housing Stock
Total	436,718	22.6%
Supply-Side	239,469	12.4
Low-rent public housing	171,585	8.9
City/State-sponsored middle-income housing*	41,394	2.1
Other federally assisted housing**	26,490	1.4
Demand-Side	197,249	10.2
Public Assistance, not living in other assisted housing	163,567	8.5
Section 8 Existing Housing Assistance	33,682	1.7

*"City/State sponsored middle-income housing" was constructed under the New York City and New York State Mitchell-Lama programs. The category also encompasses a smaller number of units under the auspices of the New York State Limited Profit Housing Program.

**"Other federally assisted housing" includes Section 221(d)(3) and Section 236 rental units, but excludes 5,020 new Section 8 units, 9,209 Section 8 substantial rehabilitation units not yet occupied, 829 Section 8 moderate rehabilitation units built with City or federal subsidies, and private construction or renovation that has received tax abatements or exemptions under the City's 421 and J-51 programs.

SOURCES: Advisory Services for Better Housing, "Profile and Inventory of FHA Mulifamily Projects in the New York Area," New York, 1978, p.7 (used to estimate number of "other federally assisted housing units"); Frank DeGiovanni and Mary E. Brooks, Pratt Institute Center for Community and Environmental Development, "Impact of a Housing Voucher Program on New York City's Population," Revised Draft, Pratt Institute Center for Community and Environmental Development, November 1981, Table A2, p.52 (number of low-rent public housing units, including federal and state or city sponsored); U.S. Bureau of the Census, 1981 New York City Housing and Vacancy Survey.

care.* Based on Census estimates, 321,000 dwelling units which were part of New York City's housing inventory in 1970 had been lost by the time of the 1981 Housing and Vacancy Survey. That is, these units had either been

---

*The loss counts provided by the Census were derived by multiplying the unweighted counts for various loss categories by an average survey weight and should be considered only as rough approximations of true losses.

demolished, condemned, withdrawn from the market and boarded-up and/or burned-out while still under private or city ownership, converted to nonresidential use or merged with other apartments. Net losses from the supply from April 1970 through March 1981 equalled approximately 11 percent of the 1970 and 1981 housing inventory. Of these 321,000 units, almost half have been demolished, while another 31 percent are still vacant, i.e., boarded-up, partially gutted by fire, and/or open to the elements (Table 9-4). Some of the demolitions may be buildings which landlords have abandoned because they have lost all hope of operating them profitably in the future. Other burned-out shells might have been apartment buildings which were profitable until they burned. It is not possible to estimate the extent of landlord

TABLE 9-4. LOSSES FROM THE HOUSING INVENTORY, BY BOROUGH AND TYPE OF LOSS, NEW YORK CITY, 1970-1981

Type of Loss	All Boroughs	Bronx	Brooklyn	Manhattan	Queens	Richmond
Total	321,000	108,498	105,288	81,855	22,149	3,210
Demolished	154,722	68,679	45,379	34,297	5,626	677
Condemned	21,186	7,703	9,897	3,438	--	337
Burned-out, boarded-up, etc.	99,189	28,426	32,113	33,806	4,253	677
Nonresidential	22,149	1,519	7,160	9,250	3,588	677
Merged with other unit	23,754	2,170	10,739	1,228	8,682	844
			Percent Distribution			
Total	100.0	100.0	100.0	100.0	100.0	100.0
Demolished	48.2	63.3	43.1	41.9	25.4	21.1
Condemned	6.6	7.1	9.4	4.2	--	10.5
Burned-out, boarded-up, etc.	30.9	26.2	30.5	41.3	19.2	21.1
Nonresidential	6.9	1.4	6.8	11.3	16.2	21.1
Merged with other unit	7.4	2.0	10.2	1.5	39.2	26.3
Total	100.0	33.8	32.8	25.5	6.9	1.0
Demolished	100.0	44.4	29.4	22.1	3.6	0.4
Condemned	100.0	36.0	46.4	16.0	--	1.6
Burned-out, boarded-up, etc.	100.0	28.6	32.4	34.0	4.3	0.7
Non residential	100.0	6.9	32.3	41.5	16.2	3.1
Merged with other unit	100.0	9.4	45.3	5.0	36.7	3.6

NOTE: Absolute numbers derived from percent distributions.

SOURCE: U.S. Bureau of the Census, 1981 New York City Housing and Vacancy Survey.

abandonment on the basis of this boarded-up, burned-out inventory. Chapter 10 discusses the problems of landlord abandonment, in rem housing and city-ownership of nearly 34,000 occupied apartments.

Location. The vast majority of the City's 321,000 losses since 1970 are concentrated in three boroughs: approximately one-third each in the Bronx and Brooklyn and one-quarter in Manhattan. Seven percent of the City's gross housing losses have occurred in Queens and 1 percent in Richmond. The spatial distribution of losses within each loss category differs from the citywide pattern. The Bronx has 33 percent of all losses but 44 percent of all demolitions and only 7 percent of all nonresidential conversions since 1970. Manhattan has a slightly lower proportion of total losses, but a higher relative percentage of boarded-up units and nonresidential conversions than its overall loss rate. Similarly, Brooklyn's share of condemnations and residential mergers is substantially greater than its share of net housing losses since 1970.

Composition of Losses by Borough. Another way of distinguishing market dynamics in the City is to assess the composition of losses within each borough (Table 9-4). Not unexpectedly, the Bronx leads the City in the proportion of demolitions since 1970: 63 percent of all losses there were demolished by March 1981, compared to 43 and 42 percent in Brooklyn and Manhattan respectively. Just 21 percent of all the losses in Richmond have been demolished, as have 25 percent of those in Queens. Manhattan leads the City in the proportion of total losses classified as boarded-up or burned-out. These account for 41 percent of all of Manhattan's net losses but only 26 and 31 percent of those in the Bronx and Brooklyn. More than 55 percent of Queens' residential losses are still in the inventory, either as nonresidential space, or as housing that is no longer separate dwelling units.

New Losses

Because of its longitudinal nature, the 1981 Housing and Vacancy Survey also contains data on losses from the inventory since the 1978 survey (Table 9-5). Of the 321,000 units removed from the stock between April 1970 and March 1981, 81,000 units, or 25 percent, were found to be new losses since 1978.

1978 Occupancy Status of New Losses. For the most part, the longitudinal component of the Housing and Vacancy Survey is based on a resurvey of previously sampled dwellings. It is therefore possible to determine, for example, the 1978 occupancy of housing units categorized as losses in 1981. Of the 81,000 new losses, 63 percent were renter-occupied and 9 percent were owner-occupied three years ago. The source of 17 percent -- 13,800 -- of all new losses in 1981 was the 1978 inventory of vacant available rental housing units. Given that the pool of available vacancies totaled 59,000 dwelling units in 1978, around 23 percent of these vacancies were removed from the inventory over the ensuing 36 months.

Returning Losses. The 1978 Housing and Vacancy survey documented returning losses to the inventory, a phenomenon that has been part of the dynamics of real estate investment markets for some time. Unlike demolished housing units which can never return to the inventory, other types of losses, including boarded-up dwellings, can. Indeed, Marcuse reported that

TABLE 9-5. 1981 LOSSES FROM THE HOUSING INVENTORY BY STATUS IN 1978, NEW YORK CITY

Status in 1978	Number	Percent
Total losses as of 1981	321,000	
Total losses, date of loss known	313,938	
Losses in 1978 that remained losses in 1981	233,046	100.0%
Demolished	99,831	42.8
Condemned	7,062	3.0
Burned-out, boarded-up	95,337	40.9
Nonresidential	12,840	5.5
Merged with other unit	11,235	4.8
Losses of indeterminant nature	6,741	2.9
New Losses since 1978	81,213	100.0%
Owner-occupied	7,062	8.7
Renter-occupied	51,360	63.2
Vacant for rent	13,803	17.0
Vacant for sale	642	0.8
Unavailable vacant	8,346	10.3
Date of loss not known	7,062	
New losses as percent of total losses		25.8%

NOTE: Absolute numbers derived from percent distributions.

SOURCE: U.S. Bureau of the Census, 1981 New York City Housing and Vacancy Survey.

38,000 housing units which had been declared losses in 1975 were back in the inventory by 1978.

The phenomenon of returning losses is also documented in the 1981 Housing and Vacancy Survey. Approximately 33,000 (13 percent) units which were found to be losses in 1978 had returned to the inventory in 1981 (Table 9-6). One can compute a rate for returning losses by subtracting the number of demolished units during the period under consideration from the total losses at the beginning of that period. Thirty-eight percent of the 262,000 units found to be losses in 1978 had been demolished by 1978. Of the remaining losses demolished since 1978 or returned to the inventory in 1981, 57 percent were demolished, 9 percent had returned to the owner-occupied housing stock and another 22 percent were back in the renter occupied inventory.

TABLE 9-6. 1978 LOSSES FROM THE INVENTORY BY STATUS IN 1981, NEW YORK CITY

Status in 1981	Number	Percent
Total losses in 1978	261,905	
Losses in 1981	228,905	
Losses for which status is known	228,643	100.0%
Demolished	143,262	62.7
Condemned	8,643	3.8
Boarded-up, burned-out	56,310	24.6
Nonresidential	10,214	4.5
Merged with other unit	10,214	4.5
Total demolitions and returning losses since 1978	76,431	100.0%
1978 losses demolished since 1978	43,431	56.8
Returned to inventory in 1981:		
Owner-occupied	7,071	9.3
Renter-occupied	17,024	22.3
Vacant for rent	786	1.0
Vacant for sale	262	0.3
Unavailable vacant	4,714	6.2
Status not known	3,143	4.1
Returning losses as a percentage of total losses, 1970-1981		10.3%

NOTE: Absolute numbers derived from percent distributions.

SOURCE: U.S. Bureau of the Census, 1981 New York City Housing and Vacancy Survey.

Source of Returning Losses. Of the 33,000 losses that returned to the inventory between 1978 and 1981, 35 percent stood vacant, boarded-up, partially burned-out or open to the elements in 1978 (Table 9-7). An equally important pool of returning losses is merged dwellings which have been reconverted into separate living quarters. Another 22 percent of returning losses were nonresidential in 1978. In short, the phenomenon of returning losses shows the physical stock to be flexible and adaptive. Given appropriate market conditions and incentives, older buildings can shift from an unused to a used state, from nonresidential to residential use and back again; they can be joined with other units to produce larger dwellings, or be subdivided into smaller apartments, all to suit changing demand and market conditions.

While most returning losses reenter the inventory as rental dwellings and each source of returning losses is heavily oriented to reuse as rental housing, losses which were classified in 1978 as either nonresidential or mergers are less likely to do this. Nearly one out of every five nonresidential losses in 1978 had reentered the residential sector as owner-

TABLE 9-7. STATUS IN 1978 AND 1981 OF UNITS RETURNED TO THE INVENTORY BETWEEN 1978 AND 1981, NEW YORK CITY

		Status in 1978				
	Total	Condemned	Burned-out, boarded-up	Non-residential	Merged	Other
Total	33,000	1,620	11,664	7,240	11,753	800
Percent of returning losses	100.0%	4.7	35.3	21.9	35.6	2.4
Status in 1981						
Total		100.0%	100.0%	100.0%	100.0%	100.0%
Owner-occupied		11.1	15.1	19.4	37.8	--
Renter-occupied		66.7	59.3	65.8	45.4	100.0
Vacant for rent		--	2.3	7.2	1.4	--
Vacant for sale		--	--	--	1.4	--
Unavailable vacant		22.2	24.4	7.2	13.7	--

SOURCE: U.S. Bureau of the Census, 1981 New York City Housing and Vacancy Survey.

occupied housing by 1981. Thirty-eight percent of all returning losses that were part of previously combined apartments are also owner-occupied. It is possible that the subdivision of larger apartments into individually owned units is part of the cooperative conversion process that has been gaining momentum in New York over the past few years. Without more data on any of these loss and return categories, however, one cannot ascertain which sector of the market they serve nor the processes through which, and auspices under which, they have reentered the inventory.

Net Loss Rates

One must first distinguish between gross and net loss rates to estimate the rate at which housing is dropping out of the inventory in New York. The 321,000 units that were in the inventory in 1970, but not at the time of the 1981 Housing and Vacancy Survey, exclude returning losses and represent net losses. The gross loss rate would include the 71,000 units which had returned to the inventory since 1975. Thus, gross losses totaled 392,000 over the 131-month period between April 1970, the time of the 1970 Census enumeration, and March 1981, the time of the 1981 Housing and Vacancy Survey. During this time, average monthly gross losses to the housing inventory were 2,992 units.* For the 95 months from April 1970 to March 1978, the average monthly gross loss to the inventory was 3,274 units.** For the most recent three years, average gross losses from March 1978 to March 1981 are 31 per-

---

*(321,000 + 71,000)/131.

**(392,000 - 81,000)/95.

cent lower at 2,250 dwelling units a month.* Thus, gross losses to the City's housing inventory are occurring at a slower rate since 1978 than at any other documented time during the seventies.

The recent reduction in gross losses can be confirmed by relating them to the size of the total inventory at different times. Thus, gross losses of 311,000 units between 1970 and 1978 equalled 1.34 percent of the 1970 housing stock and the 81,000 units which dropped out of the inventory after 1978 represented .97 percent of the City's 1978 stock. The difference between these two loss rates is around 29 percent.

The Concentration of Housing Problems at the Neighborhood Level

The Housing and Vacancy Survey is based on a sample of dwelling units that is large enough to produce very reliable citywide estimates of important market variables such as the number of vacant units, and to allow the disaggregation of data to the borough level without too much deterioration in the level of confidence attached to these statistical estimates. Sample size limitations prevent the detailed analysis of market conditions and occupancy patterns at the neighborhood level. Within the limits of the survey, however, it is possible to estimate the distribution of a few key variables across Community Planning Districts in each borough. This indicates how housing problems tend to concentrate geographically. The Census Bureau provided breakdowns of four variables by Community Districts in the Housing and Vacancy Survey: available vacancies, unavailable vacancies, *in rem* housing and losses. The percentage breakdowns for each borough were mapped and the clustering patterns were then examined. Using the simple decision rule of encompassing as many variables as possible in as few of the Community Districts as possible allows a graphic display of the resulting concentrations (Table 9-8 and Exhibits 9-1 to 9-5). The appendix to this chapter offers supplemental data on the distribution of the above variables throughout the Community Districts.

---

*81,000/36.

TABLE 9-8. PERCENT OF TOTAL VACANCIES, *IN REM* HOUSING UNITS AND LOSSES FROM THE INVENTORY WITHIN SPECIFIED COMMUNITY DISTRICTS, NEW YORK CITY, 1981

	Bronx	Brooklyn	Manhattan	Queens	Richmond
Total number of community districts	12	18	12	14	3
Community districts included in analysis	1-5	1-5, 8, 16	3, 9-11	3, 12-14	1
Percent of 1980 population included in districts	24.5	30.6	33.5	30.8	39.3
Percent of units in borough within selected districts					
Vacant for rent	72.7	50.0	50.8	42.7	28.6
Other vacant*	61.9	38.8	53.2	54.9	66.7
In rem	87.8	84.3	75.2	92.3	--
Losses	84.2	71.2	67.1	40.0	65.0

*"Other vacant" includes units that are vacant for sale, vacant not for sale or rent, and dilapidated vacant.

SOURCE: U.S. Bureau of the Census, 1981 New York City Housing and Vacancy Survey.

EXHIBIT 9-1. PERCENT OF TOTAL VACANCIES, IN REM HOUSING UNITS, LOSSES TO THE INVENTORY, AND POPULATION IN SELECTED COMMUNITY DISTRICTS, THE BRONX, 1981

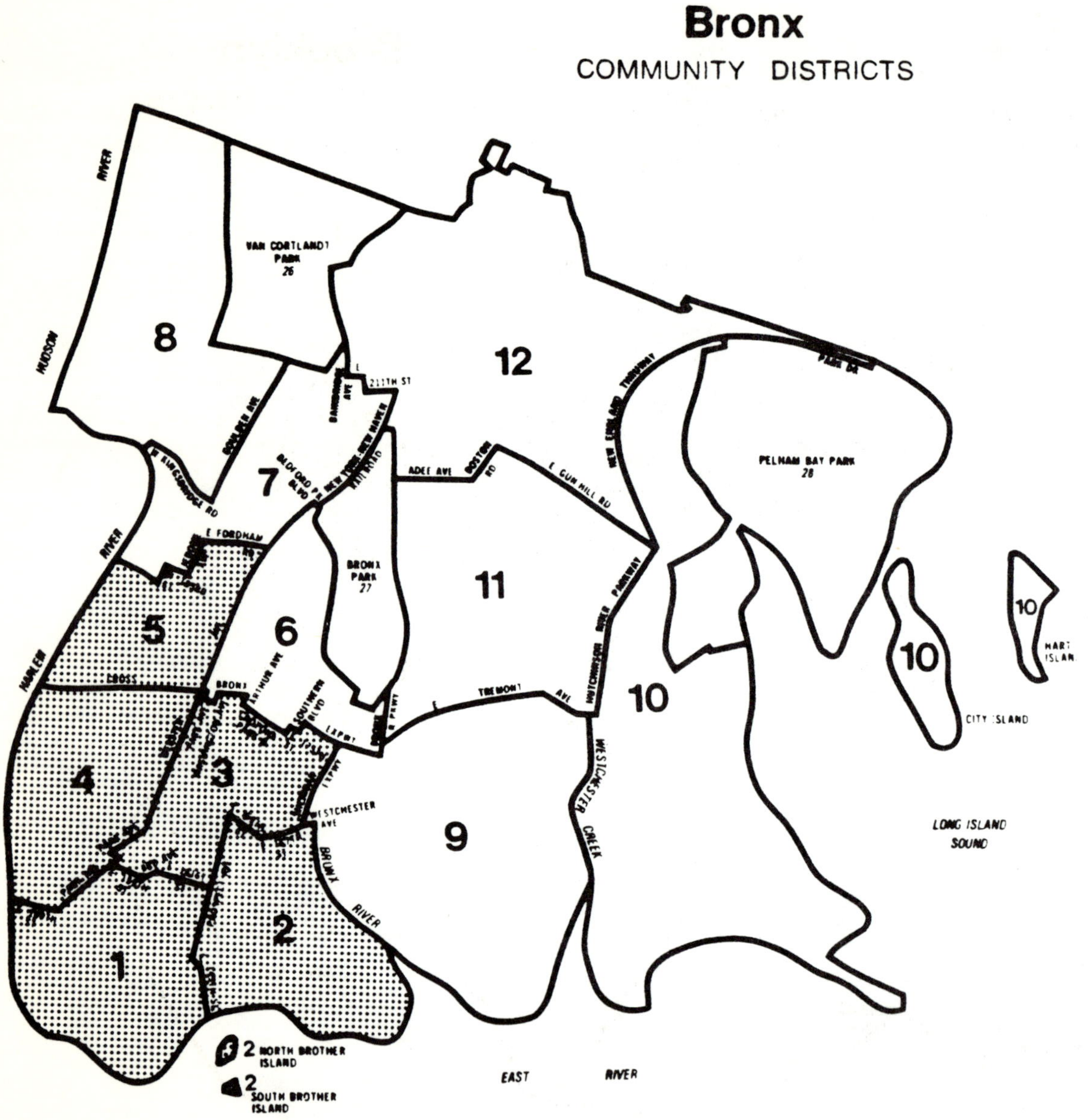

The shaded area represents the following shares of the borough's total:

Vacant for rent	72.7%
Other vacant	61.9
<u>In rem</u>	87.8
Losses	84.2
Population	24.5

EXHIBIT 9-2. PERCENT OF TOTAL VACANCIES, IN REM HOUSING UNITS, LOSSES TO THE INVENTORY, AND POPULATION IN SELECTED COMMUNITY DISTRICTS, BROOKLYN, 1981

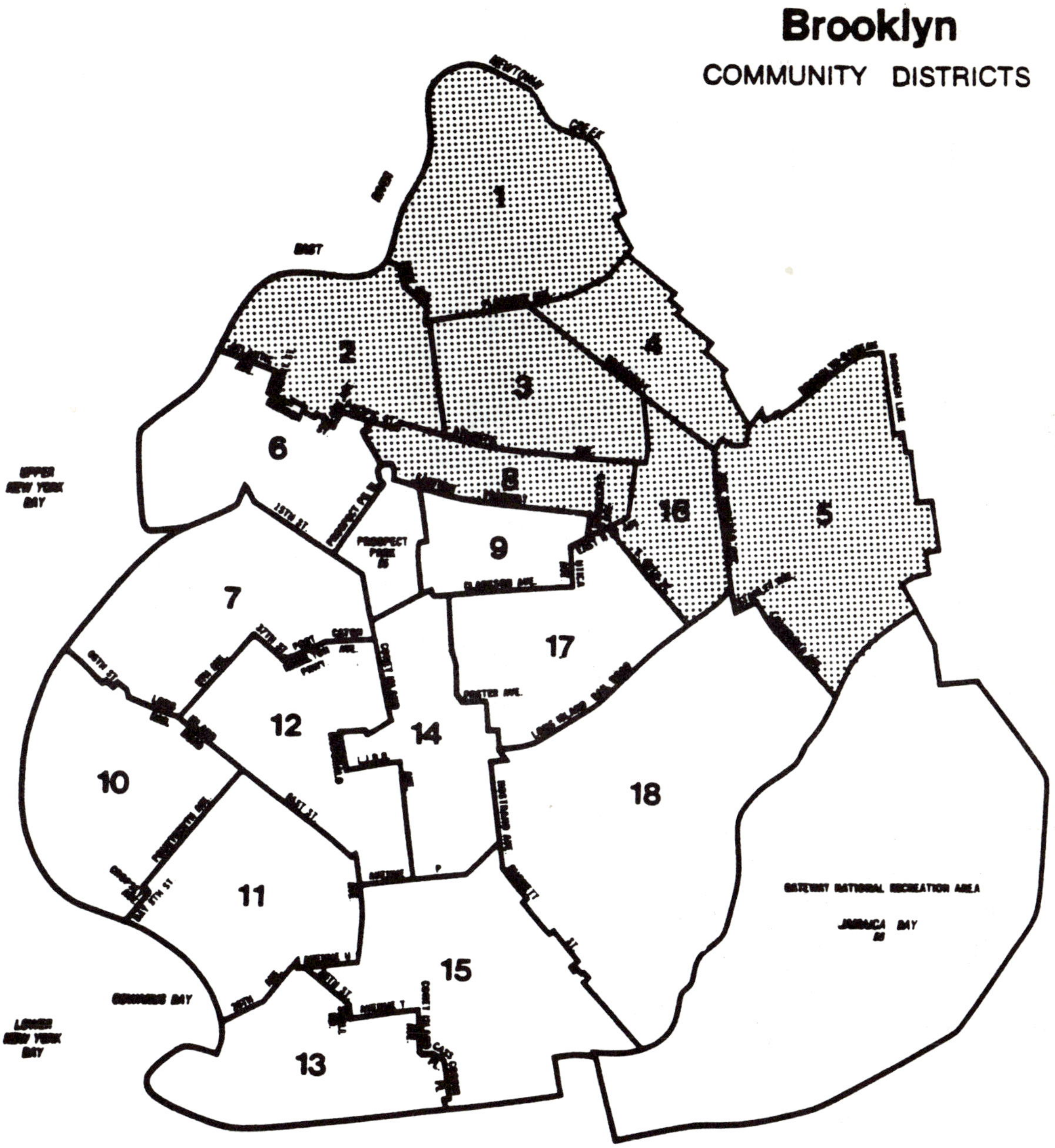

The shaded area represents the following shares of the borough's total:

Vacant for rent	50.0%
Other vacant	38.8
In rem	84.3
Losses	71.2
Population	30.6

EXHIBIT 9-3. PERCENT OF TOTAL VACANCIES, IN REM HOUSING UNITS, LOSSES TO THE INVENTORY, AND POPULATION IN SELECTED COMMUNITY DISTRICTS, MANHATTAN, 1981

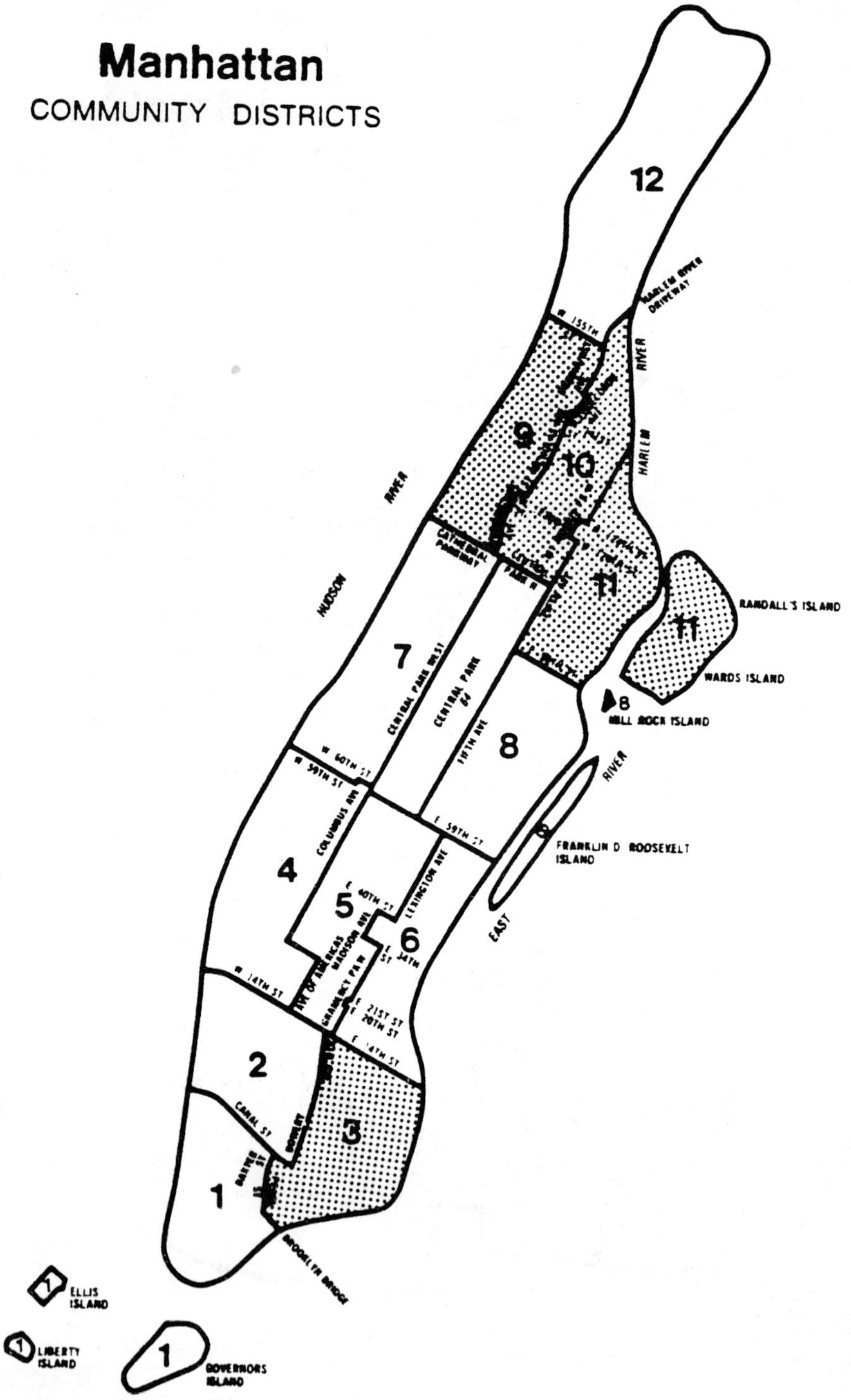

The shaded area represents the following shares of the borough's total:

Vacant for rent	50.8%
Other vacant	53.2
In rem	75.2
Losses	67.1
Population	33.5

EXHIBIT 9-4. PERCENT OF TOTAL VACANCIES, <u>IN REM</u> HOUSING UNITS, LOSSES TO THE INVENTORY, AND POPULATION IN SELECTED COMMUNITY DISTRICTS, QUEENS, 1981

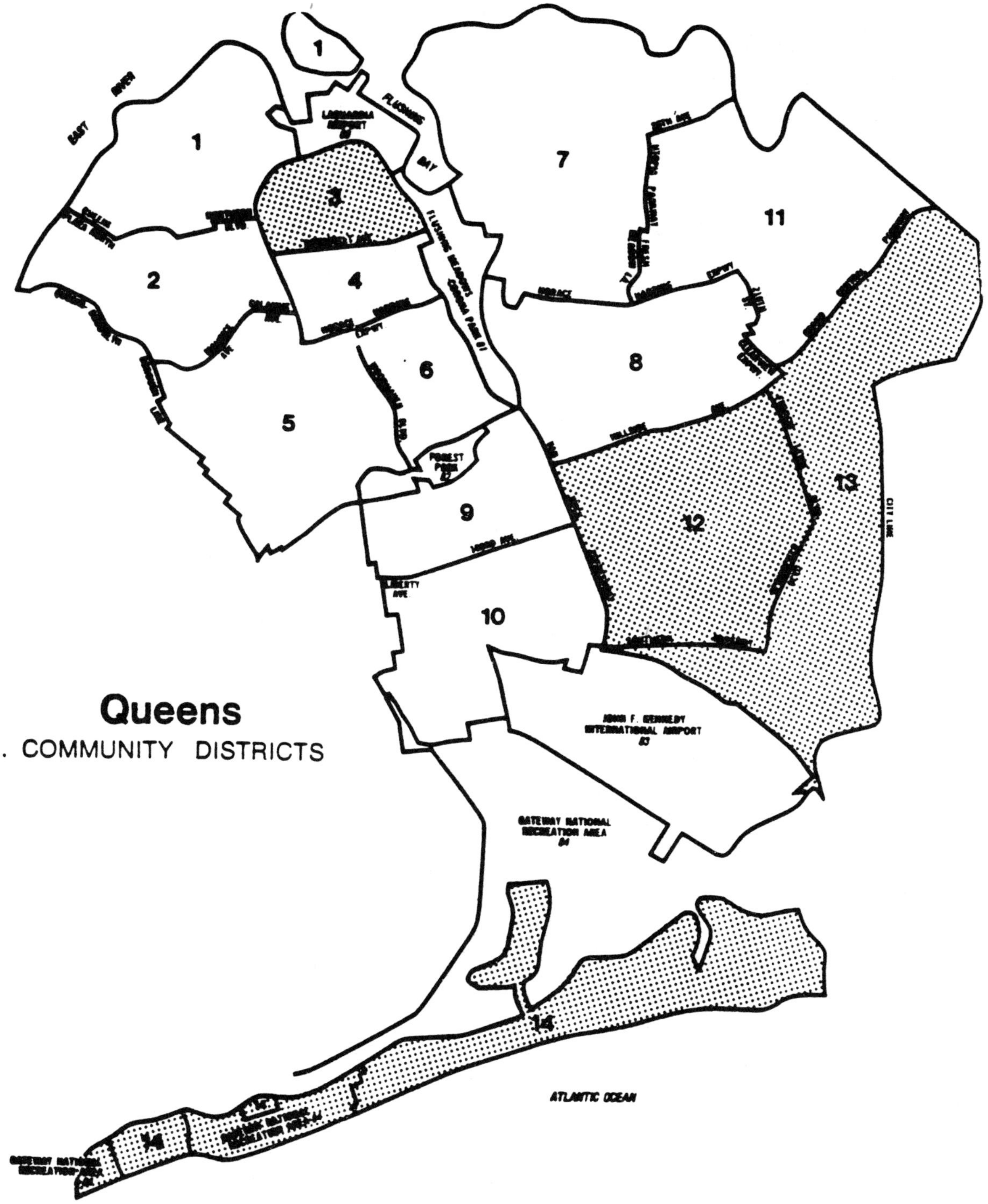

The shaded area represents the following shares of the borough's total:

Vacant for rent	42.7%
Other vacant	54.9
In rem	92.3
Losses	40.0
Population	30.8

EXHIBIT 9-5. PERCENT OF TOTAL VACANCIES, <u>IN REM</u> HOUSING UNITS, LOSSES TO THE INVENTORY, AND POPULATION IN SELECTED COMMUNITY DISTRICTS, STATEN ISLAND, 1981

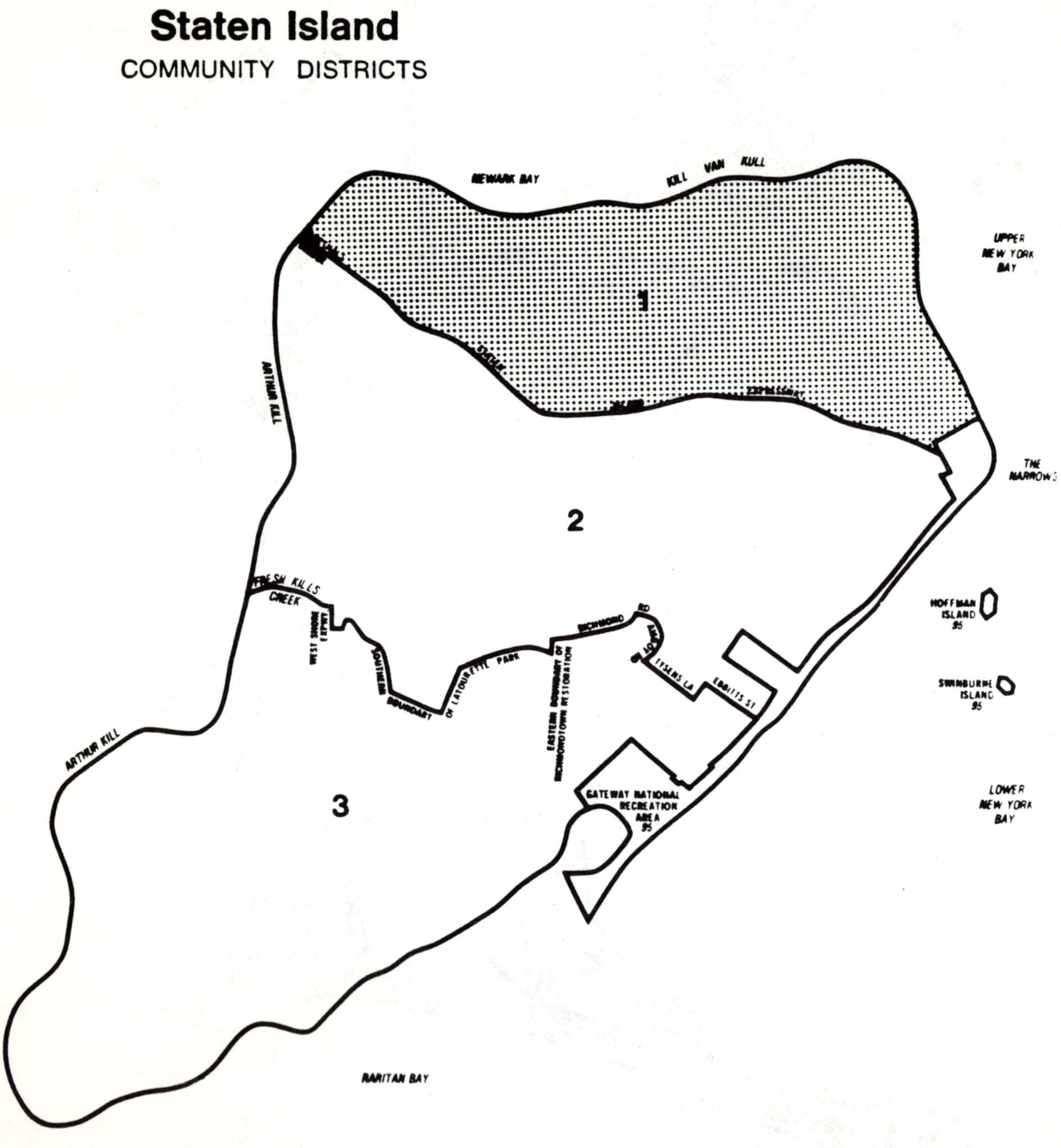

The shaded area represents the following shares of the borough's total:

Vacant for rent	28.6%
Other vacant	66.7
<u>In rem</u>	--
Losses	65.0
Population	39.3

In general, all boroughs showed substantial concentrations of problem housing in certain Community Districts. Save for the Bronx, where all four variables are highly clustered, available vacancies tend to be less concentrated than the three distress-related variables. Problem housing tends to be concentrated in a relatively small number of each borough's Community Districts, but in Manhattan and Queens, it can be found in widely separated neighborhoods. Areas of serious distress tend to be closer together in the Bronx and Brooklyn. The most significant concentrations of problems were found in less than half of each borough's Community Districts. Five Districts in the South Bronx, for example, contain 62 percent of the borough's unavailable vacancies, 87 percent of all *in rem* housing and 84 percent of all apartments considered losses by the Census Bureau in 1981. These five of the 12 Community Districts in the Bronx also contain 73 percent of all available vacancies.

The most serious areas of market distress in Brooklyn include Williamsburgh, Bushwick, Eastern Parkway and Bedford-Stuyvesant. Seven of Brooklyn's 18 Community Districts contain half of all available rental vacancies, 39 percent of unavailable vacancies, 84 percent of the borough's *in rem* housing and 71 percent of all losses from the inventory. Manhattan's two areas of intense distress are in the Lower East Side below 14th Street and in Upper Manhattan above 96th Street. The four Community Districts in these areas contain half of the borough's vacancies, three-quarters of its *in rem* housing and two-thirds of all its inventory losses.

Available rental vacancies in Queens and Richmond are more widely dispersed than in the other boroughs and are therefore less closely associated with problems such as derelict buildings, city-owned housing and the like. Queens has three noncontiguous areas of housing distress: Corona Park in Northern Queens just below La Guardia Airport; a stretch along the eastern border of the borough from the Van Wyck Expressway on the south to the Grand Central Parkway on the north; and the extreme southern tip of Queens along the ocean and the Rockaways. These three pockets, which together span four of Queens' 12 Community Districts, contain 92 percent of all *in rem* housing, but only 40 percent of all losses and 43 percent of available vacancies in the borough. Two-thirds of all unavailable vacancies and losses in Richmond are in the northern third of the borough above the Staten Island Expressway. Community District One, however, contains just 29 percent of all available vacancies.

From Rent Control to Rent Stabilization

As described earlier, the longitudinal component of the 1981 Housing and Vacancy Survey consists of all housing units enumerated in both 1978 and 1981. Because failure to respond to the survey in either year eliminates a dwelling from the longitudinal survey, the size of this "matched sample" is smaller and perhaps less representative of the stock than either the 1978 or the 1981 cross-sectional survey. However, because the matched sample captured at least 80 percent of each regulated market sector and, when properly weighted, represents more than 1.5 million apartments in the City, we can gain important insights into rental market dynamics by analyzing these data (Table 9-9).

TABLE 9-9. CONTROL STATUS OF MATCHED RENTAL UNITS, NEW YORK CITY, 1981

	All Units	Controlled	Stabilized Pre-'47	Stabilized Post-'47	Other Control Statuses*
All renter-occupied	1,933,887	285,733	615,497	312,858	719,800
Matched renter units	1,530,471	234,194	493,492	260,322	542,463
Percent of all renter-occupied	79.1	82.0	80.2	83.2	75.4

*"Other Control Statuses" includes decontrolled, public housing, state or city assisted housing, and other rental housing.

SOURCE: U.S. Bureau of the Census, 1981 New York City Housing and Vacancy Survey.

Housing Quality. The longitudinal survey permits us to consider whether there are any significant differences between controlled apartments which pass into the stabilized sector upon vacancy and those that are not vacated and remain under rent control (Table 9-10). Although there are no longitudinal data on the physical condition of the sampled dwellings, certain characteristics of the stock are known. The 1978 median rents, incidence of dilapidation, and probability of being near vacant or boarded-up buildings are almost identical for controlled apartments that have and for those that have not turned over since 1978. We can infer from this that there are no important differences in the physical and neighborhood quality of these two categories. Owners were more likely to be living in buildings of 12 or fewer apartments that have not had a turnover in occupancy since 1978 than in buildings where apartments have changed status. It should be pointed out, however, that since owner residency is inversely related to building size and previously controlled apartments in buildings with fewer than six units are decontrolled, not stabilized, owner residency figures for newly stabilized apartments may be misleadingly low since they refer only to buildings with between seven and 12 apartments.

Household Characteristics. Although there do not seem to be dramatic differences between controlled units which did and did not experience a change in occupancy since 1978, there are interesting differences in the 1978 characteristics of the households occupying these two groups of units. First, a higher percentage of tenants in units that were controlled in 1978 and 1981 were White compared to tenants in controlled apartments which turned over after 1978 (79 versus 71 percent). Controlled units which turned over after 1978 had higher proportions of Puerto Rican tenants (10 versus 5 percent) and tenants classified as "other minority."

TABLE 9-10. SELECTED CHARACTERISTICS BY CHANGE IN CONTROL STATUS OF MATCHED RENTAL UNITS, NEW YORK CITY, 1978 AND 1981

	1978 Characteristics	
	Controlled 1978/ Controlled 1981	Controlled 1978/ Stabilized 1981
Median gross rent	$167	$162
Median age	61	57
Median income	$7,529	$7,220
Owner in structure containing 12 or less units	86.6%	71.4%
Gross rent as percent of income	29.1%	28.7%
Receiving public assistance	5.0%	7.2%
Dilapidated	<1.0%	<1.0%
Boarded-up or other vacant structure on street	54.2%	51.9%
Female headed households	46.3%	45.0%
Median persons per household	1.6	1.5
Race	100.0%	100.0%
White	79.2	70.6
Black	12.6	12.7
Puerto Rican	4.8	10.4
Other	3.4	6.3

SOURCE: U.S. Bureau of the Census, 1981 New York City Housing and Vacancy Survey.

Not only are controlled apartments which turned over more likely to be initially occupied by relatively younger households and by a lower proportion of Whites, but the transition from controlled to stabilized is associated with dramatic changes in the characteristics of the occupants. One of the most striking is the age distribution of the tenants who move into previously controlled apartments. Because the rent controlled market has become so dominated by older people, turnover lowers the median household age by at least 40 percent, depending on the sex of the tenant (Table 9-11). Female household heads who move out of controlled apartments had a median age of 65 in 1978. Both male and female household heads in newly stabilized units have a median age of 35.

TABLE 9-11. MEDIAN AGE OF HOUSEHOLD HEADS IN MATCHED RENTAL UNITS, NEW YORK CITY, 1978 AND 1981

				Stabilized	
Household Head	All Renters	Controlled 1978 Controlled 1981	Controlled 1978 Stabilized 1981	Pre-47 1978 Pre-47 1981	Post-47 1978 Post-47 1981
Male					
1978	44	61	57	37	45
1981	44	62	35	39	45
Female					
1978	48	67	65	35	49
1981	45	68	35	36	46

SOURCE: U.S. Bureau of the Census, 1981 New York City Housing and Vacancy Survey.

Both controlled units which had no change in tenants after 1978 and those that did, had different household size distributions in 1981 than three years earlier (Table 9-12). Median household size in still-controlled apartments dropped from 1.61 to 1.49 people, probably due in part to the death of older family members and the fact that movers tend to be younger and have larger households. Median household size grew from 1.52 to 2.02 people in apartments that were controlled in 1978 and stabilized in 1981.

Racial and Ethnic Change. Two aspects of racial dynamics can be explored with the longitudinal data (Table 9-13). First, the proportion of Whites in previously controlled apartments fell 22 percent when these units were reoccupied as part of the pre-'47 stabilized inventory (from 71 percent White in 1978 to 55 percent in 1981). Black occupancy increased from 13 to 18 percent, while the percentage of Puerto Rican tenants in now stabilized

TABLE 9-12. PERSONS PER HOUSEHOLD IN MATCHED RENTAL UNITS, NEW YORK CITY, 1981

	Median Persons per Household 1978	1981
All renter occupied	1.93	1.90
Controlled 1978/Controlled 1981	1.61	1.49
Controlled 1978/Stabilized 1981	1.52	2.02
Pre-'47 Stabilized, 1978/ Pre-'47 Stabilized, 1981	1.92	1.92
Post-'47 Stabilized, 1978/ Post-'47 Stabilized, 1981	1.67	1.63

SOURCE: U.S. Bureau of the Census, 1981 New York City Housing and Vacancy Survey.

apartments climbed from 10 to 18 percent.

To reduce the average rate of White occupancy of controlled apartments by 22 percent requires that minorities move in to formerly White-occupied apartments in large numbers, which is the case (Table 9-14). Fully one-third of all controlled apartments occupied by Whites in 1978 and vacated since then are now inhabited by minority households. Sixteen percent of these previously controlled apartments have been rented by Puerto Rican households, 8 percent by Blacks, and 10 percent by other minority group members.

The Pre-'47 Stock. The New York City rental market is very dynamic in terms of racial and ethnic change, and especially so in the inventory of apartments that were controlled in 1978 but stabilized in 1981. Nearly 20 percent of the pre-'47 stabilized apartments that Whites were living in in 1978 are occupied by minorities in 1981. Equally striking is the fact that 9 percent of this same inventory that was occupied by Blacks, and 12 percent that was inhabited by Puerto Ricans three years ago, now houses White tenants.

The Post-'47 Stock. A substantial, though lesser, degree of racial and ethnic changes in occupancy accompanies tenant turnover in the City's newer, more costly and higher quality post-'47 stabilized housing. Nearly 10 percent of all post-'47 apartments occupied by Whites in 1978 had experienced racial or ethnic change by 1981. This pattern is even more apparent in the Black-occupied post-'47 stock. One out of every four Black-occupied apartments in 1978 had non-Black tenants in 1981, including 16 percent which were newly occupied by Whites. The rate of racial and ethnic change was even greater in Puerto Rican-occupied post-'47 housing. Less than half (45 percent) of these units are still occupied by Puerto Rican households: Whites live in nearly one-third of these apartments, and Blacks in another 10 percent of them.*

---

*It should be noted that the longitudinal sample cannot provide any insight into whether the rental market is becoming more or less segregated by race or ethnic origin since we do not know the locations of the apartments which are undergoing transition.

TABLE 9-13. RACE AND ETHNIC GROUP BY CONTROL STATUS OF MATCHED RENTAL UNITS, NEW YORK CITY, 1978 AND 1981

	Controlled/Controlled		Controlled/Stabilized		Stabilized Pre-'47/Pre-'47		Stabilized Post-'47/Post-'47	
	1978	1981	1978	1981	1978	1981	1978	1981
	Percent Distribution							
All households	100.0	100.0	100.0	100.0	100.0	100.0	100.0	100.0
White	79.2	80.2	70.6	55.0	48.3	48.4	79.3	77.8
Black	12.6	12.0	12.7	17.5	24.2	23.0	12.2	12.3
Puerto Rican	4.8	4.8	10.4	17.9	20.8	19.6	3.9	3.9
Other	3.3	3.0	6.3	9.6	6.6	9.0	4.7	6.1

SOURCE: U.S. Bureau of the Census, 1981 New York City Housing and Vacancy Survey.

TABLE 9-14. RACE OF HOUSEHOLD HEAD IN MATCHED RENTAL UNITS, NEW YORK CITY, 1981

				Stabilized	
	Total	1978 Controlled/ 1981 Controlled	1978 Controlled/ 1981 Stabilized	1978 Pre-'47/ 1981 Pre-'47	1978 Post-'47/ 1981 Post-'47
			Percent Distribution		
White in 1978	100.0	100.0	100.0	100.0	100.0
White in 1981	87.5	97.4	66.2	81.9	90.7
Black in 1981	3.6	0.7	7.5	3.4	3.6
Puerto Rican in '81	4.0	0.6	16.1	6.9	1.8
Other race in 1981	4.9	1.3	10.2	7.7	3.9
Black in 1978	100.0	100.0	100.0	100.0	100.0
Black in 1981	83.6	90.2	81.9	77.8	74.3
White in 1981	7.3	7.7	12.0	8.7	16.0
Puerto Rican in '81	6.4	--	6.1	9.3	6.5
Other race in 1981	2.7	2.1	--	4.2	3.2
Puerto Rican in 1978	100.0	100.0	100.0	100.0	100.0
Puerto Rican in '81	68.7	82.3	58.2	65.2	45.3
White in 1981	12.5	10.9	22.3	12.3	32.0
Black in 1981	11.2	3.4	12.4	12.4	10.3
Other race in 1981	7.7	3.4	7.1	10.0	12.4
Other race in 1978	100.0	100.0	100.0	100.0	100.0
Other race in 1981	33.8	36.8	39.5	30.5	47.1
White in 1981	44.4	57.4	46.3	45.1	36.7
Black in 1981	10.4	2.9	9.6	9.3	8.0
Puerto Rican in '81	11.4	2.9	4.6	15.1	8.2

SOURCE: U.S. Bureau of the Census, 1981 New York City Housing and Vacancy Survey.

Incomes. Changes in household incomes were analyzed in Chapter 8. Occupants of rent controlled apartments had median incomes 22 percent higher in 1980 than in 1977, while incomes grew by 26 percent in the pre-'47 stabilized inventory. In contrast, the longitudinal data show that median household income rose 45 percent from $7,220 to $10,440 in apartments which were rent controlled in 1978 but stabilized in 1981 (Table 9-15).

TABLE 9-15. INCOME BY SELECTED CONTROL STATUS OF MATCHED RENTAL UNITS, NEW YORK CITY, 1978 AND 1981

	Controlled 1978/Stabilized 1981	
	1978	1981
Total	100.0%	100.0%
Under $4,000	27.8	11.5
$4,000-5,999	16.6	13.2
$6,000-7,999	7.6	11.4
$8,000-9,999	11.3	11.0
$10,000-12,499	13.1	16.5
$12,500-14,999	2.8	5.1
$15,000-24,999	15.6	19.7
$25,000 or more	5.2	11.6
Median income	$7,220	$10,440

SOURCE: U.S. Bureau of the Census, 1981 New York City Housing and Vacancy Survey.

Landlords who want their new tenants to be able to afford the maximum increases permitted under Guidelines Board rent orders should look with favor on incomes that increase at more than twice the citywide rate. Transition from controlled to stabilized status, however, is accompanied by higher proportions of large households and welfare dependency (Table 9-16). Although the proportion of households receiving public assistance in pre-'47 stabilized housing has remained nearly constant at 18 percent since 1978, the proportion of welfare recipients in the 1978-controlled/1981-stabilized inventory increased more than two and one-half times, from 7 to 18 percent.

Nonelderly female-headed households with children accounted for the majority of welfare clients whether or not their housing was controlled in 1978 or stabilized three years later, but they represent a much larger fraction of all recipients in the latter category. When the apartments were under rent control in 1978, 57 percent of all welfare recipients in them were women with children, whereas now that the apartments are under stabilization, 80 percent of their welfare-dependent tenants are women with children. Similarly, 20 percent of the welfare recipients in the controlled apartments in 1978 were elderly, while only 4 percent of those in newly stabilized units were elderly.

TABLE 9-16. HOUSEHOLDS RECEIVING PUBLIC ASSISTANCE FOR MATCHED RENTAL UNITS, NEW YORK CITY, 1978 AND 1981

	Controlled/Controlled		Controlled/Stabilized		Pre-'47 Stabilized/Stabilized	Pre-'47 Stabilized/Stabilized
	1978	1981	1978	1981	1978	1981
	Percent Distribution					
All matched rental households	100.0	100.0	100.0	100.0	100.0	100.0
Percent receiving public assistance	5.0	4.0	7.2	17.9	17.1	18.2
Households receiving public assistance	100.0	100.0	100.0	100.0	100.0	100.0
Male household head under 65	14.2	16.3	22.0	15.9	19.2	16.4
Female household head under 65	59.7	56.4	56.5	80.1	77.3	81.0
Household head 65 or over	26.1	27.2	21.5	4.1	1.9	1.9

SOURCE: U.S. Bureau of the Census, 1981 New York City Housing and Vacancy Survey.

Rents. Chapter 6 cited the argument put forth by the President's Commission of Housing that measuring changes in housing cost by taking two or more readings of average marketwide rents at different times tends to result in misleadingly high estimates of rent inflation. New units entering the market and older ones dropping out of it tend to overestimate the measurement of later rents. The Commission suggests that an indicator similar to the Consumer Price Index should be used to measure actual changes in rents for a unit of constant quality and that this would give a fairer and more accurate idea of changes in rents. While not precisely identical to a price index, the longitudinal data do provide an opportunity to measure changes in rents since 1978 for the same representative sample of housing units. Since the samples are identical, the readings on actual rent changes are unaffected by gross additions to or losses from the inventory over the measurement period (Table 9-17).

TABLE 9-17. MEDIAN GROSS RENT BY SELECTED CONTROL STATUS OF MATCHED RENTAL UNITS, NEW YORK CITY, 1978 AND 1981

	Median Gross Rent		Increase	Percent Increase
	1978	1981	1978-1981	1978-1981
All units	$210	$265	$55	26.2%
Controlled/ Controlled	167	213	46	27.5
Controlled/ Stabilized	162	265	103	63.6
Pre-'47 Stabilized/ Pre-'47 Stabilized	212	265	53	25.0
Post-'47 Stabilized/ Post-'47 Stabilized	292	368	76	26.0

SOURCE: U.S. Bureau of the Census, 1981 New York City Housing and Vacancy Survey.

The change data from the longitudinal sample virtually replicate the rent changes estimated using marketwide data and presented in Chapter 6. Median gross rents for all units have increased by 26 percent since 1978. Rents in controlled apartments rose by 28 percent, while pre- and post-'47 stabilized rents increased by 25 and 28 percent, respectively. In absolute terms, rents in post-'47 units increased the most, by $76 per month. What the straightforward analysis of rent changes in Chapter 6 could not directly estimate, however, is the three-year increase in rents that accompanied a change in the regulatory status of apartments from rent controlled to rent stabilized. Actual rent changes for such apartments can be determined directly using the longitudinal data. Apartments that were controlled in both 1978 and 1981 experienced a median rent increase of $46. Apartments that were controlled in 1978 and stabilized in 1981 had a median rent $103 higher than three years earlier. The $52 difference between the two medians ($265 - $213) equals 24 percent of the 1981 median rent for apartments under rent control, and represents the additional rent increase for apartments which moved into the stabilized sector between 1978 and 1981.

Rent-Income Ratios. The longitudinal data provide few insights into changing rent burdens in the City that are not discussed in Chapter 8. As did the earlier analysis, the longitudinal data confirm that no significant changes have occurred in relative housing expense patterns since 1978 (Table 9-18). The largest increase in rent-income ratios was for previously controlled apartments which became stabilized after 1978. Even though the new occupants of these apartments have substantially higher incomes than their predecessors, the three-year rent increase of 64 percent in these units is greater than the difference in their incomes. Hence, the median rent-income ratio for apartments that were controlled in 1978 but stabilized in 1981 has risen from 29 to 31 percent since 1978, while relative expense burdens in other market sectors remained constant.

TABLE 9-18. MEDIAN GROSS RENT AS PERCENT OF INCOME, BY CONTROL STATUS OF MATCHED RENTAL UNITS, NEW YORK CITY, 1978 AND 1981

Control Status	Median Gross Rent as Percent of Income 1978	1981
Controlled/Controlled	29.1%	28.9%
Controlled/Stabilized	28.7	31.0
Pre-'47 Stabilized/ Pre-'47 Stabilized	30.9	31.2
Post-'47 Stabilized/ Post-'47 Stabilized	25.0	24.7

SOURCE: U.S. Bureau of the Census, 1981 New York City Housing and Vacancy Survey.

NOTES

1. See, for example, Louis B. Winnick, "Housing: Has There Been A Downward Shift in Consumers' Preferences?" Quarterly Journal of Economics, LXIX, February 1955, pp. 85-98; with Ernest M. Fisher, "A Reformulation of the Filtering Concept," Journal of Social Issues, VII, 1951, pp. 47-85.

2. Cited in Frank S. Kristof, "The Nation's Rental Housing Inventory: Does It Have a Future?" January 26, 1981 (mimeo), p. 2.

3. Ibid., p. 7.

APPENDIX

1981 NEW YORK CITY HOUSING AND VACANCY SURVEY

PERCENT UNITS VACANT FOR RENT, OTHER VACANT, *IN REM* AND UNITS REMOVED FROM THE INVENTORY BY COMMUNITY DISTRICTS

1981 NEW YORK CITY HOUSING AND VACANCY SURVEY

Percent Units Vacant For Rent, Other Vacant, In Rem and

Units Removed from the Inventory by Community Districts

Bronx

Community Districts	Vacant for Rent		Other Vacant[1]		In Rem		Removed from Inventory[2]	
	Percent	Standard Error	Percent	Standard Error	Percent	Standard Error	Percent	Standard Error
Total	100	(X)	100	(X)	100	(X)	100	(X)
1	9.1	5.4	4.8	3.3	13.7	2.4	14.5	2.0
2	13.6	6.3	20.6	6.2	27.3	3.1	21.4	2.4
3	11.4	5.8	4.8	3.3	16.4	2.6	13.1	1.9
4	13.6	6.3	20.6	6.2	22.5	3.0	20.0	2.4
5	25.0	7.9	11.1	4.8	7.9	1.9	15.2	2.1
6	4.5	3.9	6.3	3.8	8.2	2.1	11.6	1.8
7	9.1	5.4	7.9	4.1	-	-	1.0	0.6
8	-	-	-	-	1.0	0.7	...	...
9	9.1	5.4	7.9	4.1	3.1	1.2	1.4	0.7
10	-	-	12.7	5.0	-	-	0.7	0.5
11	4.5	3.9	-	-	-	-	...	...
12	-	-	3.2	2.7	-	-	0.7	0.5

A dash - indicates that there were no units in sample.

X indicates not applicable. Three dots ... indicate only one sample unit.

1 "Other Vacant" includes units which are vacant for sale, vacant not for sale or rent, and vacant-dilapidated.

2 "Removed from Inventory" represents those units found to be no longer in the inventory at the time of the 1981 NYCHVS. Reasons for removal include demolished, boarded up, burned out, open to the elements, became nonresidential, and merged with other units.

1981 NEW YORK CITY HOUSING AND VACANCY SURVEY

Percent Units Vacant for Rent, Other Vacant, In Rem and Units Removed from the Inventory by Community Districts

Brooklyn

Community Districts	Vacant for Rent		Other Vacant[1]		In Rem		Removed from Inventory[2]	
	Percent	Standard Error	Percent	Standard Error	Percent	Standard Error	Percent	Standard Error
Total	100	(X)	100	(X)	100	(X)	100	(X)
1	6.9	3.8	2.9	1.8	16.6	3.7	9.8	1.7
2	8.3	4.1	13.7	3.6	1.4	1.2	4.7	1.2
3	...	...	10.8	3.3	16.6	3.7	13.8	1.9
4	11.1	4.7	1.4	1.3	11.7	3.2	14.7	2.0
5	5.6	3.4	5.0	2.3	15.9	3.6	11.2	1.7
6	4.2	3.0	14.4	3.6	2.8	1.7	3.8	1.1
7	2.8	2.5	3.6	2.0	-	-	2.2	0.8
8	15.3	5.2	5.0	2.3	2.1	1.5	8.5	1.6
9	4.2	3.0	7.9	2.8	4.8	2.2	4.5	1.2
10	...	...	6.5	2.6	-	-	1.8	0.8
11	4.2	3.0	3.6	2.0	-	-	1.8	0.8
12	5.6	3.4	8.6	3.0	-	-	5.6	1.4
13	5.6	3.4	2.9	1.8	2.8	1.7	1.1	0.6
14	8.3	4.1	6.5	2.6	-	-	1.3	0.7
15	2.8	2.5	2.9	1.8	-	-	2.9	1.0
16	2.8	2.5	...	...	20.0	4.1	8.5	1.6
17	6.9	3.8	3.6	2.0	5.5	2.3	2.5	0.9
18	2.8	2.5	-	-	-	-	1.3	0.7

A dash - indicates that there were no units in sample.

X indicates not applicable. Three dots ... indicate only one sample unit.

1 "Other Vacant" includes units which are vacant for sale, vacant not for sale or rent, and vacant-dilapidated.

2 "Removed from Inventory" represents those units found to be no longer in the inventory at the time of the 1981 NYCHVS. Reasons for removal include demolished, boarded up, burned out, open to the elements, became nonresidential, and merged with other units.

1981 NEW YORK CITY HOUSING AND VACANCY SURVEY

Percent Units Vacant For Rent, Other Vacant, In Rem and Units Removed from the Inventory by Community Districts

Manhattan

Community Districts	Vacant for Rent		Other Vacant[1]		In Rem		Removed from Inventory[2]	
	Percent	Standard Error	Percent	Standard Error	Percent	Standard Error	Percent	Standard Error
Total	100	(X)	100	(X)	100	(X)	100	(X)
1	-	-	-	-	-	-	-	-
2	-	-	1.9	1.8	2.3	1.5	2.8	1.1
3	4.9	3.3	6.6	3.1	19.7	4.0	11.9	2.1
4	3.3	2.7	4.7	2.6	6.4	2.5	4.3	1.3
5	6.6	3.9	-	-	1.8	1.3	9.4	1.9
6	16.4	5.6	4.7	2.6	1.8	1.3	4.3	1.3
7	13.1	5.1	17.9	4.7	3.7	1.9	4.5	1.4
8	4.9	3.3	12.3	4.0	-	-	6.2	1.6
9	6.6	3.9	2.8	2.0	19.3	2.4	15.0	2.3
10	21.3	6.3	41.5	6.0	32.1	4.7	27.2	2.9
11	18.0	5.9	2.8	2.0	4.1	2.0	13.0	2.2
12	4.9	3.3	4.7	2.6	8.7	2.9	1.4	0.8

A dash - indicates that there were no units in sample.

X indicates not applicable.

1 "Other Vacant" includes units which are vacant for sale, vacant not for sale or rent, and vacant-dilapidated.

2 "Removed from Inventory" represents those units found to be no longer in the inventory at the time of the 1981 NYCHVS. Reasons for removal include demolished, boarded up, burned out, open to the elements, became nonresidential, and merged with other units.

1981 NEW YORK CITY HOUSING AND VACANCY SURVEY

Percent Units Vacant For Rent, Other Vacant, In Rem and Units Removed from the Inventory by Community Districts

Queens

Community Districts	Vacant for Rent		Other Vacant[1]		In Rem		Removed from Inventory[2]	
	Percent	Standard Error	Percent	Standard Error	Percent	Standard Error	Percent	Standard Error
Total	100	(X)	100	(X)	100	(X)	100	(X)
1	14.8	5.9	11.3	4.7	-	-	7.3	1.0
2	3.3	3.1	...	...	-	-	4.5	0.8
3	8.2	4.7	4.2	3.0	61.5	15.4	4.5	0.8
4	11.5	5.4	4.2	3.0	-	-	2.7	0.6
5	-	-	9.9	4.5	-	-	8.2	0.7
6	...	...	8.5	4.2	-	-	1.8	0.5
7	4.9	3.7	...	...	-	-	6.4	1.0
8	9.8	5.1	-	-	-	-	4.5	0.8
9	4.9	3.7	2.8	2.5	...	...	11.8	1.2
10	3.3	3.1	4.2	3.0	-	-	11.8	1.2
11	3.3	3.1	...	...	-	-	...	...
12	11.5	5.4	12.7	4.9	30.8	14.5	18.2	1.4
13	3.3	3.1	23.9	6.3	-	-	5.5	0.9
14	19.7	6.8	14.1	5.1	-	-	11.8	1.2

A dash - indicates that there were no units in sample.

X indicates not applicable. Three dots ... indicate only one sample unit.

1 "Other Vacant" includes units which are vacant for sale, vacant not for sale or rent, and vacant-dilapidated.

2 "Removed from Inventory" represents those units found to be no longer in the inventory at the time of the 1981 NYCHVS. Reasons for removal include demolished, boarded up, burned out, open to the elements, became nonresidential, and merged with other units.

1981 NEW YORK CITY HOUSING AND VACANCY SURVEY

Percent Units Vacant For Rent, Other Vacant, In Rem and Units Removed from the Inventory by Community Districts

Staten Island

Community Districts	Vacant for Rent		Other Vacant[1]		In Rem		Removed from Inventory[2]	
	Percent	Standard Error	Percent	Standard Error	Percent	Standard Error	Percent	Standard Error
Total	100	(X)	100	(X)	-	(X)	100	(X)
1	28.6	14.2	66.7	14.9	-	-	65.0	13.6
2	28.6	14.2	-	-	-	-	30.0	12.9
3	42.9	15.6	...	...	-	-	...	...

A dash - indicates that there were no units in sample.

X indicates not applicable. Three dots ... indicate only one sample unit.

1 "Other Vacant" includes units which are vacant for sale, vacant not for sale or rent, and vacant-dilapidated.

2 "Removed from Inventory" represents those units found to be no longer in the inventory at the time of the 1981 NYCHVS. Reasons for removal include demolished, boarded up, burned out, open to the elements, became nonresidential, and merged with other units.

CHAPTER 10

THE SPECIAL PROBLEM OF IN REM HOUSING

Introduction

Local Law 45, New York City's "fast foreclosure" law, was enacted in January 1977.[1] Besides discouraging tax delinquency, the law was intended to preserve low- and moderate-income housing by preventing further deterioration of marginal properties likely to be abandoned by their owners. By reducing, from three years to one, the minimum length of time tax delinquency is permitted before the City can foreclose, Local Law 45 has made it possible for the City to obtain title and assume effective control over marginal residential real estate before abandonment occurs. Properties obtained under Local Law 45 are referred to as in rem. Since 1978, the City has carried out seven separate sets of in rem vestings -- two each in Manhattan and Richmond and one in each of the other boroughs.[2] Excluding redemptions by landlords who eventually paid their back-taxes, these vestings have brought into city-ownership more than 16,500 residential properties.[3]

Housing abandonment is not unique to New York City. The General Accounting Office reported in a 1978 study that 113 of the 149 responding cities had an abandonment problem.[4] Many of these cities, like New York, have initiated "...creative and innovative approaches to adapting surplus or abandoned real estate to new uses consistent with the changing needs of their populations."[5] What is unique about New York's in rem problem is that many of these apartment buildings are still occupied, even though they have been abandoned by their owners.

New York's Response

Although it is not explicit City policy to own and manage landlord-abandoned stock permanently, local housing officials understand that the economics of marginal rental housing are such as to make private ownership of these properties unlikely without some form of assistance. They recognize that, distressed as it is, the in rem stock is the sole housing option for thousands of poor families in New York. Consequently, the City has embarked on an ambitious set of initiatives, including management and rehabilitation programs, several of which involve tenant organizations and community-based sponsors, and efforts to sell the properties to private owners while, in the vast majority of cases, retaining their lower rents.[6]

Of course, not all of the in rem stock is occupied or even habitable. Many thousands of apartments in New York had been abandoned by tenants and landlords alike before the City began vesting under the new law. In the past two fiscal years alone, the City demolished almost 1,600 vacant uninhabitable buildings.[7] This figure includes some of the nearly 1,200 in rem structures from which tenants had been relocated into more adequate city-owned buildings slated for repair, rehabilitation and eventual sale.[8] Despite these demolitions, more than 4,000 vacant city-owned residential buildings remain in New York. In addition, there are approximately 4,000 occupied in rem buildings.[9] The annual rent roll of the nearly 33,500 households in these occupied buildings was around $52 million, of which the City collected $39 million, or 75 percent, in fiscal year 1981.[10] In prior years the rate of collection has averaged less than 50 percent of rents billed.[11] These gross revenues, which have totaled nearly $100 million since 1978, are more than offset by program expenses estimated to exceed $342 million over the same period.[12] Nearly three-quarters of the costs of operating the City's in rem program have come from federal Community Development grants. The program costs include major capital improvements, weatherization and rehabilitation of structurally adequate and occupied buildings, emergency repairs to buildings awaiting rehabilitation and disposition, emergency fuel deliveries, management contracts with tenant groups and community sponsors, and program administration.

The City's policy is to return as many in rem buildings as possible to private ownership for continued use as low- and moderate-income housing. Including redemptions, sales and other transfers of ownership, approximately 1,600 in rem buildings containing 17,000 units have been returned to the private sector since Local Law 45 was passed.[13] New York's Commissioner of Housing recently indicated that the in rem housing program is fully operational. However, there are some housing activists who believe that the City, by slowing its rate of tax foreclosure, misrepresents the magnitude of the in rem problem. Commissioner Anthony Gliedman sees it differently. "Through our diverse disposition mechanisms," Gliedman stated, "the Office of Property Management ... actually achieved the first net reduction in the number of city-owned residential properties since 1977."[14] He went on to say that fiscal year 1981 should be remembered as the "year that the City, working with tenants, community groups and private firms, turned the in rem problem into the in rem resource."[15]

Despite the City's contention that the in rem program is "... considerably less of a drain on public resources than most ... other housing programs,"[16] the Citizens Housing and Planning Council (CHPC) of New York recently attacked the City's efforts as costly and ineffective. CHPC's analysis of the in rem program indicated that "in the absence of drastic changes, operation of these properties by the City threatens to be a permanent, costly, and highly inefficient public housing program likely to require an annual expenditure level of no less than $100 million for the balance of the decade or longer."[17]

Whether the City alters its policy in response to CHPC's criticisms and changes in federal funding, or remains committed to maximizing direct sales to tenants and community-based management groups, planning and program development efforts would be substantially enhanced if more detailed information on the occupants of city-owned buildings were available. To supplement the City's data base on the characteristics of the in rem inventory, the 1981 Housing and Vacancy Survey for the first time provides household and occupancy information on those living in in rem buildings. The remainder of this chapter describes the Survey results, and notes important differences between characteristics of privately and city-owned units.

The In Rem Housing Inventory*

As of the first quarter of 1981, the New York City *in rem* inventory totaled nearly 112,000 units, 33,816 or 30 percent of which were occupied (Table 10-1). Of the remainder, 2,000 units are classified as vacant, available for rent, while another 5,000 are considered vacant but unavailable. The remaining 70,000 or so city-owned units are classified as losses to the inventory. More than 17,500 apartments in the inventory at the time of the 1970 Census had been demolished by the time of the 1981 Housing and Vacancy Survey. Another 9,700 dwelling units in the *in rem* inventory are considered losses by reason of condemnation for urban renewal or other public purposes. By far the largest loss category is the 41,000 *in rem* apartments in burned-out or boarded-up buildings, or in structures which are open to the elements. It is not possible to determine whether the boarded-up structures are concentrated in a few buildings or are scattered throughout the *in rem* stock because the Housing and Vacancy Survey is based on dwelling units rather than buildings. While this somewhat limits the Survey's usefulness in planning for these buildings, its focus on apartment and occupancy characteristics can enlighten discussions of policies to deal with the *in rem* stock.

TABLE 10-1. THE IN REM RENTAL HOUSING INVENTORY, NEW YORK CITY, 1970-1981

	Number	Percent
Total units	111,984	100.0
Units in the inventory	41,434	37.0
Occupied	33,816	30.2
Vacant for rent	2,090	1.9
Vacant for sale	218	0.2
Vacant, not available	5,310	4.7
Units not in the inventory*	70,550	63.0
Demolished	17,693	15.8
Condemned	9,743	8.7
Burned-out, boarded-up, etc.	41,434	37.0
Other losses	1,680	1.5

*It would be incorrect to assume that these units were in the inventory at the time they were taken by the City for back taxes. Many *in rem* properties were already in burned-out, boarded-up states prior to their taking.

SOURCE: U.S. Bureau of the Census, 1981 New York City Housing and Vacancy Survey.

---

*All the *in rem* data that follows are from the 1981 New York City Housing and Vacancy Survey.

Characteristics of the In Rem Stock

Borough. The Bronx and Manhattan have disproportionately large shares of *in rem* housing. Brooklyn's share is somewhat smaller than would be expected if the city-owned stock was distributed according to each borough's share of the City's occupied rental inventory (Table 10-2). Queens is very much under-represented, while Richmond, despite two vestings, is reported by the Census Bureau to be free of *in rem* rental housing.* The Bronx also dominates *in rem* vacancies: fully three-quarters of all *in rem* available

TABLE 10-2. LOCATION OF THE IN REM RENTAL INVENTORY, NEW YORK CITY, 1981

	In Rem		All Renters	Controlled	Pre-'47 Stabilized
	Number	Percent	Percent	Percent	Percent
Occupied Units					
Total	33,816	100.0	100.0	100.0	100.0
Bronx	12,871	38.1	16.9	15.3	21.2
Brooklyn	8,352	24.7	30.1	28.8	27.6
Manhattan	11,315	33.5	30.2	36.7	38.6
Queens	1,278	3.8	20.8	19.1	12.6
Richmond	--	--	2.1	0.1	--
Available Vacancies					
Total	2,090	100.0	100.0	N.A.	100.0
Bronx	1,587	75.9	19.0	N.A.	21.3
Brooklyn	--	--	29.8	N.A.	33.9
Manhattan	503	24.1	26.9	N.A.	32.1
Queens	--	--	21.7	N.A.	12.8
Richmond	--	--	2.6	N.A.	--
Median vacancy duration (months)	2.5		1.9	N.A.	1.9

SOURCE: U.S. Bureau of the Census, 1981 New York City Housing and Vacancy Survey.

*This is a sampling problem. The list from which the Housing and Vacancy Survey sample was drawn contained 135 small *in rem* structures in Richmond. Because these were largely one- and two-family dwellings and the Housing and Vacancy Survey sampled one out of every 167 dwelling units, it is understandable that no *in rem* units in Richmond were surveyed. The City reports a total of 229 city-owned buildings in Richmond as of July 1981. This includes 77 vacant and 152 occupied buildings, with each of the latter containing an average of 1.5 households. See *The In Rem Housing Program Third Annual Report*, City of New York, October 1981, p. 33.

vacancies are in the Bronx, with the remainder in Manhattan. The median vacancy duration for available *in rem* units is 2.5 months, compared to 1.9 months citywide. Vacant unavailable *in rem* units, 43 percent of which are dilapidated, have a median vacancy duration of more than one year and most are slated for eventual demolition.

Structure Class. *In rem* units are far more likely to be in New Law tenements than are apartments in general (Table 10-3). Old Law tenements are also over-represented in the city-owned stock, though to a much lesser degree. The dominance of New law tenements in the *in rem* inventory is also reflected in larger apartment and building sizes. The median size for occupied *in rem* apartments is 4.0 rooms, compared to 3.5 in the City as a whole. For vacant *in rem* units, the median is 4.2 rooms. *In rem* buildings tend to be of medium size, with between 20 and 49 units. This is especially true for available vacancies, 90 percent of which are in New Law tenements. The median *in rem* vacant dwelling is in a building with nearly 35 apartments. Eighty-three percent of all vacancies are in buildings with between 20 and 49 apartments.

Dilapidation and Maintenance Deficiencies. As expected, the occupied city-owned stock is in far worse condition than either the total rental inventory or the controlled and pre-'47 stabilized stocks, both with respect to the extent of dilapidation and the frequency of multiple maintenance deficiencies (Table 10-4). A household in city-owned housing is nearly four-and-a-half times as likely to live in a dilapidated apartment than is the average New York renter. The need for additional heating is much greater in the *in rem* stock, and the frequency of multiple heating breakdowns is more than twice the citywide rate. More than half of all *in rem* tenants indicated that their apartments had at least three of the maintenance deficiencies specified in Chapter 6, compared to 21 percent of all renters and 25 percent of all tenants in controlled units. Not surprisingly, a very high percentage of *in rem* units are in boarded-up buildings or on blocks with such structures; the rate for the occupied stock is nearly three times the citywide average. For available *in rem* vacancies, the relationship between unoccupied apartments and abandoned buildings is even stronger. More than 90 percent of all vacant available city-owned units have boarded-up buildings nearby.

Characteristics of Tenants in In Rem Buildings

Households occupying city-owned housing are more likely than others to be poor, to belong to an ethnic minority, to be headed by a woman with children, and to have very high rent burdens. Indeed, it comes as no surprise that the City's housing of last resort shelters some of the poorest and most at-risk population groups in New York (Table 10-5).

Race and Ethnic Origin. The concentration of minorities in the city-owned stock is substantially greater than in the City as a whole. Citywide, 37 percent of the renter population is Black or Puerto Rican, compared to 78 percent of the households in *in rem* buildings. These racial and ethnic patterns are even more stark when the *in rem* and rent controlled populations are compared. Rent control, because of its long-term tenancy, affects Whites to a far greater degree than minorities. Conversely, minority populations rely on *in rem* housing to a far greater extent than do Whites.

TABLE 10-3. STRUCTURAL CHARACTERISTICS OF THE IN REM AND NON-IN REM HOUSING INVENTORY, NEW YORK CITY, 1981

Structure Type	In Rem Occupied Number	In Rem Occupied Percent	All Renter Occupied Number	All Renter Occupied Percent	In Rem Vacant Available Number	In Rem Vacant Available Percent	All Renter Vacant Available Number	All Renter Vacant Available Percent
Total reported	32,407*	100.0	1,839,142	100.0	2,090	100.0	38,570	100.0
Old Law tenement	7,332	22.6	184,629	10.0	176	8.4	3,414	8.9
New Law tenement	18,705	57.7	552,928	30.1	1,914	91.6	15,826	41.0
Post-'29 multiple	5,547	17.1	716,793	39.0	--	--	8,510	22.1
Other multiples	219	0.7	134,993	7.3	--	--	5,961	15.5
1 or 2 family houses	605	1.9	249,800	13.6	--	--	4,860	12.6
Units in Structure								
Total reported	33,632*	100.0	1,918,621	100.0	2,090	100.0	41,437	100.0
1-9 units	6,073	18.1	567,243	29.6	--	--	13,316	32.1
10-19 units	5,200	15.5	151,367	7.9	169	8.1	5,319	12.8
20-49 units	13,942	41.5	420,519	21.9	1,729	82.7	10,767	26.0
50 or more units	8,417	25.0	779,492	40.6	192	9.2	12,036	29.0
Median units	31.4	N.A.	36.7	N.A.	34.7	N.A.	25.3	N.A.
Median rooms in unit	4.0	N.A.	3.5	N.A.	4.2	N.A.	3.4	N.A.

*The total number of in rem units is 33,816; the different "total reported" figures are due to the units for which structure type and size of building were not reported.

SOURCE: U.S. Bureau of the Census, 1981 New York City Housing and Vacancy Survey.

TABLE 10-4. CONDITION OF IN REM AND OTHER SELECTED HOUSING UNITS, NEW YORK CITY, 1981

Housing Condition	In Rem Number	In Rem Percent	All Renters Percent	Controlled Percent	Pre-'47 Stabilized Percent
Dilapidated units	5,970	17.9	4.2	5.0	6.1
Maintenance deficiences					
1 or more	25,481	84.3	55.4	61.7	69.8
3 or more	15,972	52.9	20.7	25.1	32.4
Additional heating needed	15,714	49.3	29.9	35.0	36.1
Heating breakdown 4 or more times	9,913	32.2	14.1	18.8	21.1
Cracks in wall/ceiling	16,628	52.2	22.2	26.6	33.6
Holes in floor	10,037	31.7	9.4	9.9	15.8
Broken plaster	11,754	37.3	16.9	20.5	25.3
Rodents present	18,641	57.5	24.3	23.2	37.2
Boarded-up structure nearby					
Occupied units	20,734	62.0	23.3	20.4	30.8
Vacant available units	1,739	91.6	45.0	N.A.	48.9

SOURCE: U.S. Bureau of the Census, 1981 New York City Housing and Vacancy Survey.

TABLE 10-5. SELECTED CHARACTERISTICS OF HOUSEHOLDS IN IN REM RENTAL HOUSING AND OTHER SELECTED HOUSING UNITS, NEW YORK CITY, 1981

Racial/ Ethnic Origin of Household Head	In Rem Number	In Rem Percent	All Renters Percent	Controlled Percent	Pre-'47 Stabilized Percent
Total	33,816	100.0	100.0	100.0	100.0
White	5,908	18.6	57.1	77.1	49.3
Black	17,019	53.5	23.4	13.2	22.7
Puerto Rican	7,678	24.1	13.1	5.6	18.9
Other	1,203	3.8	6.4	4.1	9.1
Not Reported	2,008	N.A.	N.A.	N.A.	N.A.
Household Character- istics					
Female headed	19,567	57.9	46.9	50.3	47.4
Single person	11,262	34.4	39.9	52.2	40.5
Household with at least 1 child	14,037	41.5	28.5	10.9	31.0
Median age of head	42	N.A.	43	64	37

SOURCE: U.S. Bureau of the Census, 1981 New York City Housing and Vacancy Survey.

Seventy-seven percent of all tenants in controlled units are White, compared to just 19 percent of *in rem* tenants.

Age and Sex. The *in rem* population is also distinguished by its median age of 42 years. Although this is close to the 43 year median age of household heads in all rental units, *in rem* households tend to be much younger than those in controlled units, and older than tenants in pre-'47 stabilized units. Nearly half of all household heads in controlled housing are at least 65, while just 14 percent of all *in rem* households are that old. *In rem* households are also more likely than others to be headed by women: 58 percent compared to 47 percent of renter households overall. Similarly, *in rem* households are much more likely than others to include children. More than 20 percent of all *in rem* households have children under the age of six, while 42 percent contain youngsters under eighteen. For the renter population as a whole, the respective figures are 14 and 29 percent.

Overcrowding. Despite the fact that the in rem stock is dominated by New Law tenements which typically have larger apartments than other structure types, the higher proportion of families with children in this inventory produces a higher rate of overcrowding than the citywide rate (Table 10-6). Nearly 12 percent of all in rem households live in moderately crowded conditions (more than one person per room) compared to 7 percent of all renters. More serious overcrowding, i.e., apartments which have at least 1.51 persons per room, is a problem for 4 percent of all in rem tenants and less than 2 percent of renter households across the City.

TABLE 10-6. OVERCROWDING IN IN REM AND OTHER SELECTED HOUSING UNITS, NEW YORK CITY, 1981

Persons	In Rem		All Renters	Controlled	Pre-'47 Stabilized
Per Room	Number	Percent	Percent	Percent	Percent
1.01 or more	3,928	11.8	6.5	3.2	8.9
1.51 or more	1,428	4.3	1.7	0.6	2.3
Median	0.5	N.A.	0.5	0.4	0.6

SOURCE: U.S. Bureau of the Census, 1981 New York City Housing and Vacancy Survey.

Income. The median income of households in in rem housing is just $6,865, less than two-thirds the median income for all renters (Table 10-7). Twenty-four percent of all in rem households have incomes of less than $4,000 a year, compared to 14 percent of all renters with this low income. The rate of welfare dependency in the in rem stock is more than double the citywide average. Thirty percent of all in rem households receive public assistance, compared to 13 percent of all renters and only 5 percent of tenants in controlled units. Finally, 46 percent of in rem tenants have incomes below the federal poverty level, versus the overall city rate of 25 percent.

City Rent Levels and Subsidies

More than half of all in rem tenants have gross rent-income ratios in excess of 35 percent.* This is important, but it overstates the true rent burden shouldered by households in in rem housing: City reports indicate a rent delinquency rate of 25 percent among in rem tenants. Rather, it suggests that tenant incomes in in rem housing are insufficient to pay the higher rents required to maintain the housing in adequate condition once it is rehabilitated, without some form of long-term government subsidy. This would be true whether the housing remained in city-ownership, was sold at

---

*This percentage is lowered considerably when public assistance households are excluded from the calculation (see note to Table 10-7).

nominal cost to tenants or community-based sponsors, or was auctioned at market price to private investors.

The law permits the City to "restructure" the rents in *in rem* buildings to support necessary debt service and full operating and maintenance costs even if those charges exceed the maximum permitted controlled or stabilized rent for the apartment. Rents, however, are not typically restructured until rehabilitation is well underway and a disposition plan for the building has been completed. Nevertheless, the combination of lower tenant incomes in the city-owned inventory and the fact that existing rents are not high enough to pay post-rehabilitation costs, including fuel, insurance and taxes, means that even without any debt service payments for city-financed improvements, unaffordable rent increases will be needed to restore many *in rem* buildings to financial stability. This cannot be accomplished without substantial subsidy.

The above nothwithstanding, not all households in the city-owned stock are poor. More than 1,200 *in rem* tenants are reported by the Census to have incomes of at least $25,000 a year, while nearly 30 percent have incomes equal to or exceeding the citywide renter median of $11,001. Clearly, therefore, some amount of rent restructuring is possible in this stock without long-term assistance such as Section 8. Whether tenant incomes are correlated with the quality of the *in rem* housing, or whether the relatively better-off tend to live in the same buildings, cannot be determined from the Housing and Vacancy Survey data. Answers to these and related questions are needed in order to determine the most effective way of returning occupied city-owned buildings to the private sector and assuring their long-term viability as lower- and moderate-income housing.

TABLE 10-7. FINANCIAL CHARACTERISTICS AND INCOMES OF THE OCCUPANTS OF IN REM AND OTHER SELECTED HOUSING UNITS, NEW YORK CITY, 1981

Financial Characteristics	In Rem	All Renters	Controlled	Pre-'47 Stabilized
Median income	$6,865	$11,001	$8,918	$10,355
Median contract rent	$172	$235	$181	$228
Median contract rent-income ratio	30.0	24.9	23.5	27.6
Median gross rent	$210	$265	$213	$262
Median gross rent-income ratio	35.7	28.0	28.6	31.7
Percent of households:				
With rent-income ratio over 35%*	51.2	37.1	38.0	44.4
Receiving public assistance	29.7	13.3	5.0	18.4
Below federal poverty level	45.8	25.3	20.2	29.4

*A higher proportion of public assistance than nonpublic assistance households have gross rent-income ratios greater than 35%, and a greater proportion of tenants in *in rem* than in other housing receive public assistance. Although the Census Bureau did not provide a crosstabulation of rent-income ratios by public assistance status for *in rem* households, we do have such data for other groups of renters. We were thus able to compute the extent of high rent burdens among households not receiving public assistance, except for those living in *in rem* housing. However, we were able to estimate this incidence for *in rem* households. Because median gross rents in the controlled and *in rem* stocks are nearly the same ($213 versus $210), we applied the percentage of controlled tenants receiving public assistance who had high rent burdens to the number of *in rem* tenants receiving public assistance. This resulted in an estimate of the number of *in rem* tenants receiving public assistance who had rent-income ratios over 35 percent. We were then able to net out public assistance households with high rent burdens from the total number of households with high rent burdens, leaving us with households not receiving public assistance who had high rent burdens. Dividing this figure by the number of households not receiving public assistance resulted in the following percentages:

In Rem	All Renters	Controlled	Pre-'47 Stabilized
34.1%	31.2%	36.4%	35.1%

SOURCE: U.S. Bureau of the Census, 1981 New York City Housing and Vacancy Survey.

NOTES

1. Citizens' Housing and Planning Council of New York, Inc., In Rem: Recommendations for Reform, September 1981, p. 1.

2. City of New York, Department of Housing Preservation and Development, The In Rem Housing Program, Third Annual Report, October 1981, p. 34.

3. Ibid.

4. General Accounting Office, Housing Abandonment: A National Problem Needing New Approaches, Report CED-78-126, August 10, 1978, p. i.

5. U.S. Department of Housing and Urban Development, Adaptive Reuse Handbook, Executive Summary, June 1980, p. 2.

6. City of New York, The In Rem Housing Program, p.1.

7. Ibid., p. 35.

8. Ibid., p. 24.

9. Ibid., p. 1.

10. Ibid., p. 36.

11. Ibid., p. 8.

12. Citizens' Housing and Planning Council of New York, Inc., In Rem: Recommendations for Reform, p. 1.

13. City of New York, The In Rem Housing Program, p. 1.

14. Ibid.

15. Ibid.

16. Ibid., p. 32.

17. Citizens' Housing and Planning Council of New York, Inc., In Rem: Recommendations for Reform, p. 2.

18. City of New York, The In Rem Housing Program, p. 36.

GLOSSARY, NOTES AND DEFINITIONS

GLOSSARY

Bureau of Labor Statistics (BLS) - A division of the U.S. Department of Labor that publishes the official government statistics on the cost of living, such as the Consumer Price Index (CPI). From 1971 to 1981 the New York regional office of BLS, under contract with New York City, carried out an annual survey of operating costs which was published each year in a report entitled "Price Index of Operating Costs for Rent Stabilized Apartment Houses in New York City."

Certificate of Occupancy - Entitles the owners of a newly constructed or substantially rehabilitated building to begin initial occupancy. Issuance of a Certificate of Occupancy by the Department of Buildings indicates that the building is substantially completed and complies with all applicable City building codes and regulations.

Cohort - A component of the population, such as a particular age or ethnic group, which is being singled out for analysis.

Community Districts - Created in 1962 to increase opportunities for community participation in the planning process. As of January 1980 there were 59 districts in the City, each with a Community Planning Board and District Service Cabinet. Each Board is authorized to prepare a comprehensive plan for the growth and development of its district and to review proposals for publicly and privately sponsored development and service projects proposed for their districts prior to presentation to the City Planning Commission.

Conciliation and Appeals Board (CAB) - An independent agency created to hear and resolve applications for relief from tenants and disputes between landlords and tenants which arise under the Rent Stabilization Law. The CAB is composed of nine members: four represent tenants, four owners, and one is an impartial Chairperson.

Condominium - A multi-family building or complex where units are offered for ownership. Individual units may also be referred to as condominiums. Units are owned by individuals who may either live in them or rent them to others. At purchase, the owner acquires a proportionate interest in the common areas and voting rights in the condominium owners association.

Constant dollars - Current or nominal dollars of income, prices, costs or rents adjusted for inflation. Allows a comparison of income, etc. over time in terms of real purchasing power.

Consumer Price Index (CPI) - A statistical measure of change over time in the prices of goods and services in major expenditure groups, such as food, housing, apparel, transportation, health and recreation typically purchased by urban consumers. The CPI measures the purchasing power of consumers' dollars by comparing what a sample "market basket" of goods and services costs today with what the same sample cost at an earlier date.

Contract Rent - Monthly rent, which may or may not include payments for furnishings, utilities or services.

Control Status - Refers to those provisions of the rent regulation system which apply to a particular housing unit or groups of housing units. See controlled, decontrolled and stabilized.

Controlled (Rent Controlled) Housing - See 1981 Control Status Definitions (Prepared by New York City Department of Housing Preservation and Development, Rent Control Division).

Conventional Homeowner - An owner-occupant who neither lives in a condominium nor a cooperative.

Conversions - The creation of housing units out of nonresidential space or structures and vice-versa; also, the division of a larger apartment into several smaller individual dwellings.

Cooperative - A housing corporation in which individual households own shares entitling them to live in a particular unit in a multi-family building or complex and to use the common areas of the building or complex.

Decontrolled Housing - See 1981 Control Status Definitions (Prepared by New York City Department of Housing Preservation and Development, Rent Control Division).

Dilapidated - As used by the Census it means a housing unit having one or more serious deficiencies or of inadequate original construction so that it does not provide adequate and safe shelter. A unit is dilapidated if it has a combination of minor deficiencies which prevent it from providing adequate protection to its occupants. As noted by Marcuse (p. 146), "no matter how carefully criteria were drafted and instructions provided to enumerators, a substantial amount of variability among enumerators was bound to result. It was not surprising, therefore, to find that in a Post-Enumeration Survey after the 1969 Census, of the units a second enumerator classified as dilapidated only 38% had originally been called dilapidated, while 39% were originally classified as deteriorating and 23% were originally classified as sound."

Elderly Household Head - Refers to a person who is 65 years of age or older, except that the Senior Citizen Rent Increase Exemption applies to persons over 62.

Emergency Housing Act of 1962 - New York State law that transferred total administration of rent control to cities with populations of one million or more. It authorized enactment of local legislation, while the state bore reasonable and necessary costs, and imposed a freeze on previously established maximum rents pending transfer of rent control to local jurisdiction.

Emergency Price Control Act of 1942 - The original enabling legislation signed into law by President Roosevelt in 1942 establishing wartime rent controls.

Emergency Tenant Protection Act of 1974 (ETPA) - A law enacted by New York State which placed all vacant destabilized apartments back under stabilization effective July 1, 1974. ETPA also placed under rent stabilization all apartments in buildings with six or more units which had originally been rent controlled but were vacancy decontrolled between July 1, 1971 and June 30, 1974. Under ETPA, all future vacancies in rent controlled apartments in buildings containing at least six units will, upon reoccupancy, become rent stabilized.

Equity - The difference between the price or current market value of a property and the value of any claims or liens against the property such as a mortgage.

Federal Poverty Level - A federal index adopted in 1969 and updated annually that provides a range of income cutoffs or "poverty threshold" adjusted to account for family size, sex and age of family head, number of children and farm residence.

Foreclosure - The legal process by which a serious mortgage default is remedied by the mortgagee. It typically results in the transfer of title to the mortgaged property from the borrower to the lender. Although the form and method of the foreclosure process vary by state, in most cases a mortgage foreclosure involves an auction sale of the property under court order.

Fuel Pass-through - In 1980, Local Law 20 was adopted, allowing owners to pass 75 percent of the increased cost of heating oil through to tenants in controlled apartments. The increase is based on actual consumption, not to exceed a certain level, and average price change for the type of heating fuel used. The rent stabilization program has also had a fuel pass-through program, as ordered by the Rent Guidelines Board.

Gross Rent - See Notes and Definitions (Prepared by Housing Division, Bureau of the Census).

Gross Vacancy Rate - A vacancy rate that includes vacant dilapidated and vacant, not available apartments in the numerator and demoninator of the vacancy equation. Because it counts vacant dilapidated and unavailable units as available for occupancy,the gross rental vacancy rate will typically be higher than the net rental vacancy rate which excludes these units.

Household Income - In the 1981 Housing and Vacancy Survey, household income includes the incomes of all household members over age 14, regardless of their relationship to the householder. The 1975 and 1978 Housing and Vacancy Surveys did not use the term "household income." In these surveys, data were published separately for family incomes, which included the incomes of all household members over age 14, if related to the head by blood or marriage. Data were also collected for primary individuals who were either household heads living alone or with nonrelatives. Direct comparisons are possible, therefore, between 1980 household incomes and 1978 incomes of families and individuals. The 1981 Housing and Vacancy Survey defines primary individuals as a single person householder so that no direct comparisons between primary individuals in 1978 and 1981 are possible. (See also, Notes and Definitions prepared by Housing Division, Bureau of the Census).

Householder/Reference Person - See Notes and Definitions (Prepared by Housing Division, Bureau of the Census).

Housing Expense Burden - A synonymn for rent-income ratio.

Housing Unit - A dwelling unit, house, apartment, groups of rooms, or a single room, occupied as separate living quarters, or, if vacant, intended for occupancy as separate living quarters. Occupants must live and eat separately from other persons in the building and have direct access to their quarters from the outside.

Housing and Vacancy Survey - Conducted periodically by the U.S. Bureau of the Census under contract with New York City to measure the rental vacancy rate. This rate is then used to determine whether the threshold vacancy rate which would require the orderly decontrol and destabilization of rents in New York City has been reached. The Housing and Vacancy Survey also collects important data on rents, housing conditions, and household characteristics. The data are used for planning, program development and evaluation, as well as other purposes.

In Rem Housing - See 1981 Control Status Definitions (Prepared by New York City Department of Housing Preservation and Development, Rent Control Division).

In Rem Proceeding - Initiation of legal actions by the City against real property that is at least four quarters (one year) in tax arrears. Results in title to the property being passed from private to public hands.

Inventory Losses - Housing units that were in the inventory at the time of a prior Census enumeration or Housing and Vacancy Survey which, in 1981, were either demolished, condemned, burned-out or boarded-up, converted to nonresidential use, or which had been merged with another unit or units.

Local Law 30, 1970 - Introduced the Maximum Base Rent System (MBR) to the rent control program. Based on the concept of economic rent, the MBR system was designed to close the gap between the maximum permitted rents and the costs of providing standard housing, and to keep the gap closed. A separate, formula-based MBR is calculated for every rent controlled apartment with annual 7.5 percent rent increases allowed until the MBR is reached. Annual increases are permitted only if all rent-impairing and 80 percent of other housing code violations are corrected. The MBR is increased every two years by the Rent Control Division on the basis of a field study of operating costs.

Local Law 45 - New York City's Fast Foreclosure law, enacted in January 1977, which reduced the minimum length of tax delinquency allowed before the City foreclosed from three years to one.

Longitudinal Survey - A survey that enumerates the same units at various times. The survey sample consists of housing units that were enumerated in both 1978 and 1981. Failure to respond to the survey in either 1978 or 1981 eliminates a dwelling from the longitudinal component of the 1981 Housing and Vacancy Survey.

Maintenance Deficiencies - See Notes and Definitions (Prepared by Housing Division, Bureau of the Census).

Maximum Base Rent (MBR) - Since 1972, maximum base rents (MBR) are established for rent controlled units, based on operating costs and a fair return to owners. Rent increases are allowed as costs rise, providing the building is well maintained.

Median - See Notes and Definitions (Prepared by Housing Division, Bureau of the Census).

Mitchell-Lama Program -Under the New York State Private Housing Finance Law of 1955, the City and State made low interest loans and granted tax exemptions to limited-profit housing companies to construct or rehabilitate housing for middle-income families.

Monthly Carrying Charge - See Notes and Definitions (Prepared by Housing Division, Bureau of the Census).

Near-Poor - Households with incomes between 100 and 125 percent of the official poverty level.

Net Rental Vacancy Rate - The ratio of the number of rental units that are vacant and available to the sum of all occupied and vacant available rental units. The net rental vacancy rate excludes vacant dilapidated and vacant, not available units from both the numerator and denominator.

Other Races and Ethnic Groups - The category "other" includes those reporting "other than White or Black" heads of household and reporting neither the householder, nor the householder's father, nor mother as being born in Puerto Rico. Includes such races and ethnic groups as American Indian, Chinese, Eskimo, Filipino, Hawaiian, Aleut, Korean, Japanese, and Malayan.

"Other" Rental Control Status -In 1981 a residual category of limited analytical value. In 1972 these units were classified as "Never Regulated and Publicly Aided," or "one- or two-room units lacking specified facilities." (See also, 1981 Control Status Definitions, New York City Department of Housing Preservation and Development, Rent Control Division).

Post-'29 Multiple Dwellings - Built subsequent to 1929 and subject to the regulation of the Multiple Dwelling Code of 1929. Includes all the City's public housing as well as more contemporary luxury buildings.

Presidential Commission on Housing - A 25-member commission established by President Reagan to advise him on options for the development of a national housing policy.

Public Assistance - Defined in the 1981 Housing and Vacancy Survey as Aid to Families with Dependent Children, or Home Relief.

Real Income - Household income in current dollars divided by the Consumer Price Index for the same year in which the income was reported. Permits analysis of income in constant dollars or real purchasing power relative to a base year.

Redemption - The payment of some or all back taxes and interest on a tax-foreclosed property by a landlord before title to the property is vested by the City.

Rent Gap - A term used prior to implementation of the Maximum Base Rent (MBR) system to refer to the difference between rental income permitted under the pre-1970 rent control program and the amount of income needed to maintain housing in standard condition.

Rent Guidelines Board - A nine-member board appointed by the mayor to adminster the Rent Stabilization Law. The Guidelines Board is authorized to establish maximum permitted rent increases for lease renewals and vacancy leases for rent stabilized and newly occupied rent controlled apartments in buildings containing six or more apartments. The Board consists of two tenant representatives, two real estate representatives, and five public members from whose ranks the mayor selects a chairperson.

Rent-Income Ratio - A ratio of the monthly rent to the monthly income of the householder or individual. In all cases, the rent referred to is one year more current than the income. The 1981 Housing and Vacancy Survey, for example, collected data on 1981 rents and on 1980 household incomes.

Rent Stabilization Association (RSA) - Owners of apartments subject to the Rent Stabilization Law must join this private, self-regulating real estate industry association. The Association is responsible for enrolling owners whose apartments are subject to the Rent Stabilization Law, drafting a code to regulate the conduct of its membership, and collecting sufficient dues from its members to defray the costs of enforcing and administering the law.

Senior Citizen Rent Increase Exemption - See Notes and Definitions (Prepared by Housing Division, Bureau of the Census).

Stabilized - See 1981 Control Status Definitions (Prepared by the New York City Department of Housing Preservation and Development, Rent Control Division).

Submarkets - Refers to groups of housing units which share important features and are subject to similar price-determining influences such as rent controlled apartments, pre-'47 units, etc.

Tax Delinquency - Multiple dwelling properties which are behind at least four quarters in their property taxes are liable to be taken by the City in *in rem* proceedings.

Tenements (Old and New Law) - First built in New York City around 1833, tenement houses were buildings "... for the poorer classes of our population, so as to cover the whole or nearly the whole area of the grounds, and thus crowding a large number of families together in a space which is not sufficient for one." Formally defined by law in 1865 to mean "and include every house, building or portion thereof, which is rented, leased, let or hired out to be occupied or is occupied as the home or residence of more than three families living independently of another, and doing their cooking upon the premises or by more than two families upon a floor, so living and cooking, but having a common right in the halls, stairways, yards, water closets or privies or some of them." Old Law tenements refer to tenement houses built prior to 1901. New Law tenements, built in accordance with the requirements of the Tenement House Act of 1901, opened up the inner courts of the Old Laws, bringing more light and air into interior rooms. Maximum lot coverage was reduced to 70 percent, shafts and staircase halls had to be fireproofed and a separate water closet had to be provided for each family.

Vacancy Decontrol Law of 1971 - Authorized the decontrol of all controlled and stabilized units after a dwelling was vacated and rented by a new tenant.

Vacant Available - Nondilapidated vacant units offered for sale or rent for year-round occupancy. Newly constructed or rehabilitated units are considered "vacant available" if they are in buildings that have been issued a Certificate of Occupancy.

Vacant Housing Unit - An apartment is vacant if no one is living in it at the time of enumeration. If the occupants are only temporarily absent, the unit is considered occupied. A vacant unit may be furnished or unfurnished; offered for rent or sale; rented or sold but the new occupants have not yet moved in; or held off the market for speculation or other uses. Newly constructed units were counted as vacant only if they had been issued a Certificate of Occupancy.

Vacant, Not available - Vacant units that are intended for seasonal use; dilapidated, already rented, or sold and expecting occupancy; held for occasional use; held for painting or repair; or held for other reasons.

Very-Poor - Those households with incomes below 100 percent of the federal poverty level.

Vesting - The passing of title to a tax-foreclosed property from private to City ownership.

1981 CONTROL STATUS DEFINITIONS

Prepared by New York City Department of Housing Preservation and Development, Rent Control Division

Note: A comparison of data by categories of control status from one survey to the next may be misleading unless one reviews the definitions appropriate to each survey since there have been changes in laws and regulations over the years.

Controlled - These units are subject to the provisions of the Rent Control Law and Regulations which have jurisdiction over occupied private rental units in existence before February 1, 1947. All increases in rent are set and must be approved by the New York City Rent Control Division.

Under law, all rent controlled apartments that are voluntarily vacated after June 30, 1971 are no longer subject to the jurisdiction of the Rent Control Law. If the unit is in a building with fewer than six units it becomes decontrolled; if the unit is in a building with six units or more it is subject to the jurisdiction of the Rent Stabilization Association.

The figures shown in this Survey may undercount the full rent controlled inventory for two reasons: (1) there are an unknown but probably small number of one- and two-room units tabulated in the All Other Renter category (see below) that may be subject to the Rent Control Law and (2) some units that initially qualified for registration with the Rent Stabilization Association may not have joined or may have been expelled and now come under the jurisdiction of the Rent Control Law. For purposes of this Survey, however, these units are considered eligible for Stabilization and appear under the "Stabilized" count.

Decontrolled - Rental units in structures built before 1947, previously subject to rent control and subsequently removed for reasons permitted by law.

The number of units in this category has and will continue to increase as a result of the State vacancy decontrol provision which calls for the decontrol of rent controlled units that are voluntarily vacated after June 30, 1971 (also see definitions of Controlled and Stabilized categories).

Stabilized - Rental apartments, exclusively in structures of six or more units.

Units were classified as "Stabilized" for this Survey when (a) the unit was in a structure of six units or more that was built between 1947 and 1973 and was not Regulated; (b) the unit was in a structure of six units or more and was built in 1974 or later and received tax abatement, or the unit was in a structure converted from non-residential to residential use and received tax abatement to aid the conversion (a condition of receiving tax abatement is that the building join the Rent Stabilization Association and abide by the Rent Stabilization Law); (c) the unit was in a structure with six units or more built before 1947, and has been decontrolled under provisions of law.

The Stabilized category represents units that were eligible to join the Rent Stabilized Association and thereby come under the jurisdiction of the Rent Stabilization Law; therefore the number of units categorized as Stabilized in this survey will be higher than the number actually registered with the Rent Stabilization Association (see definition of Controlled category above).

State/City Assisted: Renter* - The majority of these units were constructed under the New York State and New York City Mitchell-Lama program. In addition the category encompasses a smaller number of units constructed under the auspices of the New York State Limited Profit Housing program.

The three programs are addressed primarily to middle income tenants; therefore occupancy is restricted to households meeting certain income limitations. The mechanisms employed to keep rents at affordable levels include tax exemption, State-provided low interest mortgages, and limitations on return of equity. In certain instances federal subsidy programs are combined with the state and local assistance measures to achieve the program's objectives.

Rentals are directly or indirectly regulated because the owner's profit is limited; adjustments are based on changes in operating costs, debt structure, and profitability in the particular project and must be approved by the appropriate State or City agency.

State/City Assisted: Owner** - These units were constructed under the New York State and New York City Mitchell-Lama program. The purpose of the program is to enable middle income families to secure decent affordable housing through cooperative ownership.

The mechanisms employed to keep both the initial downpayment and monthly carrying charges within the means of the middle income families, to which the program is restricted, are tax exemption, State or City provided low interest mortgages, and limitations on return of equity. In certain instances federal subsidies are combined with the State and local measures to achieve the program's objectives.

---

*In the 1978 Housing and Vacancy Survey these units were classified as "Never Regulated and Publicly Aided."

**In the 1978 Housing and Vacancy Survey these units were classified simply as "Owner-Coop and Condominium."

All Other Renter - A residual category encompassing anything and everything excluded from the classifications listed above; the catch-all nature of the category makes it of very limited analytical value.*

Public Housing -Rental units in structures owned and managed by the New York City Housing Authority. Only households with specified low or moderate income levels may qualify as tenants. Rentals and terms and conditions of occupancy are regulated by the Authority. Private housing leased by the Authority is not classified here as "Public Housing".

---

*In the 1978 Housing and Vacancy Survey these units were classified as follows:

(a) Never Regulated and Publicly Aided - Units with no governmental restrictions or regulation on rents or rental conditions or type of tenancy -- these units are subject to free market conditions. These units were never subject to rent regulation or control. Units in this grouping are mainly located in structures of less than six units that were completed on or after February 1, 1947, or are in non-regulated buildings of any size built on or after January 1, 1974.

(b) 1 and 2 Room Units Lacking Specified Facilities - These units lack private cooking facilities or share bathroom facilities. Most of them are located in older buildings either in rooming houses or in Single Room Occupancy Tenements. Some are high rent residential hotel units which lack complete cooking facilities. These units may fall into almost any of the control categories, except public housing, depending on the date of occupancy, year of construction and other characteristics.

Also included in this category are the following:

In Rem - Units located in structures owned by the City of New York as a result of an *in rem* proceeding initiated by the City after the owner failed to pay tax on the property for four or more consecutive quarters. Though many of these units had previously been subject to either rent control or rent stabilization they are exempt from both regulatory systems during the period of City ownership.

NOTES AND DEFINITIONS

of the

1981 New York City Housing and Vacancy Survey

Prepared by Housing Division, U.S. Bureau of the Census

b. General Limitations

c. Contract Rent as a Percent of Income by Contract Rent as a Percent of Income

I. General

a. Note regarding rounding. Detail may not add to total due to rounding.

b. Medians. The median is the middle value in a distribution, i.e., the median divides the distribution into two equal parts. For Persons and Rooms a continuous distribution is assumed, with the whole number used as the midpoint of the interval. A continuous distribution is also assumed for Units in Structure and Elevator in Structure with 4 or More Stories. If the median should fall in the "6 to 9 units in structure" interval, the range of the interval would be 5.5 to 9.5 units, and the "tenths" would be added to 5.5.

For all other items a continuous distribution is inherent. If the median income falls in the "$10,000 to $12,499" interval, the "hundreds" (of dollars) would be added to $10,000.

The medians in these tables are computed from the most detailed distribution presented for an item. This means that when a tabulation item, e.g., Persons per Room, appears in Series IA and Series III, its median for Series III will reflect a median based on the full group of categories for Series IA rather than the collapsed categories of Series III. In some cases, the medians are carried out to decimal places more detailed than is warranted for such accuracy to be meaningful.

c. Not reported. In general, these are cases in which the question or questions related to the tabulation item were blank, unanswered or refused. For three questions (Senior Citizen Rent Increase Exemption, Senior Citizen Carrying Charge Increase Exemption, and Type of Heating Fuel), a "Not reported" on the question was counted in the "Don't know" category of the respective tabulation item. Several other Not reported cases are counted as "Not applicables" or included with "Not computed" in certain combination items as explained in paragraphs d and e below.

d. Not applicable. In general, "Not applicables" appear when the detail of a table is restricted to a particular sub-universe. Those cases out of the sub-universe are included on a separate line to account for the total universe as reflected in the control total line. For example, in the item 1980 Income of Primary Individuals, the "Not applicable" line includes all households in the occupied universe that consist of 2 or more persons.

Sometimes when a tabulation item is a combination of an independent and a dependent question, and the independent question is not reported it will be (by definition) included in the "Not applicable" line. Some examples of this are: Room Access and Elevator in Structure with 4 or more Stories."

Other times, in the situation described above, the "Not applicable" line (or lines) will be clearly spelled out as to what this component of the universe includes, such as "1 or 2 family house." Examples of these items are: Purchase Price, Monthly Carrying Charge, Households Receiving Public Assistance, Households Below Specified Income Level, and New York City Structure Classification.

e. Not computed or not reported. This term is used only with the tabulation items Contract Rent as Percent of Income and Gross Rent as Percent of Income. It indicates one of two things: (1) that one or both of the questionnaire items were "Not reported," or (2) that the household had "No income or loss" and/or was occupied for "No cash rent" and therefore did not have a percentage computed.

f. Not found. This term applies only to NYC Structure Class where the address of the sample unit was not found in the Master Building Files (MBF) of New York City.

g. Data not available. This term applies to only one item, NYC Structure Class. For City Structure Class, the data on this line indicate that the City could not find the specific address in the MBF but found an address that seemed to be an alternate or part of the same complex. They entered that code elsewhere on the card in hopes that the interviewer would clarify the addresses involved and the code could then be used. If no such reconciliation occurred, the unit was tabulated as "Data not available."

h. Symbols. A dash ("-") signifies zero. A dash also appears in some of the tables for lines excluded from the distribution. An (X) means not applicable or that the figures were excluded from the distribution. A (Z) means that the base for a derived figure is too small for it to be shown (i.e., less than 0.05 percent).

II. Survey Design

a. Sample. The sample selected for the 1981 New York City Housing and Vacancy Survey (NYC-HVS) was the same as that used for the 1978 NYC-HVS (with updating for new construction). It was drawn primarily from the following sources: (1) 1970 census records, (2) New York City Certificates of Occupancy (C of O) for units constructed from April 1970 through December 1980, (3) for the boroughs Manhattan and Brooklyn, sampling was also done from a list of commercial-use structures with upper floors rented for residential use and from a list of units which were "special places"[1] in 1970 but were residential at the time of the 1981 NYC-HVS and, (4) for the boroughs Bronx, Brooklyn, Manhattan and Queens, sampling was done from a list of units constructed under the supervision of the New York State Urban Development Corporation. These units did not get C of O's from the city.

Not all housing units were in the scope of the survey. Housing units in special places were excluded from the survey.

In the 1981 NYC-HVS, special care was taken with respect to those units found to be lost from the inventory on the first visit by an enumerator. Each sample housing unit originally categorized as demolished, condemned, boarded up, burned out, nonresidential, or in a special place was rechecked on an individual unit by unit basis by Housing Division and Field Division personnel to be certain that a proper determination had been made.

b. Source of tabulation items. All data in Series I through VIII were collected by the Census Bureau during the 1981 NYC-HVS except for New York City Structure Class and Rent Control Status.[2] These data were provided by the City from their records prior to the 1975 survey. Adjustments to City control status data were made based on information collected in the 1978 and 1981 surveys. For example, if City records showed a unit as being controlled prior to 1975, and new residents moved into the unit in 1980, this unit was considered decontrolled if it was less than 6 units or stablized (pre-1947) if it was 6 or more units.

Most of the concepts and definitions incorporated in the 1981 survey are the same as those used in the 1978 survey. In addition, many of the concepts and definitions in this survey are similar to those used in the 1970 census. Section III explains those items which are not directly comparable to the Census. For more information on the 1975 and 1978 surveys, see the 1975 and 1978 New York City Housing and Vacancy Survey, Notes and Definitions. For a complete discussion of Census subjects, see the 1970 Census of Population, Series PC(1)-C, General and Economic Characteristics, and the 1970 Census of Housing, Series HC(1)-B, Detailed Housing Characteristics reports.

---

[1]Special places include hospitals, jails, mental institutions, college dormitories, and large rooming or boarding houses, etc., where large numbers of people dwell, and which require different survey procedures from those used for housing units such as private homes or apartments.

[2]Full details on definitions of New York City Rent Control Status are contained in Part B.

c. Series continuity. For this survey, as well as for other periodic surveys that the Bureau conducts, an attempt is made to keep some continuity of features in order to maintain comparability with previous surveys. For this survey, the numbers of the various series, the series tables and the many cross-tabulations are similar to those of the 1975 and 1978 NYC-HVS. The only major differences, other than those discussed in this section, reflect additions or deletions to the data items collected.

III. Items Unique to New York City Housing and Vacancy Survey, Different from Previous Surveys or Different from the Census

a. Reference Person/Householder. All current survey programs of the Census Bureau have discontinued the use of the "head of household" concept. The Bureau's longstanding practice of designating the husband in husband-wife households as the "head" of household and a respondent determined "head" in all other households, as the person for determining the relationships of other household members have become less relevant in the analysis of household and family data. To meet this change, the Bureau has developed a new approach to determining household relationship through the use of a "reference person" in the questionnaire and "householder" in the final tabulation. For purposes of this survey the reference person (householder) was defined as the household member or one of the household members who owned or rented the sample unit. If no household member owned or rented the sample unit, the first person listed was the reference person.

b. Race and Puerto Rican Birth or Parentage of Householder. The category "Other" includes those reporting other than white or Negro on the race question and reporting neither the householder, the householder's father or the householder's mother born in Puerto Rico on the birthplace question.

c. Address of Householder 5 Years Ago. In the 1978 survey no specified time limit was placed on this item; the data were based on the response to the following question: Where did the "head" live prior to moving to his/her present unit? Therefore, the data for 1981 are not directly comparable with 1978.

d. Household Members Under Age 6 and Under Age 18. These tabulations include all members of the household regardless of whether they are related to the householder or not.

e. Income of Primary Individuals. For purposes of the 1981 survey, a primary individual is defined as a householder who lives alone. This differs from the definition used in the 1975 and 1978 surveys. In these surveys a primary individual was defined as a household head who either lived alone or with nonrelatives.

f. Income of Households. Household income is the income of all members of the household 14 years old or older regardless of whether they are related to the householder or not. This item was tabulated for the first time in 1981 and replaces the tabulation on income of families.

g. Condition. Condition is classified by the interviewer as either sound, deteriorating, or dilapidated; for purposes of this tabulation, deteriorating and sound are combined into the category, "Not Dilapidated." In previous surveys condition has been combined with plumbing facilities as a measure of housing quality. However, since less than one percent of the housing inventory lacked plumbing facilities in 1978, the usefulness of this tabulation has diminished.

h. Gross Rent. The computed term gross rent is the contract rent plus the estimated average monthly cost of utilities (electricity, gas, water) and fuels (oil, coal, kerosene, wood, etc.) if these items are paid for by the renter in addition to rent. It is intended to eliminate differentials which result from varying practices with respect to the inclusion of utilities and fuel as part of the rental payment.

The four utility and fuel items are all two-part questions: (1) Is the item paid in addition to rent? and (2) If it is paid in addition to rent, what is the cost (amount)? "Not reported" includes units which did not have an amount for contract rent or which did not have amounts for two of the following three items: Electricity, gas, or fuel oil.

i. Length of Lease. A lease is defined as a contract granting use or occupation during a specified period in exchange for rent. The length of lease is from the time the lease originated, not from the time of the interview.

j. Monthly Carrying Charges. This item applies only to owners of cooperatives and condominiums. Some or all of the following components could be included in this item: Debt service, real estate taxes, fire and hazard insurance, mortgage insurance, salaries of project employees, heating expenses, utilities and reserve for major repairs, maintenance, etc.

k. Senior Citizen Rent Increase or Carrying Charge Exemption. In 1981, the inquiry on exemptions was made of all households with members 62 years of age or older. In 1978, the inquiry was limited to household "heads" 62 or over.

1. Households Below Specified Income Level. The specified income level statistics presented in these tabulations are derived from an updated poverty level index used in the March 1981 Current Population Survey supplement. This index is based on a definition originated by the Social Security Administration in 1964 and subsequently modified by a Federal Interagency Committee in 1969. This index, as applied to the NYC-HVS, provides a range of income cutoffs or "poverty thresholds" adjusted to take into account such factors as household size, sex and age of householder and number of children. These thresholds are shown in the chart below.

Basic Nonfarm Poverty Thresholds by Age and Sex of Householder,

Household Size and Number of Children

(Dollars)

Household Size	Number of Related Children Under 18						
	None	1	2	3	4	5	6 or more
Male Householder							
1 under age 65.......	4,441						
65 or over.........	3,990						
2 under 65...........	5,552	6,220					
65 or over.........	4,985	6,220					
3....................	6,464	6,674	7,054				
4....................	8,521	8,647	8,349	8,772			
5....................	10,284	10,408	10,075	9,821	10,032		
6....................	11,796	11,835	11,585	11,333	10,997	11,166	
7 or more............	14,856	14,984	14,689	14,437	14,104	13,598	13,473
Female Householder							
1 under age 65.......	4,109						
65 or over.........	3,938						
2 under 65...........	5,130	5,601					
65 or over.........	4,922	5,601					
3....................	6,255	5,958	6,590				
4....................	8,182	8,477	8,438	8,349			
5....................	9,821	10,117	10,075	9,991	9,654		
6....................	11,459	11,668	11,585	11,500	11,124	10,784	
7 or more............	14,395	14,606	14,563	14,437	14,061	13,768	13,095

m. Monthly Cost of Electricity and Monthly Cost of Utility Gas. These two items exclude those renters who heat their units with either electricity or gas. By this exclusion, the distributions of cost are not distorted by high paying/high volume users of gas and electricity.

n. Room Access. Access to other rooms without having to go through one's bedroom is a measure of privacy and therefore related to the quality of the unit. The data are shown separately for those units that have bedrooms lacking privacy when it is necessary to pass through a bedroom to get to another rooom, such as a den; and when it is necessary to pass through a bedroom to get to the bathroom.

o. Additional Heating. The data on additional heating refer to units which had to use an additional source of heat to supplement the regular system because the regular system did not provide enough heat during the winter prior to the time the survey was taken. Additional sources of heat such as kitchen stoves, fireplaces, or portable heaters, may have been used only in the mornings or on very cold evenings. Electric blankets, heating pads or hot water bottles are not considered additional sources of heat.

p. Breakdown in Heating System. The data on breakdowns or failures in heating systems are limited to units whose heating equipment broke down for six hours or longer during the winter prior to the time of the survey. The data are presented according to the number of times such a breakdown occurred. Heating equipment is considered unusable if it cannot be used for the purposes intended; the breakdown may be caused by broken pipes, electrical or gas parts out of order, or downed power lines.

q. Cracks or Holes in Walls, Ceiling or Floor. Data are presented on whether or not there are open cracks or holes in interior ceilings or walls and floors of a housing unit. Included are cracks or holes that do not go all the way through to the next room or to the outdoors. Not included are "hairline" cracks or cracks that appear in the walls or ceilings but are not large enough for a fingernail file to be inserted, and very small holes caused by nails or similar objects.

r. Broken Plaster or Peeling Paint. Data are presented on whether or not there is broken plaster or peeling paint on the interior ceilings or walls of a housing unit. Included in the "yes" category are those areas of broken plaster or peeling paint that are approximately one square foot or larger.

s. Rodent Infestation. The data on rodent infestation refers to households who reported that they had seen mice or rats or signs or traces of their presence inside the house or building during the last three months. Signs of mice and rats or traces of their presence include droppings, holes in the wall, or torn food containers. "Regularly" refers to periodic visits by a licensed company or individual who uses chemicals and sprays to control or kill pests and rodents. The regular service interval may be once a month, four times a year, or any other such interval. Other service may be on an "only when needed" basis or "irregularly" where it is known that a building is serviced but it is not known whether the service is regular or irregular. "Not at all" includes units in a house or building that has not been serviced during the 12 months prior to the taking of the survey and "Don't know" includes units where it is not known if there is any extermination service of any sort.

t. Number of Maintenance Deficiencies. The data for this item consists of a count of the households answering affirmatively to the specific maintenance deficiency items. In order to be counted in one of the five deficiency categories, all of the following items had to be reported: Heating equipment breakdown, additional heating required, rodent infestation, cracks/holes in walls/floors, and broken plaster/peeling paint.

u. Ethnic Origin of Householder. The classification by origin here refers to the origin of the householder occupying the housing unit. Origin was determined on the basis of a question that asked for self-identification of a person's origin or descent. Respondents were asked to select their origins from a "flash card." Persons classified as "other Spanish" were those who indicated that their origin was either Mexican-American or other Spanish. Persons classified as "all other" are those who indicated a choice other than those for "other Spanish" or "Puerto Rican."

IV. Cross-Tabulations for Recent Mover Households

a. Definition. Recent mover households are defined as those in which the current householder moved into the unit in 1980 or 1981.

b. General Limitations. For the cross-tabulations involving contract rent, contract rent as a percent of income, contract rent per room, and utilities paid in addition to rent, the data are limited to current residences which are renter occupied for cash rent or rent free. In addition, the "Not rented for cash rent or or NR" and "Not computed or not reported" categories for previous residence include units which are renter occupied for cash rent or rent free in current residence but owner occupied in previous residence.

c. Contract Rent as a Percent of Income by Contract Rent as a Percent of Income. Caution should be used in the interpretation of this table. The contract rent for both the current and previous residences are calculated as a percent of 1980 income of the members of the current household.

1981 NEW YORK CITY HOUSING AND VACANCY SURVEY
SAMPLE DESIGN, ESTIMATION PROCEDURE AND RELIABILITY STATEMENT

The purpose of the 1981 New York City Vacancy Survey was to measure certain vacancy rates, as well as various household and person characteristics. New York City is required by law to periodically conduct such an investigation in order to determine if rent controls should be continued. The actual enumeration occurred in February and March of 1981.

Sample Design

New York City's prime consideration is the "vacant available for rent" rate (the ratio of the vacant available for rent units to the total number of renter occupied and vacant available for rent units) for the entire city. The design required that the standard error of the estimate of the "vacant available for rent" rate for the entire city be no more than one-fourth of one percent, if the actual rate were three percent.

The survey included only housing units. The principal exclusions were living quarters classified as transient hotels, commercial and mission lodging houses, inmate living quarters in institutions, quarters for the military on military installations, and other large group quarters not meeting the definition of a housing unit. Also generally excluded were housing units in special places, such as regular housing units located on the grounds of institutions and military installations, with the exception of residential hotels and motels. Housing units for which a Certificate of Occupancy was issued for the first time after December 1980 were also excluded.

The sample was selected from four sample frames. All housing units in existence and included in the 1970 census ("old construction") comprised the first frame. Within this frame, the housing units were further classified for purposes of this survey into five strata, with each stratum consisting of housing units from one and only one borough.

The second frame consisted of all housing units constructed since the 1970 census ("new construction"). Housing units in this frame were considered to be within the scope of the survey if a Certificate of Occupancy had been issued for the structure not later than December 1980. Within this frame, the sample housing units were again obtained by sampling separately from each of the five boroughs in New York City.

The third frame was a list of units constructed since the 1970 census under supervision of the New York State Urban Development Corporation. These units were not issued Certificates of Occupancy from the City of New York.

The fourth frame consisted of a list of addresses involved in the city's J-51 Tax Exemption and Tax Abatement Program. These addresses were of two types. The first of these was a list of commercial-use structures with upper floors rented for residential use. Since this practice was illegal at the time of the 1970 census, these units had not been included in the 1970 census frame. The second was a list of addresses that were special places at the time of the 1970 census but were residential at the time of the 1981 New York City Housing and Vacancy Survey. Within the third and fourth frame, sample housing units were again obtained by sampling separately from each of the five boroughs.

ithin each frame and borough, clusters ("segments) of four housing units were elected. Each housing unit had a probability of selection equal to 1 in 167. able 1 gives the initially obtained distribution of sample sizes by old and ew construction and by borough.

ble 1.--SIZE OF SAMPLE SELECTED, 1981 NEW YORK CITY HOUSING AND VACANCY SURVEY 1/

Borough	Old Construction 2/	New Construction 3/	Total
Bronx	3,044	240	3,284
Brooklyn	5,408	209	5,617
Manhattan	4,316	332	4,648
Queens	4,244	150	4,394
Richmond	536	168	704
Total	17,548	1,099	18,647

These numbers refer to the sample as initially selected, before deletions caused by out of scope units, duplication of serial numbers, demolitions, mergers, duplication of units in the frames, multiple Certificates of Occupancy for the same structure, conversion to nonresidential use, occupancy as group quarters, etc.

These counts include units from the first and fourth sampling frames discussed previously.

These counts include units from the second and third frames.

e sample housing units were visited in February and March 1981 by a group of terviewers hired and trained for this task. The interviewers visited each mple address and completed a questionnaire, whether the unit was occupied or cant, if it qualified as being within the scope of the survey. In addition, r evaluation purposes, all vacant units were independently reinterviewed with gard to occupancy status. Any differences were reconciled by an independent ird interview.

timation Procedure

e procedure employed in estimating housing unit characteristics consists of ree parts as follows: 1) inflating the sample results by the reciprocal of e probability of selection; 2) adjusting the sample results to account for interviews (of which there were 759) and 3) utilizing known housing unit als from the 1970 census in order to adjust the estimates in a manner that creases their precision. Persons characteristics are similarly estimated, h an additional ratio adjustment employing independently estimated borough ulation totals that further increase their precision.

Reliability of the Estimates

The statistics that this survey produced are estimates derived from a sample, and hence, are apt to differ somewhat from the actual values being estimated. This occurs because there are two types of errors possible in an estimate based on a sample survey - sampling error and nonsampling error.

Nonsampling Errors: Let us suppose that a comparable complete coverage survey was conducted, that is, an interview is attempted for every housing unit in New York City. Chances are, we would still not correctly estimate every parameter (for example, the rental vacancy rate) under consideration. In this instance the difference is due solely to nonsampling errors. Nonsampling errors occur also in sample surveys and can be attributed to many sources: inability to obtain information about all cases in the sample, definitional difficulties, differences in the interpretation of questions, inability or unwillingness to provide correct information on the part of the respondents, mistakes in recording or coding the data obtained, and other errors of collection, response, processing, coverage, and estimation for missing data. Explicit measures of these errors are generally not available. However, it is believed that some of the important response and most of the operational errors were detected and corrected in the course of the Bureau's review of the data for reasonableness and consistency.

Sampling Errors: The particular sample used in the 1981 New York City Vacancy Survey is one of a large number of all possible probability samples of the same size that could have been selected using the same sample design. Estimates derived from the different samples would differ from each other. The expected deviation of a sample result from the average of all possible samples is called the sampling error. The exact sampling error is unknown, however, guides to the potential size of the sampling error are provided by the standard error of the estimate.

The standard error of a survey estimate attempts to provide a measure of this variation among the estimates from the possible samples, and thus is a measure of the precision with which an estimate from a particular sample approximates the average result of all possible samples.

The standard errors that were calculated for this survey also partially measure the effect of variable nonsampling errors but do not measure any systematic biases in the data. Obviously, the accuracy of a survey result depends upon both the sampling and variable nonsampling errors measured by the standard error, and the bias and other types of nonsampling error not measured by the standard error. Therefore, the total error, which depends upon the joint effect of the sampling and non-sampling errors, is usually of the order of size indicated by the standard error, or only moderately higher. For particular estimates, however, the total error may considerably exceed the calculated standard error.

The estimate and its associated standard error may be used to construct a confidence interval, that is, an interval having a prescribed probability that it would include the average result of all possible samples. The chances are about 95 out of 100 (95 percent) that the interval from two standard errors below the estimate to two standard errors above the estimate would include the average value of all possible samples. Of course, any particular 95 percent confidence interval may or may not contain the average value of all possible samples. But for a particular sample, one can say with 95 percent confidence that the average of all possible samples is included in the constructed interval. Also frequently used are 68 percent and 99 percent confidence intervals, which are obtained by constructing a one standard error interval (plus or minus) and a 2½ standard error.

Tables 2 through 7 present approximate standard errors for the statistics based on the sample that was used. To provide standard errors applicable to the wide variety of statistics produced, a number of approximations and generalizations have been used. Hence, the standard errors presented in these tables provide a general order of magnitude rather than the exact standard error for any specific item.

Included in tables 2 through 7 are estimates of standard errors for estimates of zero and zero percent. These estimates of standard errors are considered as overestimates of the true standard errors and should be used primarily for construction of confidence intervals for characteristics when an estimate of zero is obtained.

The several tables of standard errors are applicable to different entities. Tables 2 and 3 contain standard errors of various types of housing unit characteristics only, while tables 4 through 7 refer to person characteristics only. The standard errors shown in tables 4 and 6 are applicable to persons having a certain household characteristic only (such as the number of people living in a renter housing unit). The standard errors appearing in tables 5 and 7 are applicable to persons having a particular household characteristic and a specific person characteristic (such as the number of males living in a renter housing unit) or having a certain person characteristic only (such as the number of males).

The standard errors for estimated numbers or percents not shown in these tables may be approximated by linear interpolation.

Standard Error of a Median:

The sampling variability of an estimated median depends upon the form as well as on the size of the distribution from which the median is determined. The following procedure may be used to estimate the standard error of a median based on sample data: (1) from the appropriate standard error table (table 3 for a housing unit characteristic and tables 6 or 7 for a person characteristic) determine the standard error of a 50 percent characteristic, using the appropriate base; (2) calculate the length of the interval in which the median lies (subtract the smaller endpoint from the larger endpoint and add one); (3) determine the percentage of the base falling in the interval containing the median; and (4) multiply the standard error of the 50 percent characteristic calculated in (1) by the interval length computed in (2) and divide by the percentage of the base determined in (3). This result obtained in step (4) is the approximate standard error of the estimated median. As described earlier, the standard error can now be used to construct a confidence interval about the estimated median such that there is a stated degree of confidence that the average median from all possible samples lies within the interval.

Standard Error of a Difference or Comparison Between Two Estimates

The standard errors shown in these tables are not directly applicable to differences between two sample estimates. The standard error of an estimated difference between two figures may be approximated as the square root of the sum of the squares of the standard error of each estimate. This formula will represent the actual standard error quite accurately for the difference between estimates of the same characteristic in two different areas or for the difference between separate and uncorrelated characteristics in the same area. If, however, there is a high positive correlation between the two characteristics, the formula will overestimate the true standard error. For a difference between two sample estimates, one of which represents a subclass of the other, the tables can be used directly with the difference considered as a sample estimate.

The following two tables (tables 2 and 3) contain estimated standard errors associated with housing unit characteristics.

Table 2.—STANDARD ERROR FOR ESTIMATED NUMBER OF TOTAL HOUSING UNITS (68 chances out of 100)

Size of Estimate	Standard Error
0	250
500	360
1,000	500
2,500	800
5,000	1,130
10,000	1,590
25,000	2,520
50,000	3,550
75,000	4,340
100,000	5,000
150,000	6,090
250,000	7,780
500,000	10,710
1,000,000	14,290
1,500,000	16,390
2,000,000	17,540
2,700,000	17,900
3,000,000	17,620

Example A: In the tables presenting the survey data, table 14 of Series IIA shows 12,552 vacant housing units available for rent in Brooklyn. Table 2 above indicates, by linear interpolation, an approximate standard error of 1,750 for the estimated 12,552 vacant-for-rent units in Brooklyn. Therefore, a 95 percent confidence interval is from 9,052 to 16,052 and one can say with 95 percent confidence that the average of all possible samples is included in this interval. A 68 percent confidence interval is from 10,802 to 14,302 and so, with 68 percent confidence it can be said that the average of all possible samples lies in this interval.

Example B: Table 17 of Series IIA shows 16,086 vacant available for rent units with 10 to 49 units in structure and 12,036 vacant available for rent units with 50 or more units in structure. Table 2 above indicates, by linear interpolation, approximate standard errors of 1,970 for the estimated 16,086 vacant available for rent units with 10 to 49 units in structure and 1,720 for the estimated 12,036 vacant for rent units with 50 or more units in structure. The standard error of the estimated difference of 16,086 - 12,036 = 4,050 units is about $\sqrt{(1,970)^2 + (1,720)^2} = 2,620$ units. The 95 percent confidence interval for this difference is - 1,190 to 9,290, and since positive and negative values are included we cannot conclude with 95 percent confidence that there are more vacant for rent units with 10 to 49 units in strucuture than vacant for rent units with more than 50 units in structure.

Table 3.--STANDARD ERROR FOR ESTIMATED PERCENTAGE OF TOTAL HOUSING UNITS AND FOR ESTIMATED VACANCY RATES 1/

(68 chances out of 100)

Base of Percentage or Vacancy Rate	Estimated Percentage or Vacancy Rate (Percent)													
	0 or 100	1 or 99	2 or 98	3 or 97	4 or 96	5 or 95	6 or 94	7 or 93	8 or 92	9 or 91	10 or 90	20 or 80	35 or 65	50
2,500	9.2	9.2	9.2	9.2	9.2	9.2	9.2	9.2	9.2	9.2	9.6	12.8	15.2	16.0
5,000	4.8	4.8	4.8	4.8	4.8	4.9	5.4	5.8	6.1	6.5	6.8	9.0	10.8	11.3
10,000	2.5	2.5	2.5	2.7	3.1	3.5	3.8	4.1	4.3	4.6	4.8	6.4	7.6	8.0
25,000	1.0	1.0	1.4	1.7	2.0	2.2	2.4	2.6	2.7	2.9	3.0	4.0	4.8	5.0
50,000	0.5	0.7	1.0	1.2	1.4	1.6	1.7	1.8	1.9	2.0	2.1	2.9	3.4	3.6
75,000	0.3	0.6	0.8	1.0	1.1	1.3	1.4	1.5	1.6	1.7	1.7	2.3	2.8	2.9
100,000	0.3	0.5	0.7	0.9	1.0	1.1	1.2	1.3	1.4	1.4	1.5	2.0	2.4	2.5
150,000	0.2	0.4	0.6	0.7	0.8	0.9	1.0	1.1	1.1	1.2	1.2	1.6	2.0	2.1
250,000	0.10	0.3	0.4	0.5	0.6	0.7	0.8	0.8	0.9	0.9	1.0	1.3	1.5	1.6
500,000	0.05	0.2	0.3	0.4	0.4	0.5	0.5	0.6	0.6	0.6	0.7	0.9	1.1	1.1
1,000,000	0.03	0.2	0.2	0.3	0.3	0.3	0.4	0.4	0.4	0.5	0.5	0.6	0.8	0.8
2,000,000	0.01	0.11	0.2	0.2	0.2	0.2	0.3	0.3	0.3	0.3	0.3	0.5	0.5	0.6
2,700,000	0.01	0.10	0.14	0.2	0.2	0.2	0.2	0.2	0.3	0.3	0.3	0.4	0.5	0.5
3,000,000	0.01	0.09	0.13	0.2	0.2	0.2	0.2	0.2	0.2	0.3	0.3	0.4	0.4	0.5

1/ The base of each percentage or vacancy rate is the number of housing units (in the denominator) to which the percentage or vacancy rate applies. Standard errors are presented to the nearest one-tenth of one percentage point except when the standard error is less than fifteen-hundredths of one percentage point; in those cases, the standard error is shown to the nearest one-hundredth of one percentage point.

Example C: A computation based on the figures of Series IIA, table 16, indicates that 6.5 percent of the 41,284 vacant available for rent units that reported the year structure built have been built in or since 1970. Table 3 indicates, by linear interpolation, an approximate standard error of 2.0 percent for the estimated 6.5 percent.

Example D: Table 32 of Series IIA shows $247.92 as the estimated median monthly asking rent for vacant available for rent units. This table also shows that 21.4 percent of the base (= 34,779 after subtracting out the not reported) lies in the $200-$249 interval containing the median. Table 3 above indicates, by linear interpolation, an approximate standard error of 4.5 percent for the estimated 50 percent using the 34,779 base. The length of the interval containing the median is $249 - $200 + $1 = $50 and the percentage of the base in this interval is 21.4 percent. The standard error of the estimated $247.92 median is then approximated by:

$$\hat{\sigma}_M = \frac{4.5\text{ percent} \times \$50}{21.4\text{ percent}} = \$10.51$$

Example E: Table 32 of Series IA shows $235.06 as the estimated median monthly contract rent for renter occupied units. This table also shows that 21.0 percent of the base (= 1,872,782 after subtracting out the not reported, and the no cash rents) lies in the $200 - $249 interval containing the median. Table 3 above indicates, by linear interpolation, an approximate standard error of .6 percent for the estimated 50 percent using the 1,872,782 base. The standard error of the estimated $235.06 median is then approximated by:

$$\hat{\sigma}_M = \frac{.6\text{ percent} \times \$50}{21.0\text{ percent}} = \$1.43$$

The difference between the median monthly asking rent (see example D) and the median monthly contract rent is $247.92 - $235.06 = $12.86. The approximate standard error of this difference is $\sqrt{(\$10.51)^2 + (\$1.43)^2} = \$10.61$
Since the difference between the two medians ($12.86) is less than twice the standard error of this difference ($21.22), we cannot conclude with 95 percent confidence that the median monthly asking rent is actually greater than the median monthly contract rent.

The following four tables contain estimated standard errors associated with persons characteristics.

Table 4.--STANDARD ERROR FOR ESTIMATED NUMBER OF PERSONS HAVING A CERTAIN HOUSEHOLD CHARACTERISTIC ONLY

(68 chances out of 100)

Size of Estimate	Standard Error
0	730
5,000	1,900
10,000	2,690
25,000	4,250
50,000	6,000
100,000	8,450
250,000	13,200
500,000	18,300
1,000,000	24,770
2,000,000	31,700
3,000,000	34,240
4,000,000	33,430
5,000,000	28,970
6,000,000	18,400
6,900,000	0 1/

Table 5.--STANDARD ERROR FOR ESTIMATED NUMBER OF PERSONS HAVING A PARTICULAR HOUSEHOLD CHARACTERISTIC AND A SPECIFIC PERSON CHARACTERISTIC OR HAVING A CERTAIN PERSON CHARACTERISTIC ONLY

(68 chances out of 100)

Size of Estimate	Standard Error
0	290
5,000	1,200
10,000	1,690
25,000	2,670
50,000	3,760
100,000	5,290
250,000	8,210
500,000	11,240
1,000,000	14,800
2,000,000	17,420
3,000,000	15,910
4,000,000	8,260
5,000,000	0 1/
6,000,000	0 1/
6,900,000	0 1/

1/ The estimated total number of people in New York City is 6,872,294. This estimate corresponds to the universe of this survey as described on page 1. This total was independently estimated by beginning with the 1980 census and employing certain statistical techniques not subject to sampling error. However, the estimation procedure is subject to nonsampling error. Therefore, the estimate of 6,872,294 has no standard error but is subject to some bias.

Table 6.—STANDARD ERROR FOR ESTIMATED PERCENTAGE OF PERSONS HAVING A CERTAIN HOUSEHOLD CHARACTERISTIC ONLY 1/

(68 chances out of 100)

Base of Percentage	Estimated Percentage							
	0 or 100	1 or 99	2 or 98	5 or 95	10 or 90	20 or 80	35 or 65	50
5,000	12.7	12.7	12.7	12.7	12.7	15.2	18.2	19.0
10,000	6.8	6.8	6,8	6.8	8.1	10.8	12.8	13.5
25,000	2.8	2.8	2.8	3.7	5.1	6.8	8.1	8.5
50,000	1.4	1.4	1.7	2.6	3.6	4.8	5.7	6.0
100,000	0.7	0.8	1.2	1.9	2.6	3.4	4.1	4.3
250,000	0.3	0.5	0.8	1.2	1.6	2.2	2.6	2.7
500,000	0.14	0.4	0.5	0.8	1.1	1.5	1.8	1.9
1,000,000	0.07	0.3	0.4	0.6	0.8	1.1	1.3	1.3
2,000,000	0.04	0.2	0.3	0.4	0.6	0.8	0.9	1.0
3,000,000	0.02	0.15	0.2	0.3	0.5	0.6	0.7	0.8
6,900,000	0.01	0.10	0.14	0.2	0.3	0.4	0.5	0.5

1/ The base for each percentage is the number of people having a certain household characteristic only to which the percentage applies.

Table 7.—STANDARD ERROR FOR ESTIMATED PERCENTAGE OF PERSONS HAVING A PARTICULAR HOUSEHOLD CHARACTERISTIC AND A SPECIFIC PERSON CHARACTERISTIC OR HAVING A CERTAIN PERSON CHARACTERISTIC ONLY 1/

(68 chances out of 100)

Base of Percentage	Estimated Percentage							
	0 or 100	1 or 99	2 or 98	5 or 95	10 or 90	20 or 80	35 or 65	50
5,000	5.4	5.4	5.4	5.4	7.2	9.6	11.4	12.0
10,000	2.8	2.8	2.8	3.7	5.1	6.8	8.1	8.5
25,000	1.1	1.1	1.5	2.3	3.2	4.3	5.1	5.4
50,000	0.6	0.8	1.1	1.6	2.3	3.0	3.6	3.8
100,000	0.3	0.5	0.7	0.9	1.6	2.1	2.6	2.7
250,000	0.11	0.3	0.5	0.7	1.0	1.4	1.6	1.7
500,000	0.06	0.2	0.3	0.5	0.7	1.0	1.1	1.2
1,000,000	0.03	0.2	0.2	0.4	0.5	0.7	0.8	0.8
2,000,000	0.01	0.12	0.2	0.3	0.4	0.5	0.6	0.6
3,000,000	0.01	0.10	0.14	0.2	0.3	0.4	0.5	0.5
6,900,000	0.01	0.06	0.09	0.14	0.2	0.3	0.3	0.3

1/ Table 7 corresponds to table 6 and is to be used in the same manner, but is applicable to percentages of persons having a particular household characteristic and a specific person characteristic or having a certain person characteristic only.

It may happen that a standard error of a percentage is sought where the numerator of the percentage is of one type (e.g., table 7) and the denominator is of the other type (e.g., table 6). In this event, use the table that corresponds with the numerator (here, it is table 7).

Example F: A computation based on the figures of Series VII, table 30, indicates that 45.0 percent of the 4,517,850 persons living in renter units who reported (or had reported) sex are males. A standard error of .4 percent is obtained by linear interpolation in table 7 (the table that corresponds to the numerator, that is, the number of males living in a renter unit).

The estimated total number of people in New York City is 6,872,294. This estimate corresponds to the universe of this survey as described on page 1. This total was independently estimated by beginning with the 1980 census and employing certain statistical techniques not subject to sampling error. However, the estimation procedure is subject to nonsampling error. Therefore, the estimate of 6,872,294 has no standard error but is subject to some bias.